W9-AOK-626

MEN OF THE BIBLE.

Their Lives and Times.

Edited by Rev. J. S. EXELL, M.A.

Author of The Biblical Illustrator

"We commend the volumes of this series as useful contributions to the popularization of the results of Biblical scholarship—a tendency and movement of our time of the utmost interest and promise."—*New Englander.*

17 Volumes, 12mo, cloth.
Price reduced to 75 cents, each, postpaid.

Abraham. By Rev. W. J. Dean, M.A.
Daniel. By Rev. H. Deane, B.D.
David. By Rev. W. J. Dean, M.A.
Elijah. By Prof. W. Milligan, D.D.
Ezra and Nehemiah. By Rev. Canon Rawlinson.
Gideon and Judges. By Rev. J. M. Lang, D.D.
Isaac and Jacob. By Rev. Canon Rawlinson.
Isaiah. By Rev. Canon Driver, M.A.
Jeremiah. By Rev. Canon Cheyne, D.D.
Jesus Christ the Divine Man. By J. F. Vallings, M.A.
Joshua. By Rev. W. J. Dean, M.A.
Kings of Israel and Judah. By Rev. Canon Rawlinson.
Minor Prophets, The. By Rev. Dean Farrar, D.D.
Moses. By Rev. Canon Rawlinson, M.A.
Samuel and Saul. By Rev. W. J. Dean, M.A.
Solomon. By Rev. Dean Farrar, D.D.
St. Paul. By Rev. Prof. Iverach, D.D.

Fleming H. Revell Company,

Men of the Bible

The Kings of Israel and Judah

BY

George Rawlinson, M.A.

Camden Professor of Ancient History in the University of Oxford, and Corresponding Member of the Royal Academy of Turin; Author of "The Five Great Monarchies of the Ancient Eastern World"; "Moses: His Life and Times," Etc., Etc., Etc.

FLEMING H. REVELL COMPANY

NEW YORK   CHICAGO   TORONTO

Publishers of Evangelical Literature

PREFACE.

THE Books of Kings and Chronicles form the main source for
the History of the Kings of Israel and Judah. They require,
however, to be supplemented, especially for the later kings, by
a careful study of the Prophetical Scriptures, particularly of
Isaiah, Jeremiah, Ezekiel, Hosea, Amos, Micah, Habakkuk,
and Zephaniah. Local colouring, the life and manners of the
time, and the feelings of those contemporary with the events
described, are derivable almost wholly from this latter source,
which furnishes them often in tolerable abundance. The
"Antiquities" of Josephus supply less material than might
have been expected, and the character of all additional
material derived from this quarter requires to be weighed in
the scales of a careful and sober criticism. Considerable
light is thrown on the history of some of the kings by contemporary notices contained in the monuments of Egypt and
Assyria. It has been the endeavour of the writer, so far as
the limits of space allowed, to make full use of all these
various sources of information. His labours have been much
lightened by the excellent work done by many of his predecessors in the field of Sacred History, as especially by the
writers of the articles on the several kings in Dr. Smith's
"Dictionary of the Bible," Kitto's "Biblical Cyclopædia,"
Winer's "Realwörterbuch," and Ersch and Grüber's "Cyclo-
pädie." He is indebted also largely to the graphic and
brilliant narrative of his lamented friend, Dean Stanley,
whose "Lectures on the Jewish Church," though on some
points they "give an uncertain sound," contain the best

account of the Divided Monarchy which at present exists
in the English language. Ewald's " History of the People
of Israel" has been also consulted throughout, but more
sparingly used, the writer's absolute rejection of the miraculous rendering him an untrustworthy commentator on a
period of history wherein, according to the original authorities, the miraculous played a prominent part.

OXFORD,   G. R.
    April 30, 1889.

CONTENTS.

CHAPTER IV.

CHAPTER V.

CHAPTER VI.

CHAPTER VII.

CHAPTER VIII.

CHAPTER IX.

CHAPTER XIX.

CHAPTER XX.

CHAPTER XXI.

CHAPTER XXII.

CHAPTER XXIII.

Accession of Josiah's second son, Shallum or Jehoahaz—Further
conquests of Neco—His deposition of Jehoahaz—Feeling of the
Jews with respect to Jehoahaz—Jehoiakim reigns as an Egyptian
vassal for three years, B.C. 608–605—Character of his early
reign—Battle of Carchemish, and first expedition of Nebuchadnezzar against Palestine—Conquests of Nebuchadnezzar—His
return to Babylon—Fresh intrigues among the Palestinian
monarchs—Revolts of Judæa and Tyre—Second expedition of
Nebuchadnezzar, and execution of Jehoiakim—Estimate of his
character.

Jehoiachin made king by Nebuchadnezzar—His evil and short
reign—He is carried captive to Babylon—Zedekiah, his uncle,
made king in his place—Zedekiah's early efforts to introduce
reforms—He succumbs to the influence of the nobles—Rebels
and allies himself with Apries—Last invasion of Nebuchadnezzar—Siege of Jerusalem commenced—Advance of Apries—
Siege raised—Renewed and final investment—Jerusalem taken—
Capture and punishment of Zedekiah—His weak character.

CHAPTER I.

REHOBOAM.

Education of Rehoboam—Influence of his mother, Naamah—His early companions—His accession—Demand for a redress of grievances, how met—Consequent revolt of the Ten Tribes—Threat of war—Erection of fortifications—Exodus of the Levites from Israel—Religious corruption of Judah—Expedition of Shishak—Later years of Rehoboam —His domestic relations—His character.

THE Court of Solomon, whereat Rehoboam was brought up, has been described in a former volume of this series. A place where such wealth, such luxury, and such unrestrained polygamy were rife, was not a school apt for the formation of a strong or self-reliant character. When it is said that Rehoboam grew through boyhood to manhood in the atmosphere of an Eastern harem, enough is said to account for all that followed. In a harem princes, waited on by obsequious eunuchs, and petted by their mother and her female slaves, pass their time in softness and idleness, without any training worth the name, without the spur of emulation ; flattered, fawned upon, courted ; encouraged to regard themselves as beings of a superior kind, who can scarcely do wrong, who are to be indulged in every desire, and every fancy, and are never to be checked or thwarted. A judicious father shortens as much as possible the duration of this time of trial, early sending his sons out to the wars, or giving them civil employment, or at any rate removing them from the gynæceum, and placing them under the direction and guidance of carefully chosen tutors and instructors. But Solomon, from the time that he fell away, is not likely to have been a judicious father, or to have greatly troubled himself concerning the train-

ing of his children. There were no wars to which he could send
them, and he seems not to have employed them in civil government. Rehoboam, so far as appears, grew to manhood as a
mere hanger-on upon the Court, the centre of a group of young
men brought up with him (1 Kings xii. 8), and eager to flatter
his foibles. The enforced idleness of an heir apparent, in all
countries, and especially in the East, constitutes a severe trial
to all but the best balanced natures, and too often leads to those
evil and dissipated courses which are the great peril of youth at
every period of the world's history. We are not perhaps entitled to conclude absolutely, from the many passages of the
Proverbs where the evil doings of young men are rebuked, that
Solomon is actually glancing at the conduct of Rehoboam, or
using the expression " My son " in any other than a general
sense; but still the frequency and urgency of the remonstrances
naturally raise the suspicion that—in part at least—a personal
motive underlies them. As a personal element appears distinctly in what the wise king says (Prov. iv. 3, 4) of his own
education and instruction, so it may well be that the keen re-
proofs and reproaches addressed to the "foolish son" are
barbed by a personal sentiment of regret and disapproval.

It does not appear that Rehoboam during his youth had any
special guide or instructor. No one is indicated as standing to
him in the relation in which Nathan had, apparently, stood to
his father.[1] The prophet Shemaiah, who was the mentor of his
later life,[2] received no mission to "speak to him" until he was
king. The chief share in his early education, if it may be
allowed the name, must have been taken by his mother,
Naamah. Now Naamah was an Ammonitess (1 Kings xiv. 31).
She was one of those many foreign women, "princesses" (ibid.
xi. 3), whom Solomon took to wife very early in his reign, and
who ultimately "turned away his heart," so that he became an
actual worshipper of false gods. It was for her, principally,
that he built the High Place to Molech, or Milcom, on the hill
that is over against Jerusalem, directly in front of the Temple,
that is, on the northern crest of Olivet. According to the Septuagint translators,[3] she was the daughter of Hanun, the king of

[1] On this relation, see Dr. Farrar's remarks in " Solomon, his Life and
Times," pp. 8, 9.   [2] 1 Kings xii. 22–24 ; 2 Chron. xi. 2–4, xii. 5–8.
[3] See the Greek text of 1 Kings xii. after verse 24 : Ὄνομα τῆς μητρὸς
αὐτοῦ Νααυὰν, θυγάτηρ Ἄνα υἱοῦ Ναὰς, βασιλίως υἱῶν Ἀμμών.

Ammon, with whom David had the war provoked by the ill-treatment of his ambassadors (2 Sam. x. 1–14). Her influence over her son can scarcely have been for good. Brought up an idolatress, we cannot blame her that she remained one till her marriage and the transference of her residence to Jerusalem; but her determined adherence to the bloody rites of Molech after full acquaintance with the religion of Jehovah, indicates a moral blindness and a hardness of heart, which would make her a most undesirable instructress of youth. We can scarcely doubt but that she took her son with her when she attended the worship of Molech in the sanctuary built by Solomon for her use on the Mount Olivet, and introduced him to a knowledge of the bloody, and probably licentious,[1] rites of the Ammonite religion. The strong leaning towards the worst forms of idolatry which Rehoboam showed soon after mounting the throne is not surprising in one subjected to the influence of such a mother at the most impressible period of human existence.

It is not recorded that Rehoboam had any brothers; but we can scarcely suppose that he was without them. Solomon's wives numbered, at the least, seventy;[2] and it would be preposterous to imagine that they were all sonless. Among the "young men that grew up with him" (1 Kings xii. 10) were doubtless several who stood towards him in the near relationship, if not of full brother, at any rate of half-brother. These persons would naturally be among his earliest and most intimate companions. Brought up under the influence of their several mothers, as he of his, they would lean to their mother's cults, and practically impress upon him the syncretism, which was Solomon's idea of religion in his later life. Rehoboam can scarcely have looked on Jehovah as more than a local god, entitled to the respect of the Israelites, and to a continuous worship in the splendid temple which Solomon had built in his honour. But his own personal leanings would seem to have been towards the foreign rites which his father had established upon Israelite soil,[3] and

---

[1] Compare "Solomon, his Life and Times," pp. 146, 147. The Molech of Ammon corresponded closely with the Chemosh of Moab, one of whose names was "Ashtar Chemosh" (Moabite Stone, line 17), showing him to be the male principle corresponding to the female Ashtoreth, or Astarté.

[2] The "seven hundred" of 1 Kings xi. 3 is probably an accidental corruption of "seventy." [3] See 1 Kings xiv. 21–24; 2 Chron. xii. 1–5.

which possessed for the Israelite mind a curious fascination. We do not know, however, that, as prince, he had any great opportunity of showing his predilections, or that he shared at all in the direction of affairs under his father. The impression left by the Scriptural narrative is, that, down to his father's death, he lived a mere courtier's life, a life without serious aims or stirring circumstances.

But a time came when there suddenly devolved upon him a great and most serious responsibility. Solomon died at an age which could not have greatly exceeded sixty,[1] and Rehoboam, at the age of forty-one, found himself recognized as the natural heir to the crown, and successor to his father's kingdom in its entirety. At first no voice was raised to dispute his title, no arm was lifted to oppose him. The news indeed of Solomon's death had brought back from Egypt a discontented and ambitious refugee, who had a certain number of adherents, and who may have entertained hopes of pushing himself into notice, if trouble or difficulty should arise in connection with the transfer of sovereignty. Jeroboam, who had fled to the Court of Shishak, or Sheshonk, king of Egypt, on a mere charge of cherishing treasonable intentions, naturally returned to his own land, as Moses had done (Exod. iv. 19, 20), when the king who sought his life was dead, and attended the gathering which was to give popular sanction to a succession universally regarded as natural and proper. The gathering was held at Shechem, the chief city of Ephraim, whether by Rehoboam's appointment, or by a spontaneous movement on the part of the tribes, is uncertain. It is perhaps most probable that Rehoboam designated Shechem as the place for his inauguration in a conciliatory spirit, hoping thereby to gratify the Ephraimites, and secure their support and favour. But his concession was by some interpreted as weakness. The oppressive rule of Solomon during the later years of his reign, the heavy taxes which he imposed upon his subjects for the support of his Court (1 Kings iv. 7–23), and the forced labour which he exacted from them, had given rise to general discontent, and "the government of the Wise King had become as odious to the Israelites as that of the race of Tarquin, in spite of all their splendid works"—and indeed partly on account of them—"was afterwards to the inhabitants of Rome."[2] We may

---

[1] "Solomon ; his Life and Times," p. 157.
[2] Stanley, "Lectures on the Jewish Church," vol. ii. p. 214.

be sure that the crafty and unscrupulous Jeroboam fomented the popular ill-will ; and it was probably in consequence of his machinations, that, on the meeting of the Tribes, their complaints were formulated, and delegates named—Jeroboam being among the number (1 Kings xii. 3)—to carry them to the king, and plead for a redress of grievances. "Thy father," said their spokesman, probably Jeroboam himself, "made our yoke grievous ; now therefore make thou the grievous service of thy father, and his heavy yoke that he put upon us, lighter, and we will serve thee." The abolition of forced labour, and a reduction of taxation would, so far as appears, have contented them ; they had no thought of revolt ; they probably expected that their very moderate demands (as they considered them) would be cheerfully granted, and that the young king would be glad to purchase the popularity which most princes desire on their coronation day by the making of a few promises, which need not perhaps be altogether irrevocable.

The young king perceived, or those who were about him suggested to him, that the matter was one which required deliberation. Prerogative was in question, and prerogative is naturally dear to kings, nor have there ever been wanting, at any time or in any country, sticklers for prerogative among the hangers-on of a Court, more loth to yield one jot or tittle of it than the kings themselves. Persons of this class no doubt pointed out to Rehoboam that it was no light matter that was in question, but really the very character of the monarchy. Solomon had won for himself the privilege which the Great Monarchs of the East have always enjoyed, and which was at the time possessed and exercised by the kings both of Egypt [1] and of Assyria,[2] the privilege of exacting from their subjects as much forced labour as they pleased—was his successor to surrender the right the moment it was objected to ? If he did, might not further demands be made ? Might not the royal power be gradually cramped and limited, until it became a mere shadow, and ceased to secure to the nation the benefits with a view to which it had been set up ?[3] At any rate, the subject was one for grave debate ; and it was probably felt to be a quite reasonable

[1] Herod. ii. 124, 128.

[2] This is not exactly demonstrable, but may be concluded from the vast palaces of the later Assyrian kings.

[3] See Ewald, "History of Israel," vol. iv. pp. 308-310.

reply, when Rehoboam returned answer to his discontented subjects that he would communicate to them his decision on the third day (1 Kings xii. 5).

Rehoboam is said to have first asked the counsel of the old men,[1] the "grey-beards" who had acted for many years as his father's counsellors, and who might be expected to have derived from their contact with the " wisest of men,"[2] and from their long experience of affairs, something of that calm spirit of true worldly wisdom, which had characterized a large part of Solomon's rule.   Their advice was that he should adopt a mild and conciliatory tone, that he should "speak good words," yield, at any rate, to some extent, or seem to yield, and thus please the malcontents, who, they ventured to say, would be peaceable and tractable subjects thenceforth, if they seemed to themselves to have got their way under the existing circumstances (ibid. ver. 7).   The advice was probably not palatable.   At any rate it was not taken.   Rehoboam turned to the younger men, the men of his own standing—bold spirits, who had none of the timidity of age, and who might well seem to him more competent interpreters of the temper of their own day than persons who belonged to a generation that was just dying off.   The young men were imbued with all the contempt for popular demands, and all the pride and insolence of a narrow and exclusive aristocracy.   Their counsel was that Rehoboam should not yield an inch.   A fool was rightly "answered according to his folly."   "Thus shalt thou speak unto them," they said :   " My little finger shall be thicker than my father's loins.   Whereas my father did lade you with a heavy yoke, I will add to your yoke ; my father chastised you with whips, but I will chastise you with cat-o'-nine tails."   It was rash and foolish counsel ; but the king followed it.   He "forsook the old men's counsel that they had given him, and spake to the people after the counsel of the young men "—"roughly," rudely, cruelly (vers. 13, 14).   Not only, they were told, should there be no alleviation of their burdens, but the weight of them should be aggravated.   Rehoboam's "little finger should be thicker than his father's loins."   It was a proud, fierce, foolish answer ; and the consequences were such as any man of moderate prudence might have anticipated.   Disappointed and disgusted, the multitude burst out into the cry—

---

[1] 1 Kings xii. 6; 2 Chron. x. 6.   [2] 1 Kings iv. 41.

"What portion have we in David?
    Neither have we inheritance in the son of Jesse:
    To your tents, O Israel—
    Now see to thine own house, David! '

The tribal spirit was strong among the Hebrews. The supremacy of Judah had never been otherwise than grudgingly accepted. Reuben, Ephraim, Manasseh, perpetually kicked against Judæan sovereignty. Thus there was always a latent discontent, which any breeze might any day blow into a flame. At this time Rehoboam's silly threats were the spark which fired the train, and produced a sudden explosion. On hearing them all the tribes excepting three burst out into open revolt. Judah remained firm in its allegiance to the house of David; Benjamin, satisfied with the distinction accorded it by the emplacement of the capital within its borders, threw in its lot with Judah; Levi, thoroughly content with its grand position at the head of the religion of the kingdom, gave its sympathies to the Davidic cause, and ultimately gravitated to the southern kingdom. But Reuben, which claimed the right of the first-born; Ephraim, which had given to the nation Joshua, the conqueror, Deborah the Prophetess, and Samuel, the last and the greatest of the judges; Manasseh, which shared largely in the glories of its brother tribe, Ephraim (Gen. xlviii. 19; Deut. xxxiii. 17); Zebulun, which " sucked of the abundance of the seas " (Deut. xxxiii. 19); Gad, which "dwelt as a lion" (ibid. ver. 20); Dan, the "lion's whelp" (ibid. ver. 22); Issachar, the "strong ass couching down between two burthens" (Gen. xlix. 14); Naphtali, the "hind let loose" (ibid. ver. 21); and Asher, the dweller in the far north, threw off the Davidic yoke, declared themselves independent of Judah, and proclaimed their intention of placing themselves under a new king. Still failing to appreciate the situation, and imagining that compromise was even yet possible, Rehoboam resolved on one more effort to prevent the disruption, and sent an envoy—no doubt with an offer of some sort of compromise—to his revolted subjects; but, with the wrongheadedness which characterized all his proceedings at this period of his life, he selected for envoy one of the persons most obnoxious to the malcontents—no other than his father's chief director of the forced labours which were so unpopular—Adoram or Adoniram (1 Kings xii. 18; 2 Chron. x. 18). The rebels seem to have considered that this was adding insult to injury; and, without waiting to hear the terms which Adoniram had to offer, they threw him down and stoned him to death. Deeply shocked, and alarmed for his own safety, Rehoboam mounted his chariot, and quitting Shechem fled hastily to Jerusalem.

The Tribes proceeded to elect a king, and to constitute themselves a separate state. The condition of things was re-established which had prevailed after the death of Saul, when David reigned over Judah in Hebron, and Ishbosheth over Israel in Mahanaim. But Rehoboam was not inclined to submit tamely to this defection. From Jerusalem he sent out his mandate throughout all Judah and Benjamin, summoning to his standard the men of war of both tribes, and succeeded in gathering together an army of 180,000 men, with whom he proposed to effect the subjugation of the rebel kingdom (1 Kings xii. 21). An internecine war would have broken out ; but at the decisive moment, Shemaiah, the great prophet and historiographer of the day (2 Chron. xii. 15), received a commission to interpose, and in the name of God commanded Rehoboam to lay aside his purpose, disband his troops, and remain at peace with his Israelite brethren. "The thing," he said, "was from God." God had rent the kingdom of Solomon into two parts to punish Solomon's idolatries (1 Kings xi. 33), and it was vain for man to attempt to oppose His will. The disruption, decreed in the Divine counsels, must take effect, and it was true wisdom, as well as true piety, to acquiesce in it, and seek to make the best of the new situation established by the new circumstances.

The situation was critical. The northern kingdom, even if left to itself and not made the object of an organized attack, would necessarily be a hostile kingdom, and would require careful watching, and the perpetual maintenance of an attitude of defence. But this was not the worst. It would be supported by a southern kingdom of very much greater power, which might at any moment exchange a passive support for active intervention, and which it would be difficult, if not impossible, to resist. Egypt, which had protected Jeroboam from the hostility of Solomon (1 Kings xi. 40), would be likely to lend him effectual aid if invited to do so, and under the energetic rule of an ambitious prince, who had founded a dynasty, might even aspire to resume, on her own account, the *rôle* of Asiatic conqueror which she had laid aside for so many centuries. Awake to these perils, Rehoboam, after his return to Jerusalem, lost no time in strengthening the defences of his kingdom, more especially in the quarters which were most open to invasion from Egypt. He "built cities for defence in Judah" (2 Chron. xi. 5), "fortifying the strongholds, and putting captains in them, with store of victual, and of oil and wine" (ibid. ver. 11). Bethlehem, Etam, Tekoa, Beth-zur, and Hebron, upon the south Shocoh, Adullam, Azekah, Gath, Lachish, and Mareshah towards the south-west, Zorah and Aijalon on the west, were "made exceeding strong" (ibid. ver. 12); ample provisions and a goodly supply of spears and shields were laid up in them, and all that was possible was done to check the progress of an invader from Egypt, should one appear.

Three years of peace followed. The only notable occurrence during this tranquil interval was the gradual exodus of the Levites from the northern kingdom, where they were subject to indignities, and their concentration within the territorial limits of Judah and Benjamin, where they were respected and honoured. This exodus was followed by that of many pious Israelites, who disliked Jeroboam's religious innovations, and were attached to the worship of Jehovah, as established by David and Solomon. The northern kingdom was thus continually weakened and the southern one strengthened (2 Chron. xi. 13-17), to the great dissatisfaction of Jeroboam, who proceeded to cast about in his mind for a remedy, and ere long came to the conclusion that his best course would be to invoke the aid of his Egyptian ally against his troublesome neighbour.

Meanwhile the religious corruption introduced by Solomon was spreading itself widely among the people of the southern kingdom, unchecked by the king. "Judah did evil in the sight of the Lord, and they provoked him to jealousy with their sins which they had committed, above all that their fathers had done. For they built them high places, and images, and groves, on every high hill, and under every green tree. And there were also Sodomites in the land: and they did according to all the abominations of the nations which the Lord cast out before the children of Israel" (1 Kings xiv. 22-24). Rehoboam himself, as the author of Chronicles tells us (2 Chron. xii. 1), "forsook the law of the Lord," set an ill example to his subjects, and then "all Israel forsook Jehovah with him." The seductive rites of Phœnicia, the bloody rites of Moab and Ammon were preferred to the simple solemn ceremonies of the Jerusalem

Temple; altars blazed on every high hill; emblems of Baal and
Astarté were set up; frantic orgies absorbed and depraved the
religious sentiment of the people; the national shrine was comparatively deserted; Judah "went a-whoring" after the gods of
the nations, and practised abominations which it is impossible
to describe, or more than hint at. By the fifth year of Rehoboam's reign, the apostasy had reached its height, and provoked God to inflict on His people—even on the beloved tribe
of Judah—a terrible punishment.

In the web of mundane events woven by the hand of God,
the threads of worldly policy which men spin are taken into
account, made use of, and given their appropriate place. The
needs of Jeroboam, the ambition of Sheshonk to cover his own
name with glory, and strengthen his dynasty by conciliating to
it the affections of the military class, were made to fall in with
God's purposes, and help to work them out, in due season,
when the fitting hour was come. From the date of Solomon's
death Sheshonk had been biding his time, waiting for a
summons from Jeroboam, who would best know when he could
most effectually strike. In the fifth year of Rehoboam's reign,
just when the apostasy of Judah was complete, the summons
came, and Sheshonk hastened to obey it. Levying an army of
twelve hundred chariots, sixty (perhaps six) thousand horsemen, and footmen "without number" (2 Chron. xii. 3)—Lubim,
Sukkiim, and Cushites—he marched into Judæa "in three
columns" (Brugsch), and attacked the cities which Rehoboam
had fortified with so much care. A poor resistance was made.
Afraid to encounter his assailant in the open field, Rehoboam
shut himself up within the walls of his capital, and left the
provincial towns to defend themselves as they best could.
Probably the greater number surrendered at discretion. A few
were besieged and taken, as Shoco, Adoraim, and Aijalon.
Meanwhile the trembling king, awaiting his foe at Jerusalem,
was upbraided by the prophet Shemaiah for the sins which had
brought the visitation upon him, and warned that God had
determined to deliver him into the hands of Sheshonk. In
this strait he "humbled himself" (ibid. ver. 6), acknowledged
that he was justly punished, and deprecated the extreme anger
of Jehovah. The "princes of Judah" joined in his submission.
Hereupon Shemaiah was instructed to tell him that his self-
humiliation was accepted, and that on account of it, God would

"grant him some deliverance" (ibid. **ver. 7**). Sheshonk should not take him prisoner, but he must submit and become Sheshonk's servant, that he might learn the difference between "serving the Lord" and serving a heathen suzerain. The result was in accordance with this intimation. Sheshonk encamped before Jerusalem, but instead of forming the siege, consented to accept a ransom. Rehoboam gave him all the treasures of his palace, and all the treasures of the Temple, including the shields of gold which Solomon had made for his body-guard (1 Kings x. 16, 17 ; 2 Chron. xii. 9) ; and Sheshonk, content with this booty, and with a submission which can scarcely have been more than nominal, marched his army away to further conquests.

The remainder of Sheshonk's campaign belongs rather to the history of Israel than to that of Judah, and will be considered when we treat of the reign of Jeroboam.[1] Rehoboam's reign, after the retirement of Sheshonk, was uneventful. He continued to occupy the throne for twelve more years, and during this time was engaged in frequent, if not in continual, hostilities with Jeroboam (1 Kings xiv. 30 ; 2 Chron. xii. 15), but no important results followed, and it can only be said that the two kingdoms maintained their relative positions. In military strength they were not ill-matched, since, if Israel could bring more men into the field, the narrower limits of Judah made her able to concentrate her troops more rapidly, while the personal qualities of the men of Judah and Benjamin placed them in the front rank of Hebrew warriors. Thus, notwithstanding the invasion of Sheshonk, and the loss of strength which it must have occasioned, the southern kingdom held its ground firmly, though it can scarcely have continued to maintain any hold over the alien states upon its borders, such as Philistia and Edom, which David had subjugated, but which, probably from the date of Sheshonk's invasion, recovered their independence.[2]

The domestic relations of Rehoboam were modelled on those of his father, but without reaching the same excess of Oriental luxury and self-indulgence. The number of his wives was eighteen, of his concubines either sixty or thirty.[3] Three of

[1] See below, page 23.

[2] So Ewald, "History of Israel," vol. iv. pp. 46, 47.

[3] The present text of Chronicles (2 Chron. xi. 21) has "sixty," but Josephus ("Ant. Jud." viii. 10, § 1) gives the number as "thirty."

his wives were his near relations, Abihail, the daughter of Eliab
David's elder brother ; Mahalath, his first cousin, the daughter
of Jerimoth, Solomon's brother ; and Maachah, another cousin,
the daughter or grand-daughter of Absalom.[1] Abihail and
Maachah bore him, each of them, four sons, while his other
wives raised the number of his sons to twenty-eight, and his
daughters are said to have been sixty (2 Chron. xi. 21). His
favourite wife was Absalom's granddaughter, Maachah, whose
son, Abijah, succeeded him on the throne ; she was probably of
royal birth on both sides, descended from her namesake,
Maachah (2 Sam. iii. 3), daughter of Talmai, king of Geshur.

Rehoboam, remembering the dreariness of his own idle youth,
was careful to give his sons active employment. As they grew
to manhood, he dispersed them among the various provincial
towns, assigning to each a charge, and at the same time an establishment. The writer of Chronicles considers that, in so doing,
he acted wisely (2 Chron. xi. 23). The system which he adopted
was certainly calculated to prevent, or minimise, jealousies
among the princes, and to benefit their characters by giving
them duties to perform, instead of making them idle hangers-
on upon a Court.

Maachah survived her husband, and was Queen-mother during
the next two reigns.[2] Her influence over the kingdom was
altogether for evil, and we may, perhaps, ascribe much of the
wrong conduct of Rehoboam to the sway which she exercised
over him. Her leanings were altogether towards idolatry.
Rehoboam's character was weak and irresolute. He seems to
have had warm affections, and to have been capable of making
good resolutions under good advice (2 Chron. xi. 4 ; xii. 6) ; but
he had no stability of purpose, and his last counsellor generally
determined his actions. We are told, that "he did evil, because
he fixed not his heart to seek the Lord" (ibid. xii. 14). There
was no fixity about him ; it might have been said of him with
justice, as it was said of Reuben (Gen. xlix. 4), "unstable as
water, thou shalt not excel." Now a suppliant at the feet of
Jehovah, anon an encourager of the people in the worst forms
of idolatry (1 Kings xiv. 22-24 ; 2 Chron. xii. 1), now submitting

---

[1] She is called the daughter of Absalom in 1 Kings xv. 2, 10, and in 2
Chron. xi. 20, but in 2 Chron. xiii. 2 her designation is "Michaiah, the
daughter of Uriel of Gibeah." Probably Uriel had married an actual
daughter of Absalom's.   [2] 1 Kings xv. 2, 10, 13 ; 2 Chron. xv. 16.

himself to Shemaiah's influence, presently letting Maachah rule his conduct and his policy, he failed to set either himself or his people in any good way, and is in a great measure answerable for the halting and hesitating line pursued by the kingdom of Judah through the four centuries of its existence, a line fluctuating between good and evil, between religion and irreligion, gradually deteriorating, and at length terminating in a practical apostasy (2 Chron. xxxvi. 14–16).

CHAPTER II

JEROBOAM.

Jeroboam's parentage and birthplace—His appointment to a high post by Solomon—Prophecy made to him by Ahijah the Shilonite—His life sought by Solomon—His flight into Egypt—Condition of Egypt—Return of Jeroboam to Palestine—He is made king of the Ten Tribes—Dangers of his position—War threatened by Rehoboam averted—Danger of a desire for reunion met by Jeroboam's religious changes—Consequent exodus of the Levites and others—Aid rendered to Jeroboam by Shishak—Jeroboam warned by a man of God at Bethel—Punished by the death of a favourite son—Defeated by Abijam—His death—Estimate of his religious policy.

JEROBOAM, the son of Nebat and Zeruah, who outlived her husband, was "an Ephrathite (or Ephraimite) of Zereda" (1 Kings xi. 26), and was born a subject of King Solomon. His native place, Zereda, lay probably in the valley of the Jordan, and is reasonably identified with Zeredathah, the town or village where Solomon established the foundries for the great works in bronze, which Hiram undertook to cast for the Temple. Nebat, Jeroboam's father, seems to have died while Jeroboam was still a child, and he was brought up by his mother, "a widow woman," of whom nothing more is told us.[1]   He belonged to the middle ranks of society, and, having reached the full vigour of his youth, was among the men of Ephraim impressed by Solomon to aid in constructing the fortifications by which he was seeking to render Jerusalem an impregnable fortress. It has been surmised that he was "among the lower overseers of

[1] The author of the "Additions to 1 Kings xii." makes Zeruah, whom he calls Sarira, a woman of bad character (γυνὴ πόρνη); but this is probably a Jewish calumny.

the labourers;"[1] but the Scripture narrative gives no indication of this; and it is most natural to regard him as merely one of the many "young Ephraimites employed on the works."[2] It was as such that, on one occasion, when Solomon was inspecting the progress of the fortification of Millo, which was situated between the Temple hill and the modern Zion, he specially attracted the attention of the monarch, who, noting his vigour and activity, promoted him to the position of head-overseer over the services due to the crown from the house of Joseph. This was a vast rise in the social scale, and gave him a position equal to that of almost any other subject. Whether there is any truth in the statement, that he began at once to affect an almost regal state, maintained a retinue of three hundred chariots, and secretly aspired to the sovereignty,[3] is uncertain. The Septuagint "Additions" to the story of Jeroboam do not stand the test of a searching criticism, and if they have been accepted by some writers, as Ewald and Dean Stanley,[4] it is rather because they are picturesque and striking, than because they are entitled to be regarded as of any historical value. We *know* nothing of Jeroboam's life between his promotion by Solomon and his flight into Egypt, except that, apparently without any scheming of his own, he was the subject of a prophetical announcement, which provoked the anger of Solomon, and led him to seek the life of his too distinguished servant and subject (1 Kings xi. 40).

Ahijah the Shilonite was a prophet of repute under Solomon, who had succeeded to the position previously held by Nathan, and was Court Historiographer during Solomon's later years (2 Chron. ix. 29). Shiloh, his native town, was one of the principal cities of Ephraim; and he may have been personally acquainted with his brother Ephraimite, whom Solomon had so greatly distinguished. At any rate, as a member of the Court, he would be familiar with Jeroboam's habits and person. Having, therefore, received from God a commission to invest

[1] Ewald, "History of Israel," vol. iii. p. 304.

[2] Stanley, "Lectures on the Jewish Church," vol. ii. p. 232.

[3] See the Septuagint "Additions," and on their value, or rather want of value, see the author's note in the "Speaker's Commentary," vol. ii. pp. 561, 562.

[4] Ewald, "History of Israel," vol. iii. pp. 304-313: Stanley, "Lectures on the Jewish Church," vol. ii. pp. 232-235.

the young Ephraimite with a prospective sovereignty over ten of the twelve tribes, he took an opportunity of waylaying him on one of his numerous departures from Jerusalem in a place where they two would be alone. Here he made his meaning clear, and impressed it indelibly on the mind of his companion. by accompanying his words with an "acted parable," according to a practice not uncommon among sages and teachers in the East.[1] Jeroboam, proud of his high office, had recently clad himself in a new cloak or robe. Ahijah caught hold of this, and stripping it off him tore it into twelve fragments, one for each tribe, and retaining two, gave him the other ten, accompanying his gift with these words : "Take thou ten pieces ; for thus saith Jehovah, the God of Israel, Behold, I will rend the kingdom out of the hand of Solomon, and will give ten tribes to thee : but he shall have one tribe for My servant David's sake, and for Jerusalem's sake, the city which I have chosen out of all the tribes of Israel : because that they have forsaken Me, and have worshipped Ashtoreth the goddess of the Zidonians, Chemosh the god of the Moabites, and Milcom the god of the children of Ammon, and have not walked in My ways, to do that which is right in Mine eyes, and to keep My statutes and My judgments: as did David his father. Howbeit I will not take the whole kingdom out of his hand, but I will make him prince all the days of his life for David My servant's sake, whom I chose because he kept My commandments and My statutes : but I will take the kingdom out of his son's hand, and will give it unto thee—even ten tribes. And unto his son will I give one tribe, that David My servant may have a light always before Me in Jerusalem, the city which I have chosen to put My name there. And I will take thee, and thou shalt reign according to all that thy soul desireth, and shalt be king over Israel. And it shall be, if thou wilt hearken unto all that I command thee, and wilt walk in My ways, and do that which is right in My sight, to keep My statutes and My commandments, as David My servant did : that I will be with thee, and build thee a sure house, as I built for David, and will give Israel unto thee. And I will for this afflict the seed of David, but not for ever " (1 Kings xi. 31–39.)

It had been before this time prophesied to Solomon, though

[1] Compare Isa. xx. 2–4 ; Jer. xiii. 1–11, xix. 1–10, xxvii. 3–11 ; Ezek. iii 1–3, iv. 1, v. 1, &c.

by what prophet we cannot say,[1] that at his death his kingdom would be rent in twain, and the greater portion given to one of his "servants," one tribe only being reserved for his son (1 Kings xi. 11–13). But he had hitherto not known to whom the prophecy pointed, or which of his servants was to be especially feared. Now, however—for it was not long before the transaction between Jeroboam and Ahijah got wind, either from Jeroboam not keeping the secret or from the meeting having been observed—he found that the fated enemy of his house was the man whom he had so greatly favoured, whom he had raised from a lowly station, and set among the princes of the people. Instantly his anger was inflamed. What? Jeroboam the traitor who would rob his son! He had, then, warmed a serpent in his bosom : he had given the high position which could alone render successful treason possible to the very man who was about to use that high position to humiliate and despoil the best beloved of all his offspring. We need not wonder that, with the unpitying sternness of an Oriental despot, he at once formed the determination of taking his enemy's life (ibid. ver. 40). It is not clear, however, that Jeroboam had been guilty of any overt act of rebellion or treason. One modern writer indeed, tells us that he "openly rose against Solomon's rule," took arms, and with a band of adherents began a " contest which was not a very easy one " to put down.[2] But no Biblical writer, not even the author of the Septuagint "Additions," lends any support to this view. Jeroboam, it is probable, had done nothing more than talk of his fine prospects among his friends and followers. But in the East this is quite enough to draw down upon a subject's head the vengeance of his sovereign, and Solomon would not be shocking his people's sense of justice in seeking under the circumstances to kill Jeroboam. That he did so is plainly stated. He did not "banish Jeroboam to Egypt," as has been alleged ;[3] but formed a determination to put him to death—a determination which, coming to Jeroboam's knowledge, induced him to fly the country, and become a refugee in the foreign land which was best able to afford him protection.

[1] The assumption that Ahijah was the prophet who delivered to Solomon the message recorded in 1 Kings xi. 11–13 (Ewald, " History of Israel," vol. iii. p. 304) is one of those mere conjectures which the German writer inserts on his own sole authority into the region of historical facts.

[2] Ewald, vol. iii. p. 305.

[3] Stanley, "Lectures on the Jewish Church," vol. ii. p. 233.

Egypt, under the twentieth and twenty-first dynasties, had declined from her high estate, and was no longer the power which she had shown herself in the time of the Thothmeses and the Ramessides. Her Asiatic influence had dwindled and disappeared, and when, under the twenty-first dynasty, Solomon proposed to ally himself with a princess of the reigning house the Egyptian sovereign of the time did not regard the marriage as one of disparity. He readily acquiesced in the offer of the Israelite king, and gave his daughter a dowry suitable to her rank (1 Kings ix. 16), thus indicating his full consent to the match and approval of it. But Egypt was still, even under the twenty-first dynasty, the most powerful of all the states that bordered upon Palestine. And when Sheshonk, the founder of the twenty-second dynasty, came to the throne, she began once more, under his guidance and direction, to be something more than this. She resumed the ambitious projects which had been laid aside for three centuries, and at the same time the taste for magnificence and display which had characterized the Rames-side monarchs. Sheshonk adorned the cities of Thebes, Memphis, and Bubastis with architectural works. He held his Court commonly either at Bubastis or at Thebes, and set himself to rival the glories of other days. Egypt had from a remote antiquity been in the habit of receiving with open arms refugees from abroad; and when Jeroboam, threatened with death by his own sovereign, sought an asylum in the valley of the Nile, Sheshonk acted in accordance with Egyptian traditions in receiving him and giving him shelter. It may well be that in course of time the Israelite exile rose in his favour, and acquired an influence over him; but the doubtful tale of his having given Jeroboam an Egyptian princess in marriage seems scarcely entitled to our acceptance.[1]

In his sojourn at the Egyptian Court, which appears to have been prolonged for some years, Jeroboam would learn many new things. He would become familiar with a religion imposing by its antiquity, striking in many of its manifestations, and regarded by those who presided over it as not incompatible with a profound conviction of the truth of monotheism. He would observe the working of a firm and stable government, to

---

[1] See the Septuagint "Additions." The tale probably originated in what is related (1 Kings xi. 19) of Hadad; but it is most unlikely that, if Jeroboam had been similarly favoured, the writer of Kings would not have mentioned it.

which revolution was unknown, and which owed its permanency in a great measure to its connection with religion, and to the support lent it by a numerous and well-organized hierarchy. He would obtain a knowledge of the great military strength possessed by a kingdom which had maintained a large standing army for centuries, an army inheriting traditions of discipline, honour, and military spirit. He would contract a taste for architectural display, and an imposing religious ceremonial. It is not mere fancy which sees in Jeroboam's Egyptian sojourn the key to many of those changes which he introduced, at a later date, into the polity and worship of Israel.[1]

Occupied in observing Egyptian institutions, and in obtaining, so far as he possibly could, influence over the Egyptian monarch, Jeroboam passed, as we have said, some years. The time for a fresh movement came only when news reached Egypt of the death of Solomon, and simultaneously of a desire on the part of his friends in Palestine that Jeroboam should return to his native land, and be ready at hand in case the course of events should be such as to call for his intervention.

Jeroboam responded to the call. When the tribes assembled at Shechem to assist in the coronation of Rehoboam, but hoping at the same time to obtain a redress of grievances at the hands of the new monarch, Jeroboam was there, and acted apparently as the spokesman of the malcontents (1 Kings xii. 3). When the disappointing answer was given to the demands preferred, he was again present (ibid. ver. 12) ; and it is reasonable to suppose that either from himself or his confederates emanated the cry which was immediately raised—" To your tents, O Israel !" The rebellion broke out at once— Adoniram was murdered—and the Ten Tribes in a formal assembly (ibid. ver. 20) made Jeroboam their king. The sovereignty over Israel, as distinct from Judah, passed once more to Ephraim, and the blessing of Moses upon Joseph (Deut. xxxiii. 13-17) seemed to obtain a fresh accomplishment.

But Jeroboam, though he had now attained the object of his ambitious aims, had not thereby secured himself a bed of roses. " Uneasy lies the head that wears a crown " is true of most sovereigns, and especially of usurpers. The immediate danger against which he had to prepare was war. Legitimate monarchs do not commonly allow themselves to be

[1] Compare Stanley, '' Lectures on the Jewish Church,'' vol. ii. p. 236.

despoiled of two-thirds of their territories without at least an
attempt to punish the spoiler, and Rehoboam's first thought on
hearing of the election of the son of Nebat to the Israelite
throne was to invade his kingdom with all the troops that he
could muster, and to see if he could not stamp out the rebellion
which he had wantonly provoked by his foolish menaces. But
the prophetical order came to Jeroboam's relief. Shemaiah,
the mouthpiece of the order in Judah, made common cause
with Ahijah, its mouthpiece in Israel, and, declaring the disruption of the kingdom of Solomon to have been God's doing,
forbade the prosecution of Rehoboam's enterprise—" Ye shall
not go up," he said, " nor fight against your brethren the
children of Israel : return every man to his house ; for this
thing is from God" (ibid. ver. 24). Rehoboam did not venture
to run counter to the prophet's word, and his subjects were
probably glad to be spared a struggle in which they had nothing
to gain, and might lose their liberties or their lives. This peril,
therefore, passed off for the time, but only to be succeeded by
another, which was more secret and more insidious.

The centre of the national worship had now for seventy years
been fixed at Jerusalem. Thither "the tribes had gone up,
even the tribes of the Lord, to testify unto Israel, to give
thanks unto the name of the Lord" (Psa. cxxii. 4). Frequent
pilgrimages to the Davidic sanctuary from all parts of the
Holy Land had become an essential element in the religious
life of the people ; and this was not likely to cease, because the
political unity of the people had been broken up, and statesmen
saw in continued friendly intercourse a danger to their policy
of separatism. The danger must be admitted. " If Jerusalem
continued to be the centre of religious union for the whole
nation, if the Levites from all Palestine went up in their turns
to conduct the Temple service, and if the people continued to
flock to the Holy Place three times a year, as the Law commanded them, there could not but have been great peril of a
reaction setting in, and a desire for reunion manifesting itself." [1]
Jeroboam's forecast of the future was scarcely exaggerated—
" If this people go up to do sacrifice in the house of the Lord
at Jerusalem, then shall the heart of this people turn again
unto their lord, even unto Rehoboam king of Judah, and they

[1] See note on 1 Kings xii. 26 in the " Speaker's Commentary," vol. ii. p.
559.

shall kill me, and go again to Rehoboam king of Judah " (1 Kings xii. 27). In a worldly point of view it was necessary to meet this difficulty. Some plan had to be devised whereby the tendency to resort to Jerusalem for purposes of worship should be checked, and the subjects of the northern kingdom should find their religious aspirations met and satisfied within their own borders. It was with these objects in view that Jeroboam " resolved on creating two new seats of the national worship, which should rival the great temple of the rival dynasty." *
The policy which he adopted was "precisely that of Abd-er-Rahman, caliph of Spain, when he arrested the movement of his subjects to Mecca, by the erection of the holy place of the Zeca at Cordova ; and of Abd-el-Malik when he built the Dome of the Rock at Jerusalem because of his quarrel with the authorities at Mecca." ² The object was to provide sanctuaries within his own kingdom, at which his people would be content to pay their vows, without going further and swelling the crowd of worshippers at an alien shrine in a foreign country. Jeroboam fixed on Dan and Bethel as his two holy sites—on Bethel as possessing the prestige of an ancient patriarchal sanctuary, revered from a most remote antiquity,³ and as convenient for his southern subjects ; on Dan, as probably also the seat of a very early worship,⁴ and as suitable for his subjects in the north. At both places he erected sacred buildings of some architectural pretensions, rivals to the Temple on Mount Zion, and at both he established a ritual and ceremonies, designed as substitutes for the ritual and ceremonies which David and Solomon had under Divine guidance instituted and established at Jerusalem.

But he did not stop here. Distrustful of the attractions which his new sanctuaries would offer if they presented to the worshipper nothing new or exciting, but were mere pale and colourless repetitions of the Jerusalem model, he resolved on an innovation which should at once markedly differentiate his worship from that of the old orthodoxy, be capable of being represented as having its roots in the past, and fall in with the popular craving after a more sensuous religion than pure

---

* Stanley, "Lectures on the Jewish Church," vol. ii. p. 236. ² Ibid.
³ See Gen. xxviii. 19 ; xxxv. 14, 15.
⁴ See Judg. xviii. 29-31, and compare the remarks of Mr. Grove in Smith's "Dictionary of the Bible," vol. i. p. 386.

Mosaism, which had manifested itself almost throughout the whole course of the people's history, but had hitherto for the most part been sternly repressed by the leading spirits of the nation. It was probably his Egyptian sojourn which determined the special form of the sensuism whereto he had recourse. Bulls were worshipped as incarnations of deity both at Memphis and at Heliopolis ; [1] and, as at the time of the Exodus the Bull form presented itself most obviously to Aaron, when a visible god was wanted (Exod. xxxii. 4), so now to Jeroboam there recurred the same idea. Jeroboam even openly connected the two occasions by his address, recorded in 1 Kings xii. 28— " Behold thy gods, O Israel, which brought thee up out of the land of Egypt." He placed in his sanctuaries of Dan and Bethel two golden images of Bull-calves, as symbols of the Divine Presence, which watched over the land from one extremity to the other. These images very soon became the objects of an idolatrous worship (ibid. ver. 30) ; the creature superseded the creator in men's thoughts ; and, while bowing down to " the calves of Beth-aven " (Hos. x. 5), Israel " forgot his Maker " (ibid. viii. 14).

It was not to be expected that the Levites would approve these proceedings, or consent to take a part in the degraded worship which was thus substituted in the northern kingdom for the true religion of Jehovah. They began probably at once to " leave their suburbs and their possessions," and to " resort " to the southern kingdom (2 Chron. xi. 13, 14) in large numbers. Jeroboam would no doubt have gladly kept them in their places if they would have consented to throw in their lot with him, and to officiate in his idol-polluted temples. But this they would not do.[2] He therefore after a time determined to depose from office the whole sacerdotal order, as constituted by the Mosaic Law, and to create for his kingdom an entirely new priesthood, which should be of no particular tribe, and should be consecrated by rites of his own devising (2 Chron. xiii. 9). When it is said that Jeroboam made his new priests " from the ends " (מִקְצוֹת) " of the people," we are not to understand that he preferred

---

[1] See the author's " History of Ancient Egypt," vol. i. pp. 413-415.

[2] There was perhaps an exception in the case of the priests attached to the calf-worship at Dan, who seem to have been Gershomites, descended from Moses. (See Judg. xviii. 30, and compare Lord A. Hervey's note on the passage in the " Speaker's Commentary," vol. ii. p. 209.)

to give the office to men of low condition, but only that he took his priests from all classes, consecrating every one who applied, provided that they could furnish the necessary offering of one bull and seven rams (ibid.). This requirement would necessarily exclude the very poor. To his new order Jeroboam probably gave the consecrated lands and the right of tithes which the Levites had previously enjoyed, thus reducing the bulk of the old sacerdotal body to absolute penury. A fresh impetus was in this way given to the exodus which had already begun ; and the example of their sacerdotal guides being followed by many of the more godly among the Israelites (2 Chron. xi. 16), Jeroboam found the number of his own subjects continually diminishing, and the number of his rival's subjects increasing, through an emigration which it was almost impossible for him to stop, or even to confine within moderate limits by his own unassisted efforts.

It seems to have been under these circumstances that the Israelite monarch called in the aid of his powerful ally and protector, the Egyptian Pharaoh, Sheshonk. We may suppose his representations of his danger made and the expedition against Judah determined on, in the fourth year of the divided monarchy, though it was not until the fifth year (1 Kings xiv. 25 ; 2 Chron. xii. 2) that the great army of his ally moved to his assistance. Then, however, a severe chastisement was inflicted on the southern kingdom, and Jeroboam was effectually relieved from the fears which had disquieted him. Judah passed under a cloud, and with difficulty maintained her equilibrium with the northern kingdom. Jeroboam was relieved by the later operations of Sheshonk's army from many troublesome foes, both internal and external.[1] At the same time, he probably felt that it was a dangerous thing that he had done, to call in the aid of so powerful a monarch for the settlement of his private and almost domestic quarrels. One experience of the peril was enough for him, and Egypt's aid was never again invoked, until

---

[1] See Mr. R. S. Poole's analysis of the Inscription of Sheshonk at Karnac ("Dict. of the Bible," vol. iii. pp. 1290-1294), whereby it appears that the expedition was directed not only against the dominions of Rehoboam, but also against a number of Levitical and Canaanite cities within the territory of Jeroboam himself, and further against certain Arab tribes of the vicinity. The inference is, that Jeroboam obtained Sheshonk's aid in reducing Israelite cities that had declined to submit to him, and also in chastising Arab tribes on his borders which had given him trouble.

the northern kingdom found itself in its death throes.[1] During the remainder of Rehoboam's reign, though hostilities continued without interruption between Israel and Judah (1 Kings xiv. 30), there was no further intervention of a third power in the quarrel.

Meanwhile, however, Jeroboam found the course of affairs in his own kingdom not free from trouble. On one occasion[2] he was officiating as priest at the altar which he had set up in Bethel, on the day which he had appointed in the eighth month to be at once the Israelite Feast of Tabernacles and the Feast of the Dedication, when suddenly an unnamed prophet, who had come out of Judah,[3] stood before him, and denounced God's wrath upon his religious innovations. "O altar, altar, altar," he exclaimed, "thus saith the Lord, Behold a child shall be born unto the house of David, Josiah by name,[4] and upon thee shall he offer the priests of the high places that burn incense upon thee, and men's bones shall be burnt upon thee. And this is the sign that the Lord hath spoken this : Behold, the altar shall be rent, and the ashes that are upon it shall be poured out" (1 Kings xiii. 1–3). Instantly the sign took effect— the altar was split in twain, and the ashes upon it fell to the ground ; while Jeroboam, furious at the interruption, from his station on the altar's ledge stretched out his hand against the intruder, threatening him and ordering his arrest (ibid. ver. 4). But the stretched-out hand and arm stiffened, and could not be withdrawn ; and the king found himself a cripple, maimed and disfigured, an object that would attract every eye, and at the same time reduced personally to impotence. Thus humiliated before his assembled subjects, he lost all his pride, and stooped to intreat the prophet's intercession with God on his behalf. His prayer was granted, and his hand and arm restored ; but the wound which his pride had received could not easily have

[1] See Kings xvii. 4.

[2] Some suppose that it was on the actual day of the dedication ; but this is not so stated.

[3] Dean Stanley argues that the prophet was Iddo (" Lectures on the Jewish Church," vol. ii. p. 237) ; but this is impossible, since he died on the day when he gave his warning, whereas Iddo outlived Jeroboam, and wrote an account of the reign of Ahijah (2 Chron. xiii. 22).

[4] These words have perhaps crept in from the margin. (See the author's note on the passage in the " Speaker's Commentary," vol. ii. p. 563.)

been healed, and the insult offered to the new worship must have long remained in the minds of the worshippers.

Nevertheless, the warning, intended to turn the misguided king from his wrong-doing, was lost upon him. "After this thing Jeroboam returned not from his evil way, but made again priests of the high places from the ends of the people; whosoever would he consecrated him, and he became one of the priests of the high places" (1 Kings xiii. 33). In fact, he persisted in the course which he had marked out for himself, maintained the new altars, and the new shrines, and the self-invented feasts, and rites, and the idolatrous worship, and the unauthorized priests, and the entire system, whereof he had been the originator.

Hereupon he was visited, not in warning, but in judgment. One of his sons, a child, a favourite child, as it would seem, was suddenly smitten with a dangerous sickness. The king was greatly alarmed, and intensely anxious to know what would be the result. One way only of learning the future seemed possible. Ahijah, the Shilonite, the great prophet of the northern kingdom, was still living, though very aged and infirm, at Shiloh, and might at any rate be consulted, and would perhaps be allowed to reveal the future. Jeroboam resolved to consult him. But he feared to do so openly, lest he should bring down upon himself the denunciation of woe which he knew that he deserved. He therefore caused his wife to disguise herself as a poor country woman, and sent her to Shiloh to make inquiry of the dim-sighted prophet. But the disguise proved of no avail. Ahijah, warned beforehand who his visitor would be, made the denunciation which Jeroboam feared. The child, he said, would die as the queen set foot on her palace threshold; and not only so, but the whole house of Jeroboam would, in a little time, be cut off. God had exalted Jeroboam, and made him prince over his people, and rent the kingdom away from the house of David, and given it to him; but he had not followed the example of David : on the contrary, he had done evil above all those who had preceded him, and had made other gods and molten images, and had provoked Jehovah to anger and cast him behind his back. Therefore woe was denounced against Jeroboam, and against his house. God would bring evil against his house, and cut it off, and take away the remnant of it, *as a man taketh away dung*. Him that died of

Jeroboam in the city should the dogs eat, and him that died in the field shoulds the fowls of the air eat, for the mouth of the Lord had spoken it (1 Kings xiv. 7-11). The wife returned to her royal husband with this awful message ; and, as she put her foot upon the threshold of the palace, in exact accordance with the words of the prophet, her child died (ibid. ver. 17).

Still Jeroboam repented not, but persisted in his evil courses. He had maintained himself for seventeen years on the throne of Israel, when in the sister kingdom his rival, Rehoboam, died, and was succeeded by his son, Abijam, a warlike prince. Abijam invaded the Israelite territory with a large army, and inflicted a severe defeat on the army of Jeroboam, which was followed by the conquest of three cities, Bethel, Jeshanah, and Ephraim, with their territories (2 Chron. xiii. 3-19). The conquest of Bethel, however, cannot have been long maintained ; and altogether it may be doubted whether the relative position of the two kingdoms was much altered by Abijam's victory.[1] It was, however, a fresh blow to Jeroboam, destroying his prestige, and perhaps hastening his death, which took place within the space of three or four years afterwards, in the twenty-second year after his accession to the throne (1 Kings xiv. 20).

The Scriptural narrative brands Jeroboam as "the man who made Israel to sin."[2] He is not condemned for his ambition, for his self-seeking, or for his rebellion against the house of David, but emphatically for his religious innovations. To himself no doubt they seemed masterpieces of worldly policy. They suited the temper of his people ; they effectually secured the maintenance of his kingdom in a state of separation from that of Judah ; they remained in full vigour to the last days of the monarchy. But they had in them a root of bitterness, which proved fatal to the State. They were of human device ; they had no Divine sanction ; and they rested on falsity. The golden calves were doubtless intended as likenesses of the One True God. But to make a material image of the immaterial God is to give a false idea of God altogether (see Isa. xl. 18). And false ideas of God are fruitful of evil. As Dean Stanley

---

[1] The number in 2 Chron. xiii. 17 can scarcely be correct, even if we regard it as covering all who fell in the war. The loss of 500,000 men in a war lasting little more than two years between such petty states as Judah and Israel would be unexampled.

[2] 1 Kings xiv. 13, xv. 26, 30, 34, &c. ; 2 Kings xvii. 21.

says, "The mere fact of setting up such a likeness broke down the sacred awe which had hitherto marked the Divine Presence, and accustomed the minds of the Israelites to the very sin against which the new form was intended to be a safe-guard. From worshipping God under a false and unauthorized form, they gradually learnt to worship other gods altogether; and the venerable sanctuaries at Dan and Bethel prepared the way for the temples of Ashtoreth and Baal at Samaria and Jezreel ; and the religion of the kingdom of Israel sank lower even than that of the kingdom of Judah, against which it had revolted."[1]

Indeed, it may be questioned whether there were not from the first, in the religion set up by Jeroboam, that element of sensuality which was the worst feature of the ancient idolatries, and that which rendered them especially hateful to a pure and holy God. The worship of the Apis Bull was connected in Egypt with debasing sensualism, and when it was adopted by the Israelites in the wilderness, it was at once accompanied by unseemly and degrading origies (Exod. xxxii. 17–19 and 25). The Bull symbolized the generative power, and was chosen as a religious emblem on that account. We have no contemporary description of the festivals held at Dan and Bethel, but the terms in which the prophet Hosea speaks of them indicate that in his time they were scenes of the grossest profligacy. The calf-worship clearly "*paved the way* for those coarser and more cruel worships of nature, under the names of Baal and Ashtoreth, with all their abominations of consecrated child-sacrifices, and degrading or horrible sensuality."[2] Whether it did more, whether it actually contained the licentious element, is perhaps uncertain ; but at any rate to Jeroboam belongs the dark and evil fame of having founded his kingdom upon a false, a gross, and a sensuous system sure to blossom out into the viler and more disgusting forms of religious impurity.

[1] "Lectures on the Jewish Church," vol. ii. p. 239.
[2] Pusey, "Minor Prophets," p. 3.

CHAPTER III.

ABIJAH.

Abijah succeeds Rehoboam—Influence of his mother, Maachah — Early
assigned a high position by his father—His youthful experiences—His
successful campaign against Jeroboam—Shortness of his reign—Its
religious character.

OF Abijah,[1] the son and successor of Rehoboam, very little is
known. His mother was Maachah, the daughter, or probably
rather the grandaughter, of Absalom, and was Rehoboam's
principal and favourite wife. Her leanings were towards
idolatry (1 Kings xv. 13), and any influence which she may
have exercised upon her son is likely to have been towards
evil. Rehoboam's affection for Maachah caused him, not
only to designate Abijah, her eldest son (2 Chron. xi. 20), as his
successor, but to put him at a very early age in a position of
authority over his brethren (ibid. ver. 22), and to give him an
establishment on a scale of Oriental magnificence. Abijah,
we are told (2 Chron. xiii. 21), "waxed mighty, and married
fourteen wives, and begat twenty and two sons, and sixteen
daughters." He was probably of full age at his father's
accession, having grown to manhood during the later years of
Solomon, at a time when female influence of an evil kind was
predominant, and when there was little scope for manly virtues.
When his father came to the throne, there was an improvement
in his surroundings. He was given a position of responsibility,[2]
and no doubt bore a part in those wars which occupied so large

---

[1] Two forms of the name are given, Abijah and Abijam. The latter is
probably an intentional change (Lightfoot), resembling that of Beth-el into
Beth-aven and of Jehoahaz into Ahaz.

[2] 2 Chron. xi. 22.

a portion of the reign of Rehoboam. He must have been a witness of the invasion of Shishak (Sheshonk), have seen the environs of Jerusalem blackened by the Egyptian, Libyan, and Ethiopic host, and have shared in the fears and participated in the humiliation of his father (2 Chron. xii. 6–12). He is likely to have taken an active part in the protracted and desultory war which was waged between Rehoboam and Jeroboam "all their days" (1 Kings xiv. 30). When, upon the death of his father, he found himself king, he seems to have at once determined on a desperate effort to subjugate the kingdom of his neighbour, and so bring the schism between the Ten Tribes and the Two to an end. He "set the battle in array with an army of valiant men of war" (2 Chron. xiii. 3), who are estimated at 400,000, but was met by Jeroboam with twice the number, and brought into extreme danger. According to the writer of Chronicles, the Judæan king, like a Homeric hero, from a station upon Mount Zemaraim, a little south of Bethel, delivered a long address of rebuke and exhortation to the enemy, as the hosts faced each other ready for the conflict. He recalled the circumstances under which David was given the kingdom over *all* Israel (ibid. ver. 5); the rebellion of Jeroboam (ver. 6); the institution of the idolatry of the calves; the rejection of the legitimate priesthood and the institution of an illegitimate priesthood in its place (vers. 9, 10); and contrasting with Jeroboam's novelties the steadfast adherence of Judah to the rites and ordinances laid down in the Law[1] (vers. 10, 11); he made an appeal to the Israelites to desert the standard of Jeroboam, and "not fight against the Lord God of their fathers;" if they did so, he assured them they "would not prosper" (vers. 12, 13). It does not appear, however, that any effect was produced by this harangue. Jeroboam, wholly untouched by it, made the best disposition of his troops that was possible; his troops neither deserted, nor relaxed in their efforts, on account of the invitation addressed to them. Such was the Israelite preponderance in numbers, that it was found possible to send a large detachment to the rear of the Jewish camp, and then to make simultaneously a double attack, from the front and from behind (vers. 13, 14). The men of Judah resisted bravely, but

---

[1] It was natural, but scarcely honest, that he should make no allusion to the other worships allowed in Judah beside the worship of Jehovah, both by his father (1 Kings xiv. 22–24) and by himself (2 Chron. xiv. 3–5).

were in great distress, when the aid of God being implored with great earnestness amid the trumpet blasts of the priests, suddenly the tide of battle turned—Judah was successful, and Israel was put to flight (vers. 15, 16). A terrible carnage followed. According to the existing text, the slain on the part of the Israelites amounted to 500,000 men; but the numbers in our present Book of Chronicles are in many instances exaggerated, and it is generally agreed that the original reading in this place was probably not 500,000, but 50,000. Even this was an enormous loss; and we can well understand its having led on to the conquest of several Israelite towns, as Bethel, Jeshanah, and Ephraim, which passed for a time under the dominion of Judah (ver. 19). Abijah's triumph was, however, followed very shortly by his death. The length of his reign is said in one place to have been "three years" (1 Kings xv. 2); but as he ascended the throne in Jeroboam's eighteenth year (ibid. ver. 1), and was succeeded by Asa in the same king's twentieth year (ibid. ver. 9), the real duration of his reign cannot have much exceeded two years. He "walked," we are told, "in all the sins of his father, which he had done before him; and his heart was not perfect with the Lord his God, as the heart of David his father" (ibid. ver. 3). Though the formal worship of Jehovah at Jerusalem was not interfered with, but continued with all its legal and customary rites (2 Chron. xiii. 11), yet side by side with it numerous other worships were tolerated (2 Chron. xiv. 3), and the general condition of the nation in respect of religion was probably very much the same under Abijam as under Rehoboam. Certainly the high-place worship continued without interruption until the reign of Asa; and with this were combined image worship (ibid. ver. 5), altars to strange gods, and *ashêrah* worship, which was a form of the cult of Astarté. Abijah, in fact, would seem to have instituted no religious changes at all; but to have been content with the laxity which had prevailed during the reign of his father.

CHAPTER IV.

ASA.

Asa succeeds Abijah—Circumstances of his bringing up—Religious condition of Judah on his accession—Asa's reformation—Maachah, the
Queen-mother, degraded—Attempt made to uproot idolatry, not wholly
successful—Military organization—Invasion of Zerah, and its results
—Asa encouraged by Oded—His great festival and renewal of the
Covenant—His war with Baasha—Asa, rebuked by Jehu, son of Hanani,
imprisons him—Oppresses some of the people—Asa's general character—His illness and death.

ASA, the son of Abijah and grandson of Rehoboam, is a king
whose reign offers a strong contrast in almost every respect
to those of his father and grandfather. In length it exceeded every other Jewish reign excepting two.[1] In a military
point of view it was distinguished, and in the matter of religion
its character and tendency were directly opposite to that of the
two reigns immediately preceding it. Asa was brought up
under circumstances which seemed *à priori* most unfavourable
to the production of a pious, earnest, and zealous monarch.
Having Abijah for father, and Maachah for grandmother, and
directress of the Court, he must have been subjected to a host
of powerful influences drawing him towards the side of laxity
and idolatry, while it is difficult to see what counter-influences
could have been brought to bear upon him, or how he could
have escaped entanglement in the prevalent latitudinarian
vortex. The suggestion has been thrown out that he owed his
religious enlightenment to the efforts made by two prophets of
the period, Hanani and Azariah, the son of Oded,[2] faithful

---

[1] Those of Azariah, or Uzziah (52 years), and of Manassah (55 years).
See 2 Kings xv. 2 ; xxi. 1.

[2] Ewald, "History of Israel," vol. iv. p. 49, Eng. tr.

teachers of the true religion then resident at Jerusalem. But
very little is known of these prophets ; and there is certainly no
proof, that, during the impressible years of boyhood, and early
manhood, Asa was brought into contact with them. Still, the
"Schools of the Prophets" were undoubtedly at work under
Solomon, Rehoboam, and Abijah, labouring to counteract the
pernicious Court influence, and to impress on all, to whom they
could obtain access, the importance of maintaining a strict
observance of the ancient faith. Asa, if he did not come into
contact with Azariah or Hanani at the court of his father, is
almost sure to have come into contact with some persons, to
whom the modern laxity and latitudinarianism was detestable,
an "accursed thing," an "abomination." He had, beyond a
doubt, a good natural disposition ; and, while evil influences had
little effect upon him, such good influences as fell across his
path, strongly affected his mind, and moulded his character.
When he ascended the throne, probably at about the age
of twenty, he was already a determined adherent of the old
faith, and a stern opponent of the laxity, the idolatry, and the
heathenism, which had been tolerated or promoted by the
three preceding sovereigns.

He found the laxity and heathenism rampant. Everywhere
the "high places" attracted a worship which sufficed for most
men, and caused the Temple service at Jerusalem to be coldly
regarded and attended but by few. Jehovah was nominally
worshipped at these sites, but rather as a local than as a universal God, and with rites that were unauthorized, and perhaps
even tinged with heathenism. On some of the "high hills"
the cult of Baal and Astarté was openly practised ; "images"
or rather pillars, and "groves," or rather sacred trees, were set
up (1 Kings xiv. 23), and the lewd orgies of Phœnicia and Syria
were the favourite religious ceremonies of the worshippers.
The sacred groves and Temple precincts were the scenes both of
ordinary profligacy and of unnatural vices (ibid. ver. 24 ; comp.
ch. xv. 12), men's natural repugnance to such a degradation
being overcome by a supposed religious sanction.[1] Asa set himself against all these various forms of moral evil ; and if he did
not succeed altogether in suppressing the Jehovistic high-place
worship (1 Kings xv. 14), which the people would not give up,
at any rate he swept away the grosser forms of sensuous

[1] See Döllinger's "Jew and Gentile," vol i. pp. 425-431.

religion—the images, the phallic symbols of Baal, the Astarté emblems, the lewd rites, the companies of abandoned men and abandoned women attached to the chief sites of Baal and Astarté worship. His reformation was extensive, sweeping, so far as his intention and his will went, complete. In Ewald's words, "As far as he could, he removed from the kingdom all traces of the heathenism which had been either tolerated or promoted by the three preceding sovereigns." [1]

The first step towards the accomplishment of his designs, and, perhaps, the most difficult one, was the removal and degradation of the Queen-Mother. Maachah, the grand-daughter of Absalom, had been the leading spirit of the Court during two reigns. As his favourite wife, she had directed the religious policy of Rehoboam ; and as his mother, she had exercised a complete domination over his successor, her son, Abijah. A devotee of the Syro-Phœnician religion, she had established her own shrine of Astarté-worship in Jerusalem, and had erected in it an idolatrous emblem, probably of a sensuistic character (1 Kings xv. 13). Asa "destroyed this idol and burnt it by the brook Kidron." Probably he calcined the metal whereof it was made, and reducing the image to powder, cast the powder upon the waters of the brook Kidron, that the whole might be dispersed and lost. [2] Maachah herself he degraded from her lofty position, depriving her of all authority, and, perhaps, removing her from the Court over which she had so long exercised a baleful influence (1 Kings *l. s. c.* ; 2 Chron. xv. 16). He in this way got rid of a centre of religious corruption which, unless removed, would have vitiated all his efforts after reform, and have afforded a rallying point for the heathenizing party, against which it would have been most difficult to struggle.

Having thus set his own house in order, he proceeded, during the first ten years of his reign, which was a time of continuous peace (2 Chron. xiv. 1, 5), gradually to effect his reforms wherever he found it possible, through the length and breadth of the land. It is clear that he met with much opposition, but not very clear who were its leaders. The prophetical order must undoubtedly have been on his side ; [3] and the Levitical priesthood, which had flocked into the southern kingdom from all parts

[1] "History of Israel," vol. iv. p. 49, Eng. tr.
[2] Compare 2 Chron. xv. 16 with 2 Kings xxiii. 12
[3] See 2 Chron. xv. 1-7 ; xvi. 7.

of Israel during the reign of Jeroboam (2 Chron. xi. 14), would also lend him their aid. His chief difficulty must have been in overcoming local associations and prejudices, engrained by long habit into the hearts of the people, who were everywhere attached to their old provincial shrines and sanctuaries, hallowed to them from a remote antiquity, and endeared by a thousand tender memories. New rites were, comparatively speaking, easy to deal with—"he took away the altars of the strange gods, and brake down the images, and cut down the groves" (ibid. chap. xiv. 3)—but the old ancestral rites connected with the high-place worship would not be rooted out, and whatever steps might be taken by the monarch to destroy and remove and abolish, still the result was, that "the high places were not removed" (1 Kings xv. 14)—"the people offered and burnt incense yet in the high places" (ibid. xxii. 43). Worships which Asa viewed as "abominations" continued in many parts of Judah and Benjamin, as well as in the cities won by his father from Israel (2 Chron. xiii. 19 ; xv. 8), during the whole of the ten tranquil years which constitute the first period of his reign.

The religious reforms of Asa, though occupying so large a share of his attention, still did not entirely engross him, or prevent him from doing his duty as a sovereign in other respects. Particularly, he gave serious thought to the military position of his kingdom, which was without an ally, and surrounded on all sides by enemies. Egypt, his neighbour upon the south, was especially to be feared, as had been sufficiently proved by the expedition of Sheshonk. That prince was now dead ; but he had left his crown, and his ambitious projects, to descendants in the direct line,[1] and Asa seems to have felt that at any time an attack might come upon him from this quarter. Accordingly he made great efforts to place his little territory in a posture of defence. First of all, like Rehoboam (2 Chron xi. 5–11), he endeavoured to secure his frontier by carefully fortifying all the principal cities, which he strengthened with "walls and towers, gates and bars" (ibid. xiv. 7), to the best of his ability. Then, fully aware that "fenced cities"—"walls and towers" are of no avail without gallant defenders, he collected and organized an army, which is said to have numbered 580,000 men. More

---

[1] Sheshonk was succeeded by his son Osarkon I., and then by his grandson, Takelut I., who was the father of Osarkon II. The direct line can be traced for six generations.

than half of them were "men of Judah," well equipped with
spears and large shields; while the remainder were "men of
Benjamin," who carried small round targes, and were expert in
the use of the bow. The entire force was held in readiness to
meet attack, and was probably disposed chiefly in the frontier
towns which had been fortified with so much care. All this
was done during the tranquil period of Asa's reign, through the
wise foresight of the king, who knew that national defence is
far better organized when peril is remote than when immediate
danger threatens.

It was not very long before the prudence of these proceedings
became apparent. In the fifteenth year of Asa's reign Judæa
was suddenly invaded by "a huge host, with very many chariots
and horsemen" (2 Chron. xvi. 8), under the command of a
leader who is called "Zerah (or Zerakh [1]) the Ethiopian." The
number of the invading army is estimated at "a thousand
thousand" (ibid. xiv. 9), or a million of men. It was composed
mainly of Ethiopians and Libyans, and it fell upon Judæa on
the south or rather the south-west. There can be no reasonable
doubt that the army issued from Egypt, and was sent or led by an
Egyptian Pharaoh with the view of effecting conquests in South-
western Asia. It was a sequel to the expedition of Sheshonk.
As Sheshonk had attacked Rehoboam with an army chiefly
composed of mercenary soldiers, Ethiopians, Libyans, and Sukkiim (2 Chron. xii. 3), so now an army almost identically composed
(ibid. xvi. 8), was sent against Asa. It is impossible to determine
absolutely who was the leader. The Hebrew "Zerakh" may,
perhaps, represent the Egyptian "Usarkin" or "Osarkon," and
the expedition may have been conducted by Osarkon the Second
in person, as that against Rehoboam was conducted by Sheshonk. Or Zerah may have been an Ethiopian general, employed by the Egyptian Pharaoh to take the command of his
troops and attempt the subjugation of Judæa.[2] The march
appears to have lain along the usual coast route, by way of Gaza
and Ascalon. This route conducted to the valley of Zephathah
—the broad plain at the foot of the Judæan hills west of Zeîta

[1] The Hebrew form is זֶרַח, Zĕrakh, which the LXX. soften into Zaré.
The guttural ח may represent the Egyptian _k_.

[2] Some have seen in Zerah an independent Ethiopian prince sufficiently
powerful to march his troops through Egypt and wage war in Asia on his
own account; but the records of the twenty-second dynasty contain no
trace of such a condition of things.

and Marash (Mareshah). It was here that Asa met his enemy. From the high ground, whence he commanded a full view of the hostile army, after prayer to God (2 Chr. xiv. 11), he poured down gallant bands of free Jews and Benjamites upon the mercenary host opposed to him, which was at least double his strength ; and, after a short combat, gained a complete and decisive victory. The Ethiopians were smitten, and fled before Asa and before Judah (ibid. ver. 12) ; their host melted away, and rapidly withdrew beyond the borders of Judæa into the comparative desert south of Gaza, where was the Philistine city of Gerar, which gave a shelter to the shattered remnant. Asa pursued them up to the walls, conquered all the small towns in the neighbourhood of the city, captured a vast number of cattle, sheep, and camels (ibid. ver. 15), and returned with an immense booty to Jerusalem.

The victory had most important consequences. It put an end to Egyptian schemes of Asiatic conquest, if not for ever, at any rate for three centuries.[1] It relieved Judæa from all pressure on her southern frontier, and enabled her to turn her whole attention towards the north. It so weakened the Bubastite dynasty of the Sheshonks and Osarkons, that, within a short time, they lost their hold on large portions of Egypt. Rival dynasties arose. Disintegration set in. Soon the balance of power between Egypt and Ethiopia was shifted. The swart tribes of the south began by asserting their independence, and then proceeded to claim and exercise a sovereignty over their former masters. Napata and Meroe became the centres of African power, instead of Memphis and Thebes. Egypt grew friendly towards Judæa instead of hostile, and the Israelite kingdom learnt to lean upon the Pharaohs for support[2] instead of dreading their ambition.

On Asa's return to Jerusalem he was met and congratulated by a prophet. Azariah, the son of Oded (perhaps the same as Iddo[3]), by Divine direction, went out to meet him as he approached the city (2 Chron. xv. 2), and assured him and his people of God's favour, so long as they should continue His faithful servants. At the same time he exhorted them not to relax in their efforts against the enemies of true religion, but to

[1] Till the expedition of Neco, B.C. 609.
[2] 2 Kings xvii. 4, xviii. 24 ; Isa. xx. 5, 6, xxx. 2–7.
[3] In the Hebrew Oded and Iddo are almost identical.

be strong and determined (ibid. ver. 7). Asa seems upon this to have braced himself up to a fresh crusade against the " abominations," which he cast out now " from *all* the land of Judah and Benjamin," as well as from the cities which his father had taken from Israel. At the same time he " renewed the altar of the Lord " which stood before the great porch of the Temple, either because in the course of sixty-five years it had suffered some decay, or because sacrilegious hands had desecrated it.

Not long afterwards he held a great festival. The signal victory which he had gained over Zerah caused his fame to be spread abroad, and large numbers of Israelites from the northern kingdom quitted their homes, and emigrated into Judæa, preferring to cast in their lot with the portion of their nation which was able to exhibit such manifest proofs that the Lord their God was with them (2 Chron. xv. 9). Not only Simeonites, who from their geographical position could with difficulty maintain a connection with the rest of the Ten Tribes, but men of Ephraim and Manasseh, who constituted the very heart of the Secession, left the Israelite kingdom, and "fell to Judah in abundance" (ibid.), increasing at once the military strength, and the prestige, of the Judæan state. Asa thought it advisable to attach this fluctuating population, so far as the circumstances permitted, firmly to his own community and his own religion. He therefore proclaimed a feast for the third month of his fifteenth year, directly after Zerah had retired, and offered from the spoil which he had captured an immense sacrifice — no fewer than seven hundred oxen and seven thousand sheep— hecatombs on hecatombs—at the same time calling upon the nation, and the newly joined foreigners, to renew the covenant with Jehovah, and bind themselves by a vow, whereof the infraction should be punishable by death (ver. 13), " to seek the Lord God of their fathers with all their heart and with all their soul," and to be faithful henceforth under all circumstances to the true religion. Enthusiasm was deeply stirred. " They sware unto the Lord (Jehovah) with a loud voice, and with shouting, and with trumpets, and with cornets ; and all Judah rejoiced at the oath ; for they had sworn with all their heart, and sought him with their whole desire" (vers. 14, 15).

The emigration of his subjects into Judæa was highly displeasing to the reigning Israelite monarch, Baasha.[1] Border

---

[1] Baasha had ascended the throne of Israel in the third year of Asa (1 Kings xv. 22).

warfare had continued to prevail between the rival kingdoms
from the time of his accession (1 Kings xv. 16) ; but hitherto no
important expedition had been undertaken by either country
against the other since the days of Abijah (2 Chron. xiii. 3–20).
Now, however, Baasha thought it necessary to assume a more
aggressive attitude. Provoked by the continual movement of
his people across the frontier, he determined to erect a great
fortress upon his southern border, which should command the
entrance into Judæa, and effectually put a stop to the emigration
that was in progress. Having collected an army, he marched
southward, recovered his own cities of Bethel, Jeshanah, and
Ephraim,[1] and invading Judæa, seized on the important position
of Ramah (Er-Ram), on the high ground half-way between
Bethel and Jerusalem, and proceeded to fortify it (1 Kings xv.
17 ; 2 Chron. xvi. 1). The action was not purely defensive.
It effected the lodgment of a hostile force in Judaea itself ; it
was a menace to Jerusalem. Asa would seem to have fully
appreciated the gravity of the danger. He saw that the enemy
must be dislodged, and that speedily, but distrusted his own
ability, if he were unaided, to dislodge him from the strong position. He therefore called in to his assistance the Syrian king,
Benhadad, of Damascus, the most powerful monarch in the
region between Egypt and the Euphrates, purchasing his friendship by the gift of such treasures as had accumulated in the
Temple since it was stripped to gratify the greed of Sheshonk
(1 Kings xv. 18 ; 2 Chron. xvi. 2). Benhadad, whose interest
it was to trim the balance between Israel and Judah, and to
prevent either kingdom from becoming too powerful, readily
responded to the appeal, and, invading the Israelite kingdom
with a large force, subdued the whole of the northern extremity
of the dominions of Baasha, on both sides cf the sources of the
Jordan (1 Kings xv. 20). It was understood that his invasion
was made for the benefit of Asa, and Baasha found it necessary
to desist from his Judæan enterprise, and withdraw his troops
within his own frontier, in order to content the Syrian king ;
who thereupon retired from the territory of Israel and gave
Baasha no more trouble (ibid. ver. 21 ; 2 Chron. xvi. 5). Asa,
finding that Baasha's troops were withdrawn, "raised a levy of
the whole nation for the destruction of the works" which Baasha

[1] This is not stated ; but it seems to be a necessary preliminary to the
occupation of Ramah.

had commenced, and, occupying Ramah, tore down the constructions of his adversary, and " employed the stores of stone and timber which thus fell into his hands in fortifying the two adjacent cities of Geba and Mizpah against a repetition of the inroads of the king of the Ten Tribes. He further took the opportunity to provide Mizpah with a plentiful supply of water in case of a siege ; and it was at this time that the great well was constructed in it, which gained such a melancholy celebrity in the days of Jeremiah " [1] (Jer. xii. 7–9).

On his return from this triumphant progress, which probably seemed to him almost as glorious as the Ethiopic war, Asa was confronted by a second prophet, one " Jehu, the son of Hanani," who rebuked him for his want of faith in calling Benhadad to his aid, instead of simply trusting in the Lord, and told him that " he had done foolishly " (2 Chron. xvi. 9). It is not surprising that the king was enraged at the prophet's boldness. Rebuke is always an offence to the great ones of the earth, and especially when it is thought to be unprovoked and undeserved. Asa, no doubt, was pluming himself on his own wisdom and discretion. He had gained his end without it costing him a single drop of Jewish blood. At a small expenditure of gold and silver he had got his adversary chastised by a neighbouring monarch, and had then recovered his territory without needing to strike a blow. What a triumph of kingcraft and statesman-like sagacity over the clumsiness of brute force ! What a gain tó have not only foiled, but despoiled, his adversary, to have turned the very stones and timber of the intended Israelite advanced post into additional strength for Jewish defences ! But from the prophetical standpoint the whole aspect of the affair was different. Asa, Jehu considered, had shown distrust of God. He had put himself under obligations to a heathen king. He had given the sanction of his example to the practice of calling in foreigners to decide the internal quarrels of God's people. He had thus acted both wickedly and foolishly. But the king did not see things in this light. He thought the prophet had been guilty of great presumption in condemning a policy which had been justified by its success. He was angry because the rebuke was delivered openly, and because it caused a certain amount of dissatisfaction with his conduct among the people (2 Chron. xvii. 10). He therefore had Jehu arrested and thrown

[1] Ewald, "History of Israel," vol. iv. p. 35, Eng. tr.

into prison. From the time of the establishment of the monarchy there had frequently been a certain degree of friction and
struggle between the royal and the prophetical authority,[1] but
never as yet had a king ventured on visiting a prophet with
punishment.[2] It is a considerable blot on Asa's character, that
he set the example of a persecution which ultimately proceeded
to the extremest lengths, and which, more than anything else,
brought down the vengeance of God upon His chosen people.[3]

It was, no doubt, in connection with the prophet's rebuke, and
the dissatisfaction which it occasioned, that Asa, about this same
time "oppressed some of the people" (2 Chron. xvii. 10). How
far his severities extended we are not told ; but it cannot be
denied, that towards the close of his reign this generally pious
prince tarnished, to some extent, the excellent character he had
previously acquired, by acts indicative of a weakening of faith,
and a failure of self-control. "To his own master each man
must stand or fall" (Rom. xiv. 4) ; and God doubtless balanced
Asa's long years of piety and faithfulness against his weaknesses
and shortcomings towards the close of his life. His countrymen showed towards him a fair and equitable spirit. The
general character which he left behind him among his contemporaries was that of a brave, warlike, and pious prince, one who
"did right in the eyes of the Lord, as did David his father"
(1 Kings xv. 11), and whose "heart was perfect all his days"
(2 Chron. xv. 17). His faults and "follies" were condoned in
consideration of his earnest desire to do God's will, and his
persistence in the championship of true religion. It was
thought a high eulogy on Jehoshaphat, his son, to say that "he
walked in all the way of Asa his father ; he turned not aside
from it, doing that which was right in the sight of the Lord"
(1 Kings xxii. 43), and it was deemed right to bury the good
king with great solemnity, and with every circumstance of
honour, in the tomb which he had prepared for himself in the
city of David (2 Chron. xvi. 14), adjacent to the sepulchres of
his fathers (1 Kings xv. 24).

---

[1] Compare 1 Sam. xv. 14-29 ; 2 Sam. xii. 1-14, xxiv. 11-17 ; 1 Kings
xi. 29-39, xii. 21-24.

[2] Saul's vengeance on Ahimelech, and his companions fell upon the
priestly, not the prophetical, order (see 1 Sam. xxii. 11-19).

[3] See 2 Kings xxi. 16, xxiv. 4 ; 2 Chron. xxxvi. 16 ; Jer. li. 30, xxvi.
15, 23 ; &c.

Asa was for some time before his death "diseased in his feet." The author of Chronicles makes it a reproach to him, that in his sickness "he sought not to the Lord, but to the physicians" (2 Chron. xvi. 12). We may conclude from this, that he placed an undue reliance on the aid to be obtained from man, and did not address his prayers for recovery with sufficient fervour to the heavenly throne; but moderns will scarcely blame him greatly for his recourse to ordinary human means of cure in preference to means involving something like the expectation of a miracle.

Asa "died in the one and fortieth year of his reign" (2 Chron. xvi. 13), at about the age of sixty.

CHAPTER V.

NADAB.

Want of materials for a biographical sketch of Nadab—He is murdered by
Baasha after a reign of a few months.

OF Nadab, the son and successor of Jeroboam, nothing is
recorded except that he ascended the throne of Israel in the
second year of Asa king of Judah (1 Kings xv. 25), and was
murdered in the year following (ibid. ver. 20) by Baasha the son
of Ahijah, of the tribe of Issachar, at Gibbethon, a Philistine
town which the Israelites were besieging. No particulars are
given of his age or actions. It is merely said, in the most
general way, that "he did evil in the sight of the Lord, and
walked in the way of his father, and in his sin wherewith he
made Israel to sin" (ibid. ver. 26). Thus there are no materials
for a biographical sketch of this monarch, whose reign probably
did not cover the space of more than a few months.[1]

[1] In 1 Kings xv. 25 a reign of "two years" is assigned to him; but the
writer counts any part of a year as "a year"; and all that we can distinctly gather from him is, that Nadab began to reign in some part of
Asa's second year, and was murdered in some part of his third.

CHAPTER VI.

BAASHA.

Baasha's humble origin—His courage and daring—He murders Nadab, and is accepted as king—He exterminates the house of Jeroboam, yet continues Jeroboam's religious system—His military policy, aggressive —Alliance with Benhadad and attack on Judæa—Seizure and fortification of Ramah—Asa successfully counterplots him—He is denounced by a prophet—His death.

BAASHA, the third Israelite monarch, had a reign of twenty-four years (1 Kings xv. 33). He was the son of a certain Ahijah, of whom nothing more is known, and belonged to the very undistinguished and unimportant tribe of Issachar—the "ass crouching down between two burdens" of Jacob's prophecy (Gen. xlix. 14). It would seem that he was originally of very humble rank (1 Kings xvi. 2) ; and, at the siege of Gibbethon, where he conceived the design of murdering his master, Nadab, and seating himself upon his throne, he was perhaps no more than a common soldier. But he was "a man of distinguished bravery," ambitious to excess, and of extraordinary audacity. Without, so far as appears, any prophetic encouragement, without claim of any kind to the kingly office, he ventured to organize a conspiracy against the reigning sovereign, the son of a valiant sire, who must have had the support of many powerful interests. What circumstances favoured his attempt we do not know. It is a mere conjecture of Ewald's that Nadab's war with the Philistines was proving unsuccessful, and that therefore dissatisfaction had arisen among the soldiers engaged in besieging Gibbethon, who were thus ripe for revolt, and ready to accept for sovereign any one whom they regarded as a more competent leader. No doubt the conjecture is plausible, but it is only one out of a thousand possibilities; and it may be questioned whether it is the historian's business to indulge in conjectures where he possesses no data. All that we know is, that Baasha succeeded in his enterprise, that he slew Nadab at Gibbethon, and was accepted as king in his stead (I Kings xv. 28), obtaining the throne, as it would seem, without any civil war or long struggle. The nation, which the house of Jeroboam had in no way attached to itself, acquiesced in his rule, probably preferring the firm hand that had seized the reins of government to the feeble one from which they had slipped.

In firmly establishing himself upon the throne, and consolidating his power, Baasha showed the same vigour and unscrupulousness that he had exhibited in making himself king. Unmoved by any stir of compassion or pity, he relentlessly exterminated the entire house of Jeroboam. In thus acting he could claim, to a certain extent, prophetic sanction; since Ahijah the Shilonite, who had originally designated Jeroboam for his kingly office (I Kings xi. 29-39), had also at a later date declared that God would bring evil on the house of Jeroboam, and take away all that should remain of it, with the special curse attached, that

> "Whoso of Jeroboam died in the city should the dogs eat;
> And whoso died in the city should the fowls of the air eat."

Baasha is distinctly said to have accomplished this prophecy (I Kings xv. 29), so that we must regard him as not only putting the entire seed of Jeroboam to death, but as doing so with all those circumstances of ignominy which especially impress Orientals, and which are usually reserved for the worst grade of malefactors.

It might perhaps have been expected that the new king, having shown himself inimical in the highest degree to the royal house which had preceded him upon the throne, would have headed a reaction against the religious innovations which Jeroboam had introduced; innovations which must have been extremely distasteful to the Prophetical order, as well as to a considerable section of the nation. But in this direction he appears to have made not the slightest change or improvement. Baasha, we are told, " did evil in the sight of the Lord, and *walked in the way of Jeroboam*, and in his sin wherewith he made Israel to sin" (1 Kings xv. 34). He " provoked God to anger with the work of his hands in being *like the house of Jeroboam*" (ibid. xvi. 7). Religious feeling therefore was in no sense the motive of his usurpation, and religion profited nothing by the change of dynasty. The worship of the calves remained unchanged at Dan and Bethel; the unauthorized priesthood was maintained in office; Jehovistic Israelites were hindered from carrying their offerings to Jerusalem or participating in the Temple worship (2 Chron. xvi. 1); Jeroboam's system was, in fact, continued without the slightest modification,[1] and the Prophetical order can have been no better pleased with the rule of the house of Ahijah than with that of the house of Nebat.

It is in military, rather than in religious, matters that a difference can be traced between the policy of the first, and that of the second, Israelite dynasty. The house of Nebat had been, on the whole, content to stand on the defensive against Judah; to seek to repel attack rather than to make it; and to look to self-protection rather than to self-aggrandisement. It had even submitted under Jeroboam to the loss of territory (2 Chron. xiii. 19), and had subsequently made no effort to recover the captured cities. Baasha's military policy was the exact opposite of this. Having strengthened himself by an alliance with his northern neighbour, Benhadad, king of Damascus (ibid. xvi. 3), he challenged Judah to the combat; he collected an army, marched southward, crossed the Judæan border, reconquered the territory taken from Israel by Abijah in the reign of Jeroboam,[2] and pursuing his victorious march seized and occupied a position of the utmost importance in Judæa itself, which he endeavoured rapidly to convert into a fortress of the first class. The object, as Ewald sees, was to "annihilate" Judah.[3] Ramah was an ἐπιτειχιαμὸς against Jerusalem.[4] If it could have been maintained for a few years in the hands of Judah's bitter foes, Jerusalem must have succumbed, and with the loss of Jerusalem the Judæan state must have collapsed. It has been

[1] See the remarks of Ewald, " History of Israel," vol. iv. p. 33, Eng. tr.
[2] This is not directly stated, but is necessarily implied by the general course of the campaign. [3] Ewald, " History of Israel," *l. s. c.*
[4] Compare Mr. Grote's remarks on the occupation of Deceleia by the Spartans—a parallel case (" History of Greece," vol. v. p. 311).

already related [1] how Asa met the daring plan of his adversary, how he bribed Benhadad to change sides and turn against Baasha, with the consequent failure of Baasha's plan, and the recovery by Asa of the fortress which had threatened him with ruin. Thus Baasha's attempt to re-establish the unity of the monarchy by absorbing Judæa into his own territories, came to nought; his bold conception and near approach to execution of his project were of no avail; an unexpected impediment frustrated his designs, and caused them to be given up as impracticable.

The invasion of Israel on the north by Benhadad, and the speedy capture not only of the towns of Dan, Ijon, and Abel-beth-maachah, but of "all Cinneroth, with all the land of Naphtali" (1 Kings xv. 20), revealed the weakness of the Israelite kingdom in respect of its northern frontier, which was dominated by the more elevated tracts about Lebanon and Hermon that never formed any part of the actual territory of the chosen people, excepting under the brief dominion of David and Solomon. This weakness showed itself at other periods of Israelite history besides the present one,[2] and must have caused Baasha some alarm. He seems to have hurriedly granted all the demands which Benhadad preferred, and to have thenceforth carefully abstained from provoking his hostility. A necessary result was the complete relinquishment of his aggressive designs against the kingdom of Judah, and a resumption of the defensive attitude towards it, which had been maintained by Jeroboam and Nadab.

Thus any hopes that had been entertained in any quarters of an increment of military glory as a consequence of the change of dynasty, were disappointed, and Baasha found himself no whit further advanced on the path of military success than his predecessors. The honour and power of the kingdom would indeed seem to have "sunk lower under the new dynasty than under its predecessor."[3] Discontent consequently showed itself. A prophet denounced the murder by which Baasha had attained the throne (1 Kings xvi. 7), reproached him for his slavish adherence to the sins of Jeroboam, and prophesied for him and his house the very same fate which, a quarter of a century

---

[1] Supra, p. 38.   [2] See 2 Kings x. 32, 33; xv. 29.
[3] Ewald, "History of Israel," vol. iv. p. 35, Eng. tr.

earlier, had been prophesied for the house of the son of Nebat—

"Him that dieth of Baasha in the field," he said, "shall the dogs eat;
And him that dieth of his in the field shall the fowls of the air eat."

Baasha, however, maintained his power, like Jeroboam, till his death, and left his crown to his son Elah, who at once and without difficulty mounted the throne. The scene of Baasha's death was Tirzah, which Jeroboam had made the capital (1 Kings xiv. 17); and there he was laid to rest with the customary honours.

CHAPTER VII.

ELAH.

Elah a shadowy figure in the sacred history—Comparison of his reign with that of Nadab—Compared with Nadab, he shows to advantage—He is murdered at a drinking-bout by Zimri.

THE figure of Elah, the son and successor of Baasha, is as shadowy in the sacred history as that of Nadab, the son and successor of Jeroboam. Of neither are we told his age at his accession, or any special trait of disposition. Both have short reigns, little if at all exceeding a year; both "continue in the way of Jeroboam, the son of Nebat" (1 Kings xvi. 2, 13), and "provoke God to anger with their vanities;" both, moreover, engage in a war against the Philistines within a short period of their accession; and in both reigns the special scene of the war is the Philistine city of Gibbethon (ibid. ver. 15). The only important difference between their histories is, that whereas Nadab put himself at the head of his army and proceeded to encounter the hardships of the siege in person, Elah sent against Gibbethon the captains of his host, Zimri and Omri, while he himself remained in the capital, Tirzah, drinking and revelling in the palace of the steward of his household, a certain Arza. We may assume that Zimri was kept acquainted with the king's unkingly conduct, and saw in it his own opportunity. The associations of Gibbethon suggested that kings were not unassailable, and the special circumstances of Elah's position were such as at once to provoke attack and to facilitate it. Zimri, without informing Omri or the army of his intention, withdrew himself from Gibbethon, and, returning to Tirzah, surprised the wretched monarch at his drinking-bout, and succeeded in assassinating him. Arza was probably privy to his design, and his helper in it. Elah, who began to reign in the twenty-sixth year of Asa (1 Kings xvi. 8), perished in the same king's twenty-seventh year (ibid. ver. 15), so that he probably did not hold the throne for more than a few months.

CHAPTER VIII.

ZIMRI.

Accession of Zimri—His destruction of Baasha's relatives and friends—
Revolt of the army under Omri—Zimri besieged in Tirzah—Tirzah
taken—Zimri sets the royal palace on fire, and perishes in the flames—
Zimri's character.

THE bold soldier, who, imitating Baasha, brought the second
Israelite dynasty to an end by the assassination of its second
monarch, proceeded to follow up his first success by a further
imitation of his model, and was no sooner seated upon the
throne than he " destroyed all the house of Baasha " (1 Kings
xvi. 11), not sparing any, either of his kinsfolk, or of his close
friends. This extreme severity may have rendered him unpopular.
At any rate, when the army which was at Gibbethon heard of
his insurrection and of the bloody deeds by which he had
followed it up, they were so exasperated that they broke out
into revolt, refused to acknowledge Zimri as their monarch, and
invested Omri, who had been left at Gibbethon in sole command,
with the sovereignty. Omri was prompt in action. He did
not hesitate for a moment to accept the rank conferred upon
him; and he at once took steps to dispossess his rival of
the throne. By his orders, the army broke up from before
Gibbethon, raised the siege, and marching with all speed to
Tirzah, besieged the pretender in his capital (1 Kings xvi. 16, 17).
Zimri seems to have had no troops with him on whom he could
depend. He did not dare to venture a battle, but remained
within the walls and simply stood on the defensive. The siege
did not last many days. Within a very short time the defences
were forced, the town entered, and the place, for all practical
purposes, taken (ver. 18). Zimri, however, was of too stubborn
a spirit to submit himself. He had worn the crown, albeit but

for seven days (ver. 15), and scorned the idea of descending to
a private station. Neither would he trust his future to the
tender mercies of the conqueror. Brave, fierce, and obstinate
to the last degree, he took a desperate resolve, and throwing
himself into the royal palace, which was no doubt a sort of
fortress within a fortress, he there stood at bay, and, when
further resistance was hopeless, gave orders that the palace
should be set on fire, and burnt it over his head. So far, he
resembled the traditional Sardanapalus, with whom Ewald has
compared him,[1] but there are no grounds for concluding that
the resemblance extended any further. We have not the
slightest evidence that Zimri was "effeminate" or sunk in
luxury. On the contrary, the conception that we naturally form
of him from the Scriptural narrative is that of a bold, brave, and
reckless desperado, who, thinking that he saw an opportunity for
seizing the crown, made his venture, and finding that he had
failed, preferred death by his own hand to the chances that
might possibly be offered him through the clemency of his
conqueror. It would appear that Zimri, even in his short reign
of seven days, found occasion to give formal approval to the
religious system of Jeroboam, since it is declared of him
(1 Kings xvi. 18, 19) that "he died for his sins which he
sinned in doing evil in the sight of the Lord, in walking in the
way of Jeroboam, and in his sin that he did, to make Israel to
sin."

[1] "History of Israel," vol. iv. p. 36, Eng. tr.

CHAPTER IX.

OMRI.

THE rule of Omri over Israel was not established without a further struggle. Scarcely had he got the better of his first antagonist, Zimri, before a new antagonist, with far superior pretensions, showed himself. Tibni, the son of Ginath, or Gonath (LXX.), must have been a man of some rank or position, since he was chosen by a considerable section of the people as a preferable monarch to the late commander-in-chief, and had so large and so sturdy a following that he maintained an equal contest with his rival for four years.[1] The opportunity must have been tempting for Asa to intervene in the quarrel, and attempt the subjugation of a state divided against itself; but Asa was now advanced beyond middle age, and probably felt that he had done enough for military glory and might allow himself a season of repose. Accordingly, the two combatants were left to themselves to fight out their contest—a result which was ultimately arrived at in the thirty-first year of Asa (1 Kings xvi. 23), when Omri put down his adversary and became sole monarch. Tibni, and his brother Joram (according to the Septuagint), were, according to the usual custom of the time, put to death (ibid. ver. 22).

The new king was a man of much vigour and energy. No sooner was he settled in his kingdom than he determined on the removal of the capital to a new site. Tirzah was stained with

[1] See 1 Kings xvi. ; compare ver. 15 with ver. 23.

a series of royal murders, and would long be associated in the popular thought with crime and conspiracy, unstable dynasties, civil feuds, war, bloodshed, and revolution. Omri hoped to establish a stable and permanent dynasty. He wished to remove from the popular mind the associations of the past, to make a clean sweep of them, and himself to start afresh, as from a new beginning. Moreover, there were objections to Tirzah as the capital from its situation, which was neither sufficiently central, nor sufficiently strong. Omri cast about for a place, near the middle of the land, which should be strong in a military point of view, capable of being fortified, productive, sufficiently watered, and accessible from the various parts of the kingdom. This he found in the "hill of Shomerôn," a few miles to the north-west of the old capital, Shechem, which he accordingly purchased, and on which he built his town. The situation is remarkable. "In the heart of the mountains of Israel, a little west of their watershed, and rather nearer their northern than their southern extremity, occurs a deep basin-shaped depression, apparently surrounded by hills, but really communicating towards the west by a narrow valley with the great maritime plain. In the midst of this basin rises an oblong hill with steep but not inaccessible sides, and a long flat top. This was the site which Omri chose for his new capital. Politically, it was rather more central than Shechem, and probably than Tirzah. In a military point of view it was admirably calculated for defence. The country round it was peculiarly productive. The hill itself possessed abundant springs of water. Probably it would have been difficult to find in the whole territory a place combining so many advantages, or so suited to become the seat of government."[1] As Dean Stanley observes,[2] "it combined in a union not elsewhere found in Palestine, strength, beauty, and fertility. It commanded a full view of the sea and the plain of Sharon on the one hand, and of the vale of Shechem on the other. The town sloped down from the summit of the hill ; a broad wall with a terraced top ran round it. . . In front of the gates was a wide open space or threshing-floor, where the kings of Samaria sat on great occasions. The inferior houses were built of white brick, with rafters of sycamore ; the grander of hewn stone and cedar (Isa.

[1] "Speaker's Commentary," vol. ii. p. 582.
[2] "Lectures on the Jewish Church," vol. ii. p. 242.

ix. 9, 10). It stood amid a circle of hills, commanding a view of its streets and slopes, itself the crown and glory of the whole scene. Its soft, rounded oblong platform was, as it were, a vast luxurious couch, in which its nobles securely rested, propped and cushioned up on both sides, as in the cherished corner of a rich divan."

Omri, we are told (1 Kings xvi. 24), "called the name of the city which he built, after the name of Shemer, owner of the hill, Shomerôn, or Samaria." The word, however, means etymologically "a watch-mountain," or "a watch-tower,"[1] and was probably generally understood in this sense by the inhabitants. In neighbouring countries it was at first replaced by the descriptive epithet " Beth-Khumri," " House or Palace of Omri,"[2] though afterwards we find it represented by Sammirin, or Tsammirin.

It must have been early in his reign that Omri, desirous of military fame, invaded the territory of Moab. The Moabites, reduced to subjection by David, and treated with extreme severity, would seem to have recovered their independence at the separation of the Israelites into two hostile kingdoms, and to have maintained it until Omri's attack upon them. Omri, as we learn from the Moabite Stone,[3] quarrelled with Chemosh-Gad, the father of the Mesha mentioned in 2 Kings iii. 4. He made his first assault on Medeba, a Moabite city about seven miles to the south of Heshbon, marked by the ruins of the modern Mâdeba. Having conquered this place and occupied it, he proceeded to overrun the entire Moabite country, which he subjugated and attached to his own kingdom as a dependency. The Moabite royal family was indeed maintained on the throne and continued to govern the country, but a heavy tribute was required from the nation, which was felt as a grievous " oppression."[4] We do not know the exact amount during Omri's reign, but under his son and successor it reached the almost incredible total of 100,000 sheep and 100,000 lambs annually (2 Kings iii. 4). Moab submitted to the

[1] See Dr. Smith's "Dictionary of the Bible," *ad voc.* Samaria (vol. ii. p. 1,099).

[2] "Ancient Monarchies," vol. ii. p. 365 ; G. Smith, "Eponym Canon," p. 115, l. 12, &c.

[3] See "Records of the Past," vol. xi. p. 165, l. 5 ; p. 166, l. 8.

[4] Mesha says, "Now Omri, king of Israel, he *oppressed* Moab many days. . His son succeeded him ; and he also said, I will *oppress* Moab."

burden, but with the greatest reluctance, and only waited for a fitting opportunity to repudiate her obligations, revolt from Israel, and reclaim her independence.

Omri appears also to have carried on a war, but an unsuccessful war, with Syria of Damascus. Its result was the cession to the Damascene kingdom of a number of cities (1 Kings xx. 34), among them probably Ramoth-Gilead,[*] the most important of the Trans-Jordanic towns, and the further grant to the Syrians of a right to "make streets in Samaria." This must either have meant permission to the Syrian merchants to carry on their trade freely in the Israelite capital, and for that purpose to have a quarter in it assigned to them, as the Tyrians occupied a quarter in Memphis ; or else must have involved a quasi-military occupation, the maintenance in Samaria, that is, of a permanent embassy in a large and fortified house, with its own servants, guards, &c., so as to be able to exercise a surveillance over the allied, but half-subject country, which submitted to be thus watched and observed. Though Ewald inclines to this latter supposition, the former one seems, on the whole, more probable ; and we must regard Omri as having received into his capital a Syrian population, and as having made over to it a considerable portion of the city. Such concessions imply a very serious antecedent defeat ; and we must thus, in estimating the military talents of this king, set against his Moabite victories, which were no doubt brilliant, the grave losses that he suffered on his northern and north-eastern frontier, which must have seriously crippled the strength of his kingdom in that quarter.

The religious policy of Omri differed little from that of his predecessor, but was, if anything, characterized by greater thoroughness. He "wrought evil in the eyes of the Lord, and *did worse than all that were before him*" (1 Kings xvi. 25). We hear in later times of the "*statutes* of Omri" as still kept by the Israelites (Micah vi. 16) ; and we may gather from this that he reduced the calf-worship into a regular formal system, whereto all were required to render obedience. Whether, as Ewald supposes, he was especially harsh in his treatment of the Prophets, and "severely chastised their remonstrances," is perhaps doubtful ; but it is clear that he adhered to Jeroboam's system (1 Kings xvi. 26), and rigidly carried it out, so as to leave a worse name behind him in respect of religion than even

[*] So Ewald, "History of Israel," vol. iv. p. 38, Eng. tr.

the worst of his predecessors. Still, it does not appear that he introduced any religious novelties, or "promoted the influx into the country of heathen cults and heathen manners." He was contented with Jeroboam's system, and with enforcing it strictly upon all his subjects by new "statutes," which he required them to "keep" and observe under heavy penalties.

There is some doubt with regard to the length of Omri's reign, but the various statements on the subject seem to be best reconciled by supposing that his entire reign lasted twelve years (compare 1 Kings xvi. 23 with verses 15 and 29), from the twenty-seventh to the thirty-eighth of Asa. During the first six of these years he resided at Tirzah, and during the last six at Samaria. During the first four he contended for the throne with Tibni; during the last eight he was sole monarch.

CHAPTER X.

AHAB.

AHAB, the son and successor of Omri, is the most famous of the kings of Israel. He had considerable military ability; he was, in a worldly sense, politic in his alliances; while, so far as religion was concerned, he took an entirely new departure, discarding the system of Jeroboam, and bending all his efforts towards the introduction into Israel, and the establishment as the State religion, of an entirely new cult—that of Baal and Ashteroth, the deities worshipped by the Phœnicians (1 Kings xvi. 31). It is impossible to estimate too highly the importance of this change. Hitherto Israel had declared herself faithful to Jehovah—with whatever practical shortcomings, she had maintained Jehovah as the sole true deity, and had excused her seeming idolatry by representing it as merely a symbolical worship, through material emblems, of the One true, perfect, and absolutely spiritual God. "The change from a symbolical worship of the One True God, with the innocent rites of sacrifice and prayer, to the cruel and licentious worship of the Phœnician divinities, was," as Dean Stanley observes, "*a prodigious step downwards*, and left traces in Northern Palestine which no subsequent reformations were able entirely to obliterate."[1]

[1] "Lectures on the Jewish Church," vol. ii. p. 245.

Some idea of the general nature of the Phœnician worship has been given already in the sketch of the life of Rehoboam ; but a more exact account seems to be now needed. The reader must be placed face to face with the horrors of the new cult for the situation to be realized, and the fierce antagonism between the Prophets of Jehovah and the votaries of Baal and Ashtoreth to be understood. As the subject is one of great delicacy, and requires most cautious treatment, the well weighed words of the careful and judicious Döllinger will be preferred to any words of the writer's own. "In earlier times," says Döllinger,[1] "Baal had been worshipped without an image in Tyre and its colonies ; but for a long time now his worship had grown into an idolatry of the most wanton character, directed by a numerous priesthood, who had their headquarters at Tyre. . . . His statue rode upon bulls ; for the bull was the symbol of the male power of generation ; and he was also represented with bunches of grapes and pomegranates in his hands. As the people of Asia distinguished, properly speaking, only two deities of nature, a male and a female, so Baal was of an elemental and sidereal character at once. As the former, he was god of the creative power, bringing all things to life everywhere, and, in particular, god of fire ; but he was Sun-God besides, and, as such, to human lineaments he added the crown of rays about the head peculiar to this god. In the one quality as well as in the other, he was represented at the same time as sovereign of the heavens (Baal-samin) and of the earth by him impregnated. . . . The Canaanitish Moloch (king) was not essentially different from Baal, but the same god in his terrible and destroying aspect, the god of consuming fire, the burning sun who smites the land with unfruitfulness and pestilence, dries up the springs, and begets poisonous winds. When the prophet says (Jer. xxxii. 35) —'Such as in the valley of Ben-Hinnom built high-places of Baal, to lead their sons and their daughters through the fire to Moloch,' and again (ibid. xix. 5)—'The Jews had built high-places to Baal, to burn their children by fire as a burnt-offering to Baal'—there is no mistaking the essential identity of the two. Besides the incense consumed in his honour, bulls also were sacrificed to Baal, and probably horses too : the Persians at least sacrificed the latter to their Sun-God. But the principal

[1] "Heidenthum und Judenthum" (N. Darnell's translation), vol. i. pp. 425–429.

sacrifice was children. This horrible custom was grounded in part upon the notion that children were the dearest possession of their parents, and in part that, as pure and innocent beings, they were the offerings of atonement most certain to pacify the anger of the deity ; and further, that the god of whose essence the generative power of nature was, had a just title to that which was begotten of man, and to the surrender of their children's lives. The sacrifices were consumed by fire ; the life given by the fire-god he should also take back again by the flames which destroy being. The Rabbinical description of the image of Moloch, that it was a human figure with a bull's head and outstretched arms, is confirmed by the account that Diodorus gives (xx. 14) of the Carthaginian Cronos, or Moloch. The image of metal was made glowing hot by a fire kindled within it ; and the children, laid in its arms, rolled from thence into the fiery lap below. Voluntary offering on the part of the parents was essential to the success of the sacrifice ; even the firstborn, nay the only child of the family, was given up. The parents stopped the cries of their children by fondling and kissing them, for the victim ought not to weep, and the sound of complaint was drowned in the din of flutes and kettledrums. Mothers, said Plutarch ('De superstione,' § 13), stood by without tears or sobs ; if they wept or sobbed they lost the honour of the act, and their children were sacrificed notwithstanding. Such sacrifices took place either annually on an appointed day, or before great enterprises, or on the occasion of public calamities, to appease the wrath of the god. This primitive custom is traceable in the myth of Theseus and the Minotaur. The Cretan monster with human body and bull's head, to whom young men and maidens were sacrificed, was the Moloch who had come from Phœnicia ; and the overcoming of him by Theseus was the destruction of the bloody rite. Thus too the rape of Europa into Crete from Phœnicia, through means of the bull, was a symbol of the colonization of that island by Phœnicians. The bull on which Europa sat was the Sun-God, and she herself was the Moon-Goddess, Astarté.

"Another form of Baal was Melkarth, or 'city king,' tutelary god of the city of Tyre, whose worship was carried far and wide by the colonies proceeding thence to the shores of the Mediterranean. This protector and archegetes of Tyre was the Phœnician Heracles, god alike of sun and fire (whence a perpetual fire was kept up upon his altars), a race-king and hero-leader of the people's expeditions. From him have the Asiatic features of the contest with the lion, the self-immolation by fire on the pile, and others, passed over into the Greek saga of Hercules.

"In the Astarté (Ashtoreth) of the Western Asiatics we recognize that great nature-goddess standing by Baal's side, who is the regent of the stars, the Queen of Heaven, and goddess of the moon, the mother of life, and deity of woman's fecundity. Under the name of Ashtoreth she was the guardian-goddess of Sidon, and not essentially distinct from the Baaltis of Byblus and Urania of Ascalon. The Greeks and Romans sometimes take her for Juno, as she was the supreme female deity of the Asiatics; sometimes for Aphrodite, on account of the worship of unchastity sacred to her; and again for Selene, for she was pictured as the goddess of the moon with horns, representing the lunar crescent. . . . As highest goddess, or Queen of Heaven, Astarté was, as already observed, accounted as Hera by the Greeks; yet they also recognized in her something of Athene, Aphrodite, Selene, Rhea, Artemis, Nemesis, and the Moirai. In fact she came nearest to the Phrygian Cybele. Sceptre and spindle in hand, she wore rays and a mural crown on her head, and the girdle too—an ornament only beseeming Aphrodite-Urania. Her golden statue rode next to that of Baal-Zeus, in a chariot drawn by lions; a precious stone, placed upon her head, illuminated the whole temple at night. She was considered as one with Atergatis or Derketo, who was honoured under the form of a fish on the coast of the Philistines. A combined worship was offered to the two, Baal and the goddess. Her temple at Apheka was so exceedingly rich, that Crassus spent several days in weighing all the gold and silver vessels and precious things that it contained. These gifts were the combined offerings of Arabia, Babylonia, Assyria, Phœnicia, Cilicia, and Cappadocia, and therefore of all the people of the Semitic tongue. In the court of the temple there were sacred beasts in a tame state in great numbers, and also a pond containing holy fish. Priests and temple-ministers were present in such numbers that Lucian counted above three hundred employed in one sacrifice: besides these there were troops of flute-blowers, Galli, and women frenzied with inspiration. At the spring festival, called by some 'the brand feast,' by others 'the

feast of torches,' which was attended by streams of visitors from
every country; huge trees were burnt with the offerings sus-
pended on them. Even children were sacrificed; they were
put into a leathern bag and thrown the whole height of the
temple to the bottom, with the shocking expression that they
were calves and not children. In the fore-court stood two
gigantic phalli. To the exciting din of drums, flutes, and
inspired songs, the Galli cut themselves on the arms; and the
effect of this act, and of the music accompanying it, was so
strong upon mere spectators, that all their bodily and mental
powers were thrown into a tumult of excitement; and they too,
seized by the desire to lacerate themselves, inflicted wounds
upon their bodies by means of potsherds lying ready for the
purpose. Thereupon they ran through the city, and received
from the inhabitants a woman's attire. Not chastity, but
barrenness, was intended by this act, whereby the Galli only
desired to be like their goddess. The relation, which they
thenceforth occupied towards women, was regarded as a holy
thing, and was generally tolerated."

It was a religion of this kind, not perhaps quite so far deve-
loped, but essentially the same, unchaste, impure, permissive of
the vilest abominations, which Ahab introduced among the
Israelites, led thereto by his marriage with a Phœnician
princess. It is probable that motives of policy had brought
about the matrimonial alliance wherefrom so many evils
flowed. The time was one when the isolation of tribe from
tribe, and nation from nation, seemed no longer possible.
Assyria was threatening to impose her yoke on the whole of
south-western Asia, and the instinct of self-preservation drove
the states and kingdoms, among whom the soil was partitioned,
to make preparations for resistance by uniting in leagues and
alliances. The most important of these leagues was one, which
the Assyrian Inscriptions make known to us,[1] between the
Hittites, the Hamathites, and the Syrians of Damascus. The
league between Phœnicia and Israel, of which Judæa after a
short time became a member (2 Kings xxii. 4, 48), must be
regarded as resulting from the same motives. It is uncertain
whether the marriage of Ahab with Jezebel was proposed by the
Phœnician or by the Israelite king. Both were equally concerned to guard against a common danger. If Phœnicia was

[1] G. Smith, "Eponym Canon," pp. 109-112.

the more exposed by her geographical position, Israel was probably the weaker state of the two. For Phœnicia was at this time under the rule of a powerful prince, king of Sidon, according to the author of Kings (1 Kings xvi. 31), king of Tyre, according to the native historians,[1] therefore probably lord paramount over the whole of Phœnicia from Ramantha in the north to Akko or even Dor towards the south. Ithobalus or Eth-baal had made himself monarch by the murder of his brother, and united the royal office with the High-Priesthood of Ashtoreth or Astarté. He was thus a Priest-King, who would probably be moved as much by religious as political motives, and we may regard Jezebel as either inheriting from him a fanatical spirit, or as an instrument in his hands for spreading the faith which he was desirous of propagating. In either case she certainly became the ruling spirit of the Israelite court,[2] and by her means were brought about, both in Israel and ultimately in Judah, changes of the most disastrous character—changes which lowered the spirit and weakened the moral fibre of both nations—changes which in the end brought down the vengeance of God, first on Samaria and then on Jerusalem, resulting in the terrible calamities of the two Captivities.

Jezebel was "a woman in whom, with the reckless and licentious habits of an Oriental queen, were united the fiercest and sternest qualities inherent in the old Semitic race."[3] Bold, unscrupulous, firm of purpose, resolute in action, she was the Lady Macbeth of Israelite history, complete master of her husband, who was a mere tool in her hands, and the evil genius at once of her dynasty and of her country. Eth-baal, her father, seems to have sent her to the Israelite Court accompanied by all the pomp and attendance that were regarded as suiting the dignity of a Phœnician princess. Like Pharaoh's daughter in the time of Solomon,[4] she was (of course) to have the free exercise of her religion in the Israelite capital; but it was certainly not necessary that she should have carried with her to her new abode the enormous number of four hundred and fifty priests or prophets of Baal[5]—much less that at another occasional residence she should have maintained a further band of four

[1] Menander ap. Joseph. "Ant. Jud." viii. 13, § 2; "Contr. Apion." l. 18.
[2] 1 Kings xxi. 25.
[3] Stanley, "Lectures on the Jewish Church," vol. ii. p. 245.
[4] 1 Kings iii. 1; vii. 8; ix. 24.　　　[5] Ibid. xviii. 19.

hundred " prophets of the groves." [1] These numbers indicate, without at all fully expressing, the vast size of her *entourage*, which must have been such as to give her a distinct nucleus of physical strength in support of her projects. It probably took her but a short time to effect the complete subjugation of her husband's will to her own. Ahab was of a weak and yielding disposition, not ill-inclined if left to himself, and certainly not of a temper to devise and carry through great schemes involving violence and bloodshed, such as those in which we find Jezebel engaged very early in her married life. It is to her initiative that we must ascribe the religious persecution which soon broke out—the " FIRST GREAT PERSECUTION " for opinion, as the historian of the Jewish Church reminds us,[2] which the annals of the world bring to our notice. Not content with being at liberty to worship her national deities at Jezreel and Samaria with all the grandeur and magnificence to which she had been accustomed in her own country, Jezebel set herself, with her husband's tacit connivance, to extirpate the religion of Jehovah from the land of Israel, and to substitute in its place open and avowed Paganism—the worship of Ashtoreth and of Baal. First, every effort was made to seduce the votaries of the old religion from their pure, strict creed and lofty standard of morality. Splendid shrines were built, especially one of vast size in the capital,[3] and the rites and ceremonies of the new cult were exhibited on a grand scale, with sensuous accompaniments of all kinds—music, statuary, processions of robed priests, victims, incense, bands of fanatics worked up to frenzy by religious excitement, and the like. Astarté's emblems were erected, [4] and license was given under cover of her worship to the grossest sexual excesses. A people whose "hearts were gross " (Matt. xiii. 15), and on whom the external and the sensuous had always enormous power, was naturally attracted by such influences, and won over in thousands to the new religion. But there were some who could not be gained in this way ; and with these another method had to be tried. Persecuting bands were let loose, armed with sword and lance, and bearing the commission of the Queen (1 Kings xviii. 4),

---

[1] 1 Kings xviii. 19.
[2] Stanley, " Lectures on the Jewish Church," vol. ii. p. 246.
[3] See 1 Kings xvi. 32 ; 2 Kings x. 21.
[4] 1 Kings xvi. 33 ; xviii. 19, &c.

who traversed the land from end to end, passing from hill to hill, and destroying the many altars which existed, as in the south, so in the north, to the One True God—Jehovistic altars, never desecrated by the service of false deities, ancestral centres of worship to the various localities. Woe to the followers of the Old Religion if they ventured upon resistance—Jezebel's myrmidons had scant respect for anything but the will of their mistress, and would crush resistance by force. The Prophets especially suffered. With respect to them, an order seems to have been given, that they should be searched out and hunted down.[1] " Now began those hidings in caves and dens of the earth (Heb. xi. 38)—the numerous caverns of the limestone rocks of Palestine—the precursors of the history of the Catacombs."[2] When the persecution was at the hottest, a brave "servant of Jehovah," Obadiah,[3] one attached to the Court (1 Kings xviii. 3) but faithful to his Divine Master, found a refuge for two bands of fifty each in spacious caverns, "probably among the clefts of Carmel."[4]

When the night is darkest the day verges towards dawn. God seemed to have forsaken His people. Religion seemed at its last gasp. The Prophets were slain, or else dispersed and silent. In all Israel there were but seven thousand persons who had not openly enrolled themselves among the worshippers of Baal (1 Kings xix. 18). And these seven thousand were in hiding, or at any rate dared not openly avow themselves. But God was still with His Church, and had not forsaken His inheritance. Suddenly there rose up a light in the darkness (Psa. cxii. 4). In Israel's utmost need, God sent His people the very chief of the Prophets. Elijah appeared—" the loftiest and sternest spirit of the True Faith raised up face to face with the proudest and fiercest spirit of the old Asiatic Paganism "[5]— Elijah raised up to confront Jezebel.

We know little of Elijah's early years. Tishbi in Gilead, the place of his birth according to most critics, is otherwise unmentioned in the history, and cannot possibly be located. Gilead, however, to which he certainly belonged, is a region of a marked character, wild and secluded. The Trans-Jordanic

---

[1] 1 Kings xviii. 4 ; xix. 10.
[2] Stanley, "Lectures on the Jewish Church," vol. ii. p. 247.
[3] Obadiah is Ebed-Jah (עֹבַדְ-יָהּ), "Servant of Jah" or "Jehovah."
[4] Stanley, l. s. c.   [5] Ibid.

tribes were altogether less civilized than their brethren, harsher, with habits more like those of their Arabian neighbours. Gilead was a region of deserts and forests, and its inhabitants had a semi-Bedouin character; they lived a wild life, in their deep ravines and mountain glades; "their faces were as the faces of lions, and their feet swift as the roes upon the mountains" (1 Chron. xii. 8). It was probably their ordinary outward appearance which Elijah made famous, and with which he familiarized his countrymen on the western side of the river—an appearance like that of many modern dervishes, who allow their hair to grow to any length, and for clothing wind a leathern girdle around their loins,[1] over which they occasionally throw an undressed sheepskin. " In Elijah's simple garb," says one very familiar with the East,[2] "his wild aspect, abrupt address, wonderfully active habits, and movements so rapid as to evade the search of his watchful and bitter foes, we see all the characteristics of the genuine Bedawy, ennobled by a high prophetic mission."

The first task set Elijah was to announce to Ahab the coming of a drought. Drought in Eastern lands means famine and severe suffering, the loss of cattle, the general impoverishing of the nation, the untimely death of thousands of the inhabitants. It was doubtless understood that the judgment was on account of the recent change of religion ; and it was openly announced, that no removal or modification of the scourge would take place, except at Elijah's word (1 Kings xvii. 1). At the same time Elijah disappeared. In vain did the perplexed king, incited doubtless by his infuriated wife, send out emissaries to scour the land, and even to go beyond its borders (ibid. ver. 10), in order to find the Prophet who held the issues of life and death in his hands, and might conceivably be bribed or forced to grant some relief. The Prophet was not to be found. At one time the brook Cherith (ibid. vers. 3–7), at another the Sidonian town of Zarephath or Sarepta, sheltered him (ibid. vers. 9–24) ; and the king's, or rather the queen's messengers, could not discover his hiding-place. It was not until the third year (1 Kings xviii. 1) that it was known where he was ; and then he himself came forward from his retirement and sought

[1] Morier's "Manuscript Notes," quoted by Stanley, "Lectures," vol. ii. p. 251, note.

[2] The Rev. J. L. Porter, "Dict. of the Bible," vol. i. p. 699.

an interview with his sovereign. The drought having grown worse and worse, Ahab had set out, accompanied by his chief minister, to seek throughout the land for such patches of vegetation as might suffice for the sustenance of the royal "beasts" (ibid. ver. 5). On a sudden Elijah showed himself to the chief minister. "Go, tell thy lord," he said, "behold, Elijah is here" (ibid. ver. 8). Reluctantly the minister obeyed, doubting whether Elijah would really venture on the interview. But the Prophet had made up his mind—he had resolved on an act of vengeance. The king, he felt, brought down to despair by the long continuance of the drought, and with no Jezebel near him to lean upon, would be as clay in his hands, would do whatever he wished. So he reassured Obadiah, who fetched the king, and the interview took place. At first Ahab takes the tone of an offended prince—"Art thou here?" he asks, "thou that troublest Israel." But the tone cannot be maintained. Elijah, far from quailing before him, boldly asserts himself, and meets the charge with a counter-charge—" I have not troubled Israel, but thou ! " This drought from which Israel suffers is not my doing, but thine : it is the punishment for thy sins, and the sins of thy house. The king has no reply ready, and authority passes from him to his subject. Elijah issues his commands, and Ahab does not venture to dispute them. "All Israel" is to be gathered together (1 Kings xviii. 19)—a great assembly is to be held. The scene is to be Carmel, one of the special haunts of Elijah. There, on the eastern summit of that lofty ridge, "commanding the last view of the Mediterranean Sea, and the first view of the great plain of Esdraëlon, just where the glades of forest sink into the usual barrenness of the hills of Manasseh,"[1] was a rocky eminence, on which stood an altar of Jehovah, one of those probably which had been dismantled in the recent persecution. " Close beneath was an upland plain, round a well of perennial water, which from its shady and elevated situation seems to have escaped the effects of the recent drought."[2] Hither Ahab, at Elijah's bidding, summoned Israel. The four hundred and fifty prophets of Baal, who ministered in the great Idol Temple of Samaria, were specially sent for and came. Jezebel's four hundred prophets of Astarte likewise received a summons, but appear to have disregarded it. The people sent their representatives. On the upland plain of

[1] Stanley, "Lectures on the Jewish Church," vol. ii. p. 256.   [2] Ibid.

Carmel was abundant room for the gathering ; and here, standing alone on the one side over against the four hundred and
fifty priests of Baal on the other, in the sight of king and people,
the Prophet who had convened the meeting proceeded to
address the assembled multitudes.

It was early morning. From the lofty upland the assembly
looked down upon the Esdraëlon plain, the great battlefield
of Palestine. No mists swept across it ; no passing vapours
obscured its well-known features, for the drought was such that
the night brought no dew. Northward rose the hills of Galilee ;
eastward, on its distant eminence, might be discerned "the
stately city of Jezreel, with Ahab's palace, and Jezebel's temple
embosomed in its sacred grove ; " through the plain wandered
in countless windings, but now carrying a mere thread of water,
"that ancient river, the river Kishon ; "[1] to the south-east rose
the low range of the Manasseh hills. In the still clear air the
Prophet's voice sounded, inviting his adversaries to a trial
which should end the long controversy. "How long," he said,
addressing himself to assembled Israel, "halt ye between two
opinions? If the Lord (Jehovah) be God, follow Him ; but if
Baal, then follow him." Do not attempt to reconcile the irre-
concilable. Make your choice once for all. Either throw in
your lot with the servants of Jehovah, or with His adversaries.
And then he proposed a test, whereby it should be known who
was God. Here was he himself, alone, on one side ; on the
other were the prophets of Baal, "four hundred and fifty men"
(1 Kings xviii. 22). They should build an altar and prepare a
sacrifice, and put no fire under, and call upon their god to send
fire from heaven and consume it ; and he would build another
altar, and prepare another sacrifice, and put no fire under,
and call on Jehovah, his God, to do the like—"and the God
that answereth by fire, let him be God" (ibid. vers. 23, 24).
The people, silent hitherto, now burst out in loud acclamations.
So let it be ; no fairer test could be proposed ; Elijah had "well
spoken" (ver. 24) ; and the Baal priests could not for very
shame decline the contest, to the terms of which it was impossible to make objection.

Then began the "grand ordeal" so well known to all of us,
and so excellently described by one whose loss all Christendom
deplores, that his words cannot be bettered, but may well be

[1] Judges v. 21.

borrowed by all who have occasion to treat the subject. "On the one side [1] is the exact picture of Oriental fanaticism, such as may still be seen in Eastern religions. As the Mussulman Dervishes work themselves into a frenzy by the invocation of 'Allah! Allah!' until the words themselves are lost in inarticulate gasps ; as Eastern Christians will recite the 'Kyrie Eleison,' the 'Gospidi Pomilou,' in a hundredfold repetition ; as the pilgrims round the church of St. John at Samaria formerly, and round the chapel of the Holy Sepulchre now, race, and run, and tumble, in order to bring down the Divine Fire into the midst of them [2]—so the four hundred and fifty prophets of Baal (for the prophets of Ashtaroth seem to have shrunk from the contest) performed their wild dances round their altar, or upon it, springing up, or sinking down, with the fantastic gestures which Orientals alone can command, as if by an internal mechanism, and screaming with that sustained energy which believes that it will be heard from its much speaking—from morn till noon, '*Hear us, O Baal, hear us!*' A larger spirit of Christian insight, or Christian compassion, either perceives under these desperate forms of superstition some elements of a nobler faith, or else is oppressed, even to tears of pity, by the thought of this dark abyss of human corruption. But there is a ludicrous side, on which, in this instance, the Biblical narrative fixes our attention, in one of those bursts of laughter, which form rare exceptions in the Hebrew annals, and which when they do occur need special notice. There is, for the moment, a savage humour, a biting sarcasm, in the tone of Elijah which forms an exception alike to the general humanity of the New Testament, and the general seriousness of the Old. He had already, in addressing the assembled people, placed before them in one sharp truculent question the likeness—it might almost be said the caricature—of their stumbling, hesitating gait—'How long are you to halt and totter, first on one knee and then on the other? If Jehovah be your God, walk straight after Him; if Baal, walk straight after him!' It was the very action and gesture represented in the grotesque dances, first on one foot and then on another, round the Pagan altars. It is noon, when gods and men under that burning sun may be thought to have withdrawn to rest. And 'Elijah the Tishbite' (so he is

---

[1] Stanley, "Jewish Church," vol. ii. pp. 257–261.

[2] Compare the same writer's "Sinai and Palestine," ch. xiv. pp. 460–464.

described in his full human personality) cannot restrain himself, and cheers them on—'Cry with a loud voice, louder and louder yet, for he is a god; for he has his head full, and is too busy to hear your prayer; or perchance he has his stomach full, and has gone aside into retirement; or perchance in the heat of the day he is asleep and must be awakened.' The prophets of Baal took Elijah at his word. Like the Dervishes, who eat glass, seize living snakes with their teeth, throw themselves prostrate for their mounted chief to ride over them; like the Corybantian priests of Cybele; like the Fakirs of India, they now, in their frenzied state, tossed to and fro the swords and lances which formed part of their fantastic worship, and gashed themselves, and each other, till they were smeared with blood; and mingled with their loud yells to the silent and sleeping Divinity those ravings which formed the dark side of ancient prophecy. The midday heat is now past: the altar still remains untouched; even fraud, if there were fraud, has been unsuccessful. And now comes the contrast of the calmness and tranquillity of the true Prophet. Elijah bade the hostile prophets stand aloof, and called the people round him. He was standing amid the ruins of the ancient altar. With his own hands he gathered twelve stones from its fragments. The sacred character of the northern kingdom, as representing the twelve tribes of Israel, the ancient Patriarchal Israel, was not forgotten. These twelve sacred blocks were piled up; the sacrifice duly prepared; the water brought from the adjacent well. And then, as the hour of the evening sacrifice drew near, and as the sun began to descend towards the western sea, with no frantic gesticulation, or vain reiteration, he sent up into the evening heaven four short cries to the God of his fathers :—

'Jehovah, God of Abraham, Isaac, and Jacob, hear me:
Jehovah, hear me this day in fire, and let all the people know that Thou art Jehovah, the God of this Israel, and that I am Thy servant, and through Thee have done all these things:
Hear me, O Jehovah:
Hear me, and let this people know that Thou, Jehovah, art the God, and that Thou hast turned their hearts back again."

"On the open mountain top, and to the few words needing not more than a few seconds to utter, the answer came which had been denied to the vast concourse of prophets, to their many hours of eager application and self-inflicted torture. It was the difference between the vain and unmeaning superstition of fana- tics, 'which availeth nothing,' and the 'effectual fervent prayer of one righteous man, which availeth much.' 'Then fell fire from Jehovah from heaven.'

"There is an exultant triumph in the words in which the sacred historian describes the completeness of the conflagration. The fragments of the ox on the summit of the altar first disappear; then the pile of wood heaped from the forest of Carmel; next the very stones of the altar crumble in the flames; then the dust of the earth that had been thrown out of the trench; and lastly the water in the deep trench round the altar is licked up by the fiery tongues, and leaves the whole place bare. The altar itself had been an emblem of the tribes of the sons of Israel. Its envelopment in this celestial fire was an emblem no less of the reconstruction of the kingdom—a token that 'the God of Israel had turned their hearts back again.' So for the moment it seemed. 'JEHOVAH, *HE is God!* JEHOVAH, *HE is God!*' was the universal cry; as if turning (by a slight inversion) the name of the Prophet himself into a war-cry, 'Eli-Jah-hu,' '*My God, He is Jehovah.*' Before him the whole multitude lay prostrate on the mountain-side. He was now the ruler of the nation. His word was law. In that sudden revulsion of feeling 'the wheel had come full cycle round.' The persecu- tors became the victims. The prophets of Baal were seized; they were swept away by the wild multitude. Elijah himself led them down the mountain slopes to the gorge of the Kishon. As Phinehas, as Samuel before him, so Elijah now took upon himself the dreadful office of executioner. Sword in hand he stood over the unresisting prophets, and in one swift and terrible slaughter they fell by the sacred stream. The name of the ' Hill of the Priests ' possibly commemorates their end.

"On the peaceful top of the mountain the sacrificial feast was spread ; and to this, at Elijah's bidding, the king went up ; for already in the Prophet's ear there was 'the sound of the tread of rain' (1 Kings xviii. 41, LXX.). At 'the top of the mountain,' but on a lower declivity, Elijah bent himself down, with his head, in the Oriental attitude of entire abstraction, placed between his knees, whilst his attendant boy mounted to the highest point of all, whence, over the western ridge, there is a wide view of the blue waters of the Mediterranean Sea. The sun must have been now gone down. But the cloudless sky would have been lit up by the long white glow which succeeds an Eastern sunset. Seven times the youthful watcher ascended and looked ; and seven times 'there was nothing.' The sky was still clear ; the sea was still calm. At last out of the far horizon there rose a little cloud, the first that for days and months had passed across the heavens ; and it grew in the deepening shades of evening, and quickly the whole sky was overcast, and the forests of Carmel shook in the welcome sound of those mighty winds which in Eastern regions precede a coming tempest. Each from his separate height, the King and the Prophet, descended. The cry of the boy from his mountain watch had hardly been uttered when the storm broke upon the plain, and the torrent of Kishon began to swell. The king had not a moment to lose lest he should be unable to reach Jezreel. He mounted his chariot at the foot of the hill. And Elijah was touched as by a supporting hand : and he snatched up his streaming mantle and twisted it round his loins, and, amidst the rushing storm with which the night closed in, he outstripped even the speed of the royal horses, and 'ran before the chariot' —as the Bedouins of his native Gilead would still run with inexhaustible strength—to the entrance of Jezreel, distant, though visible, from the scene of his triumph."

So the vengeance was accomplished ; God's honour was vindicated ; the nation was checked in its irreligious course, warned, roused, to a certain extent turned to Jehovah (1 Kings xviii. 37). Elijah had carried all before him. The king had been alarmed ; the people wrought up to enthusiasm ; the Baal priests destroyed ; the entire Paganizing party shattered and cowed. But there was still one force which had not been reckoned with—there was the indomitable spirit of the implacable Queen. Jezebel was not one to quail or blench. The shivering Ahab, safe within his harem walls, tells to his wife the events of the memorable day ; but they strike no fear into her heart—they do but elicit a burst of uncontrollable fury. "So let the gods do to me," she exclaims, "and more also, if I make not thy life, Elijah, as the life of one of them by to-morrow about this time" (1 Kings xix. 2). And she sends the Prophet this message ; and he, not doubting that she will keep her word, flies from before her in the greatest haste, takes refuge in Judæa, in Arabia, at Horeb, and altogether disappears from the Israelite kingdom for several years. We may not tax him with cowardice, for his movements were Heaven-directed (ibid. vers. 7, 8, 15) ; but the result was that Jezebel remained mistress of the situation, able to work her will throughout the entire kingdom, and, though baulked of the revenge which she had hoped to take, practically triumphant.

It would seem to have been at this period, when Elijah was in some distant land, or at any rate in hiding, that a war with the Syrians of Damascus was forced upon Ahab, much against his will. A "Benhadad, king of Syria," probably the son or grandson of the ally of Asa, suddenly and without warning "gathered all his host together," having under him thirty-two subject kings, with numerous horses and chariots, and "went up and besieged Samaria, and warred against it" (1 Kings xx. 1). The attack was, apparently, unprovoked, and a mere wanton aggression. Ahab was unprepared to resist it ; and when the Syrian monarch proposed, as the price of his retirement, the forfeiture of the royal treasures and of Ahab's wives and children, he meekly answered, " My lord, O king, according to thy saying, I am thine, and all that I have" (ibid. ver. 4). But mere submission was not what the invader wanted—his intention was to sack Samaria and conquer the whole country. Accordingly, on receiving Ahab's answer, he raised his terms, and required the admission of his army within the walls, with free liberty to plunder at their pleasure. This demand was necessarily resisted ; and on an engagement taking place in the hilly tract about Samaria, the Syrians were defeated with great slaughter, and Benhadad forced to save himself by a hasty flight on horseback (ibid. vers. 20, 21). His repulse, however, did not bring the war to an end. It was thought by the Syrians that they were defeated because they had attacked the Israelites among their hills, and that the fortune of war would probably be different if a battle were fought upon an open plain —the God of Israel, they declared, was " god of the hills, but not god of the valleys "—Syria would be victorious if the hills were avoided for the future. So the next year an invasion was made on the eastern side of the Jordan, in the champaign country parallel with the Sea of Galilee, where Aphek (now Fik) was the object of attack (ibid. ver. 26). Benhadad's army was very numerous, while the Israelites opposed to them appeared, in comparison, no more than " two little flocks of kids " (ver.

27); but still the viciory was once more with the assailed party, who "slew of the Syrians an hundred thousand footmen in one day" (ver. 29). A further loss was suffered within the defences of Aphek, where the city wall, shaken by an earthquake, fell and crushed a large number; and Benhadad, seeing that further resistance was impossible, surrendered himself to Ahab at discretion, with the remnant of his army. A treaty of peace followed. Ahab obtained the same right of having "streets" in his adversary's capital assigned to his subjects, as had been imposed by Benhadad's father on his own father Omri, and allowed the Syrian monarch to return to his own country—an act of clemency for which he was rebuked by a prophet (ibid. vers. 35-42). The spirit which led Samuel to hew Agag in pieces still prevailed among the Jehovistic prophets of Ahab's time, and it was thought that piety required the enemies of God to be devoted to "utter destruction" (ver. 43).

The reign of Ahab must be regarded as, on the whole, a time of material prosperity for Israel. Besides the two triumphs over Syria which have just been mentioned, we find the kingdom otherwise advancing in wealth and consequence. New towns of importance arose both in the north and in the south, as Jezreel in the Esdraëlon plain, and Jericho, low down in the Ghor or Jordan valley. Joshua had in the olden time laid a curse on the man who should rebuild this city (Josh. vi. 26)—the first in Canaan to resist Israel—and the menace had been effective for centuries; but in Ahab's reign, a certain Hiel, a native of Bethel, set the curse at nought, and raised Jericho from its ruins, paying, however, in the deaths of two of his sons, the penalty affixed prophetically (1 Kings xvi. 34). The site of Jericho was most favourable, and the "city of palm-trees" soon became a flourishing place, but was not for a long time of the same importance as Jezreel. Jezreel, "planted on a gentle eminence, in the very centre of the rich plain—commanding the view of Carmel on the west and of the valley of the Jordan on the east,"[1] was made a royal residence; strengthened with walls and towers; adorned with a palace, a temple, and perhaps an "ivory house "[2] (ibid. xxii. 39); and continued till the end of the dynasty the ordinary seat of the Court and place of abode of the sovereign (2 Kings viii. 29; ix. 15-37).

[1] Stanley, "Lectures on the Jewish Church," vol. ii. p. 244.
[2] It is not distinctly stated that Ahab's "ivory house" was *at Jezreel*.

It was in connection with Jezreel that the event happened which brought down upon Ahab, his wicked queen, and his entire house, that final curse of God from which there was no recovery. On the eastern slope of the hill of Jezreel, looking towards the Jordan, and not far from the town wall, was a fertile plot of ground, cultivated as a vineyard, on which Ahab cast a covetous eye. It was close to his own residence, and would (he thought) make him a most convenient "garden of herbs" (1 Kings xxi. 2). He wished, therefore, to purchase it from the owner, who was a Jezreelite, Naboth by name. But that individual, with the sturdy independence often seen in peasant proprietors, and perhaps actuated to some extent by a religious motive (for the Law forbade the alienation of landed property [1]), positively refused to part with "the inheritance of his fathers" (ver. 3). The king himself viewed the refusal as terminating the business, and, deeply disappointed, took to his bed and sulked ; but there was one in the palace whose spirit opposition roused, who was absolutely devoid of all scruples, and whose breeding had probably familiarized her with the principles and practices of a more thoroughgoing despotism than had ever yet been established in Israel. Jezebel, when she heard of her husband's grief and despondency, took matters into her own hands. "Why is thy spirit so sad ?" she said to him. " Art thou the ruler of Israel or no ? Arise, and eat bread, and let thine heart be merry : *I will give thee* the vine-yard of Naboth the Jezreelite." And she proceeded to carry out her boast. Having obtained possession of the royal signet, she wrote letters in Ahab's name to the municipal authorities of Jezreel, had Naboth arrested, accused of treason, and judicially murdered. His whole family was involved in his ruin (2 Kings ix. 26) ; and, as the property of a felon, his estate escheated to the crown. Jezebel then bade Ahab " arise and take possession," which he gladly did, but only to bring on himself, and wife, and house, God's final judgment. To pass the sentence, Elijah once more came forth from his obscurity. " Hast thou killed," he said, " and also taken possession ? Behold, thus saith the Lord, In the place where dogs licked the blood of Naboth shall dogs lick thy blood, even thine. I will bring evil upon thee, and will take away thy posterity, and will make thy house like the house of Jeroboam the son of Nebat, and like the house of

---

[1] See Lev. xxv. 23-28 ; Num. xxxvi. 7.

Baasha the son of Ahijah. Him that dieth of Ahab in the city shall the dogs eat; and him that dieth in the field shall the fowls of the air eat. And of Jezebel also hath the Lord spoken, saying, The dogs shall eat Jezebel by the wall of Jezreel" (1 Kings xxi. 19–24). The irrevocable doom was pronounced; and the king heard, and trembled with self-condemnation, and remorse, and affright. Owning his sentence just, he "rent his clothes, and put sackcloth upon his loins, and fasted, and lay in sackcloth, and went softly" (ibid. ver. 27). The tardy repentance met with Divine recognition, and the fiat went forth— "Because Ahab humbleth himself before me, I will not bring the evil in his days; but in his son's days will I bring the evil upon his house" (ibid. ver. 29).

But still, though the great evil—the extinction of his house and Jezebel's awful fate—were deferred to the days of his son,[1] Ahab himself was not wholly to escape. The punishment of an untimely end was to fall upon him. He was still in the vigour of life, probably not yet fifty years of age; and his successful campaigns against Benhadad had woke in him a desire for further military glory. It seemed to him a disgrace, that Ramoth-Gilead, an Israelite town, assigned to Gad after the victories of Moses,[2] and held uninterruptedly for above four centuries,[3] should have been allowed to remain in the possession of Syria for the space of twenty years or more, and that no effort should have been made during that time to recover it. An occasion came, about three years from the close of the war described in 1 Kings xx. 26–34, which seemed to present an opportunity for recovering the lost town, which, Ahab felt, was not to be neglected. Jehoshaphat, son of Asa, king of Judah, who had already contracted affinity with Ahab by marrying Ahab's daughter, Athaliah, to his own son Jehoram, came on a visit to his near connection at Samaria. Jehoshaphat was known to have great resources (2 Chron. xvii. 5, 11–19; xviii. 1), and was accompanied to Samaria by a considerable escort (ibid. xviii. 2). If he could be induced to join in the war, success appeared to Ahab to be certain. Accordingly, the subject was introduced at the close of a grand entertainment given to his royal guest by Ahab; and Jehoshaphat, his heart warmed by wine and his vanity flattered by the magnificence of his reception, readily

---

[1] 2 Kings ix. 24, 33; x. 7, 11, 17. [2] Deut. iv. 43.
[3] Josh. xx. 8, xxi. 38; 1 Kings iv. 13; 1 Chron. vi. 80; &c.

came into the project, and yielded a complete acquiescence—
"I am as thou art, my people as thy people, my horses as thy
horses ; and we will be with thee in the war " (1 Kings xxii. 3 ;
2 Chron. xviii. 3). One only condition does he make, if so we
may regard it—"Enquire, I pray thee, of the word of the Lord
to-day " (1 Kings xxii. 4). Then followed the scene with which
we are all familiar—a second contest between four hundred
Baal-prophets and a single " Prophet of the Lord," Micaiah the
son of Imlah, in which the One Prophet obtains the victory.
"Go up to Ramoth-Gilead and prosper," cry the Baal-prophets
with one mouth ; "go up, secure of success, for the Lord shall
deliver it into the hand of the king." " Go up," says Micaiah
at first, in bitter irony, mocking them (ver. 14) ; but, when
adjured to drop his mockery, he declares in a tone not unlike
that of Isaiah or Ezekiel,—" I saw all Israel scattered upon the
hills, as sheep that have no shepherd : and the Lord said,
These have no master : let them return every man to his house
in peace " (ver. 17). In vain does the king reproach him ; in
vain do the Baal-prophets flout and even strike him : Micaiah,
one against a host, retains his calmness, and holds to his
prophecy. Ordered off to prison by the king " until he returns
again in peace," his last words are—" If thou return at all in
peace, the Lord hath not spoken by me : hearken, O people,
every one of you " (ver. 28).

Ahab's part in this scene is contemptible and pitiable.
Clearly his habits of alternate bullying and truckling have told
upon his character, and, now that he is becoming advanced in
years, there remains to him scarcely anything of dignity, or
fairness, or even decent reticence. He "hates" God's prophets ;
he desires to hear nothing but smooth words ; he calmly looks
on, while his myrmidons deride and maltreat one whose only
offence is that he is faithful and true, simple-minded and out-
spoken ; he punishes with prison discipline of a severe type the
single man in Samaria who has dared to tell him the truth.
We see plainly the effect of long persistence in sinning against
light, both on the moral temper and upon the moral perceptions.

But the end has still to come. Elated by his success in
winning over Jehoshaphat to be his ally, and encouraged by the
voices of his false prophets, who have bidden him "go up to
Ramoth-Gilead *and prosper*," Ahab leads his army across the
Jordan, and marches against the city which he desires to

recover. Jehoshaphat accompanies him, feeling that he is bound in honour to do so by the promise which he has made (1 Kings xxii. 4). But Benhadad is on his guard, and has marched in full force to defend the place. The armies meet. Ahab, either because he thinks to baffle the prophecy by not taking the position of commander-in-chief, or because he has heard that Benhadad specially seeks his life, enters into the battle as a private soldier, not in the royal, but in an ordinary, chariot. The disguise brings Jehoshaphat into danger; he escapes, however, on being recognized by his war-cry. But the doomed king of Israel, despite all his precautions, cannot escape. Early in the battle "a certain man" of the Syrian host "drew his bow at a venture," and the arrow "smote the king of Israel between the joints of his harness " (ver. 34), and Ahab could fight no more. With a braver and nobler spirit, however, than we should have looked for in him, he uttered no cry, called for no assistance, but merely quitted the field, and, "stayed up in his chariot" (ver. 35), awaited the result. It came with evening. The battle increased and raged during the whole day ; each side had held its own ; neither was victorious ; but about sunset, when both armies had retired a little, it became known to the Israelites that their king was dead, that towards the close of the day he had expired, having bled to death. The camp was at once broken up, and the army dispersed itself. Jehoshaphat returned to Jerusalem. The body of Ahab was conveyed in his blood-stained chariot to Samaria, and there received honourable burial (ver. 37) ; but the chariot in which he had died, being washed in the pool of Samaria, stained its waters with his gore, so that, when "the abandoned outcasts of the city "—votaries, probably, of Ashtoreth— "came, according to their shameless usage, for their morning bath in the pool, they found it red with the blood of the first apostate king of Israel." [1]

So ended the reign of Ahab. His widow, Jezebel, survived him ; and he left behind him a large number of sons, the offspring of his various wives and concubines. Two of them only are known by name, Ahaziah and Jehoram : of these the former succeeded him. Ahab is said to have reigned twenty-two years (1 Kings xvi. 29) ; but both his first and last year were probably incomplete.

---

[1] Stanley, "Lectures on the Jewish Church," vol. ii. p. 271.

CHAPTER XI.

JEHOSHAPHAT.

JEHOSHAPHAT, the son of Asa, succeeded his father on the throne of Judah in the fourth year of Ahab, king of Israel, at the age of thirty-five (1 Kings xxii. 41, 42). In the earlier part of his reign he was under the apprehension that Ahab would invade his territories, in order to recover the disputed cities upon his northern frontier, which were held sometimes by one of the two powers, sometimes by the other. He therefore made it his first business to " strengthen himself against Israel " (2 Chron. xvii. 1). He carried on with great vigour the work of fortification, which had been begun by Rehoboam (ibid. xi. 5-11), and continued to some extent both by Abijah and Asa (ibid. xiii. 19 ; xiv. 6, 7 ; xvi. 6) ; at the same time placing strong garrisons in the various fortified towns, and especially in the disputed frontier cities (ibid. xvii. 2). In some parts of Judæa he erected isolated castles, as places of refuge in case of invasion (ibid. ver. 11), and throughout the whole country he built " cities of store," or magazines of arms and provisions. In Jerusalem he collected a large military force, under five chief captains, Adnah, Jehohanan, Amasiah the son of Zichri, Eliada, and Jehozabad, who were placed at the head of five distinct *corps-d'armée* (ibid. vers. 13-18) ; but the numbers

assigned to the several corps in the present text of Chronicles
are incredible. Over the garrisons in the other towns he
placed his own sons as commandants, or else princes chosen
out of the host, supplying them in abundance with "the sinews
of war," in the shape of silver, and gold, and precious things
(ibid. xxi. 3).

The extent of these preparations seems to have alarmed most
of the neighbouring kingdoms, and neither Ahab, nor any of
the other chiefs of tribes or nations, ventured for many years to
measure their strength with that of the Jewish monarch. "The
fear of the Lord fell upon all the kingdoms of the lands that were
round about Judah, so that they made no war against Jehoshaphat" (2 Chron. xvii. 10). On the contrary, they in many cases
made friendly overtures, either accepting a position of dependence,
or seeking to conciliate his favour by valuable presents. The
Arabians, on at least one occasion, presented him with flocks
and herds, 7,700 rams, and the same number of he-goats (ibid.
ver. 11) ; while the Philistines, who since the disruption of
Solomon's kingdom had asserted their independence, voluntarily placed themselves under his dominion and agreed to pay
him an annual tribute. It was probably at this time, when he
"had riches and honour in abundance" (ver. 5), that the Jewish
monarch conceived the idea of still further strengthening his
position by entering into an alliance with the most powerful of
his neighbours, and commenced the negotiations which terminated in his "joining affinity with Ahab" (2 Chron. xviii. 1).
Ahab was well satisfied to give his daughter, Athaliah, in
marriage to Jehoshaphat's eldest son, Jehoram ; and a connexion was thus established, which in course of time became
a political confederation—a *quasi*-reunion of the divided kingdoms. Jehoshaphat, as we have seen, readily joined the king
of Israel in his last Syrian war, declaring that "he was as Ahab,
his horses as Ahab's horses, his people as Ahab's people"
(2 Kings xxii. 4), and went up with him against the Syrians to
Ramoth-Gilead to battle. The venture nearly cost him his life
(ibid. vers. 31, 32), since he was mistaken for Ahab, and became
the object of special attack, but he was fortunately recognized
before it was too late, and so escaping without even a wound,
"returned to his house in peace to Jerusalem" (2 Chron. xix. 1).

It was soon after this, probably in the next year, that Jehoshaphat experienced the only attack that was made upon his

territories during his long reign of twenty-five years. Moab, which had recently rebelled against the northern kingdom, and shaken off the yoke of the house of Omri, having entered into alliance with the Ammonites and a portion of the Edomite nation, came against Judah with a "great multitude" (2 Chron. xx. 2) from the country beyond the Dead Sea, and marching round the southern end of the Sea through the plain known as the "Valley of Salt," encamped on the heights opposite the mouth of the Arnon, by the abundant fountain, fruitful vineyards (Cant. i. 14), and dense palm-groves of Engedi. Jehoshaphat hastily collected troops to meet the invaders, and held a solemn service in the Temple to implore God's assistance in the dangerous crisis, after which he marched out from Jerusalem into "the wilderness of Tekoa" (2 Chron. xx. 20)—the bare table-land south and a little east of the city looking down upon the Dead Sea. It had been announced to him by the prophet Jahaziel, that he would have no need to engage the enemy—Israel need only "stand still, and see the salvation of God" (ibid. ver. 17)—the battle would be the Lord's and not theirs (ver. 15); and the result was in accordance with the announce-ment. The army, marching south-eastward in joyful fashion, singing hymns of praise, came suddenly at the edge of the high ground upon a scene of carnage and confusion, such as has rarely met the eye of one threatened by an assailant. All over the slopes of the rocks along the whole ascent of Ziz lay "dead bodies fallen to the earth," heaps upon heaps, corpses piled one upon another. There was not a man left alive. A panic or an impulse of madness had seized upon the entire host, and first the swords of Moab and Ammon had been turned against their allies from Edom—then, when Edom was destroyed, Moab and Ammon had attacked and slaughtered one another. Every-where corpses laden with golden ornaments and rich jewels strewed the ground, and it took the army of Jehoshaphat three days to gather the spoil. On the fourth day a solemn thanks-giving was offered to Jehovah for the mercy vouchsafed; the spoil was blessed and distributed; and the opening in the hills where the distribution was made received the name, which long attached to it, of 'Emek Bĕrachah, "the Valley of Blessing." "Then they returned, every man of Judah and Jerusalem, and Jehoshaphat in the forefront of them, to go again to Jerusalem with joy . . . And they came to Jerusalem with psalteries and harps and trumpets unto the house of the Lord" (2 Chron. xx. 27, 28).

In one other war only do we find Jehoshaphat engaged. In his eighteenth or nineteenth year, an invitation reached him from Jehoram, son of Ahab, and king of Israel, to join in an expedition which he was about to undertake against the Moabites, with the object of chastising their rebellion. Mesha, king of Moab, had revolted from Israel at the death of Ahab, expelled the Israelite garrisons from his towns,[1] and re-established Moabite independence. Jehoram, newly come to the throne, determined on making a great effort to re-subjugate the nation, and distrusting his own unassisted strength, resolved to call in the aid of his two principal neighbours, Judah and Edom. Jehoshaphat answered his invitation as he had answered that of Ahab—" I will go up: I am as thou art, my people as thy people, my horses as thy horses" (2 Kings iii. 7). And the king of Edom was also induced to join the confederacy. It was arranged that the attack should be made from the south-west, where it would be least likely to be expected. A combined Israelite and Jewish army proceeded through southern Judæa into Edom, where an Edomite contingent joined it, and the augmented force, rounding the southern extremity of the Dead Sea from west to east, passed through the " wilderness of Edom," or the arid Edomite country south-east of the sea to the deep wady, which separated between Edom and Moab, where they expected to find water. But it happened that the torrent-bed was dry. There were no wells in the neighbourhood, and no torrent-course so likely to yield water as the one which they had found dried up. It seemed to the kings that they and their whole army must die of thirst. Under these circumstances, Jehoshaphat bethought himself of inquiring whether there was not a prophet of Jehovah in the camp, to whom application might be made for assistance, or at least for advice (ibid. ver. 11). That he had not put the question before, shows the corrupting influence of evil company. It turned out that a prophet had accompanied the expedition, though without the knowledge of its leaders—namely, Elisha the son of Shaphat, whom Elijah during the lifetime of Ahab had appointed to be his successor in the prophetical office (1 Kings

[1] See the " Inscription of Mesha" on the " Moabite Stone" (" Records of the Past," vol. xi. pp. 166–168).

xix. 16, 21); and the kings, humbling themselves in their
necessity, went in a body to the tent where Elisha was, and
represented their need.   At first the prophet replied roughly,
bidding Jehoram "get him to the prophets of his father and
to the prophets of his mother" (2 Kings iii. 13); but after a time
he relented, on account of Jehoshaphat's general piety, and,
being visited by the divine *afflatus* under the influence of music,
he at once gave advice and predicted relief.   The kings were
recommended to open trenches in the dry soil of the torrent-
bed, and promised that, though they should "neither see wind
nor rain," yet soon all the valley would be full of water, so that
they should have abundance to drink.   Moreover they should
defeat the Moabites, and overrun their country, which they were
commanded to devastate to the utmost (ibid. ver. 19).   All
happened as Elisha had foretold.   In the night a rush of water,
caused probably by a storm at some little distance, came down
the torrent-course, filling the trenches with a liquid which "had
the red tinge of the soil of Edom."[1]   The thirsty host refreshed
itself, and returned to camp.   When morning came, the
Moabites, advancing to the attack, saw the red liquid in the
standing pools, and—the morning sun assisting the illusion—
imagined that what they saw was blood.   A quarrel must, they
supposed, have broken out in the enemy's camp, as in their
own so recently,[2] and the soldiers of the three nations must have
slain one another (ibid. ver. 23).   Elated by these false hopes,
and inspired by the wild greed that always animates the
nomadic warriors of the East, they rushed hastily across the
intervening space and fell upon the camp of Israel, which they
expected to find undefended and full of spoil.   But they found
it well watched and guarded.   The three kings rose up boldly
against their assailants, repulsed them, and inflicted upon them
a severe defeat; after which they crossed the border, entered
Moab, and marched through the entire country, devastating
and destroying.   The towns they laid in ruins; the arable land
they "marred" by scattering stones over it; the fruit trees they
cut down; and the springs of water they stopped.   We have
here a picture on a small scale of the injuries commonly
inflicted by an Oriental army of invasion on the districts
which it traversed, injuries not unfrequently represented in the

[1] Ewald, "History of Israel,' vol. iv. p. 88, Eng. tr.
[2] See above, p. 80.

sculptures of the Assyrians.[1] One stronghold only held out against the forces of the three kings. This was Kir-Haraseth, a mountain fortress very strongly situated on a lofty peak about ten miles from the south-eastern corner of the Dead Sea, and now known as Kerak. It is surrounded on all sides by a deep and narrow valley, which again is completely enclosed by mountains rising higher than the town. From these heights the slingers were able to send their missiles into the place, and greatly to harass the defenders, who, after one desperate sally which failed, had recourse to the religious rite of child-sacrifice so familiar to the Moabite and Ammonite nations. The king of Moab himself took his firstborn son and successor, and in the full sight of the besieging armies publicly offered him up to Chemosh upon the ramparts of the fortress, in the desperate hope that his god, pleased by the sacrifice, would interfere, and somehow or other avert the impending surrender. The desired effect was produced, but not (probably) in the way that he had expected. The besiegers, horror-stricken at the sight, and alarmed at the thought that they had driven the king to the commission of his fearful deed, drew off their forces and gave up the siege, recrossing the frontier and returning to their several countries (2 Kings iii. 25–27).

The religious policy of Jehoshaphat was modelled on that of his father, Asa, but was even more determined and thorough-going. He was a firm opponent of idolatry of every kind. It must not be supposed that the alliance and affinity into which he entered with the house of Omri had any other than a political motive. The Phœnician religion possessed not the slightest attraction for him. "He sought not unto Baalim" (2 Chron. xvii. 3); and it is doubtful whether his son's wife, Athaliah, was indulged during his lifetime with any facilities for even the private exercise of the idolatrous cult whereto she was so much attached. He set himself, moreover, to root out from Judah all those remains of the ancestral high-place worship and grove worship which had escaped the reforming zeal of Asa, and still maintained themselves in various parts of the Judæan territory. A complete extirpation of these rites was beyond his power (2 Chron. xx. 33); but whatever a strong will and untiring vigilance could effect towards reducing the evil

[1] See Layard, "Monuments of Nineveh," second series, pl. 40; Rawlinson, "Ancient Monarchies," vol. ii. p. 84.

to a minimum was effected by Jehoshaphat (1 Kings xxii. 43; 2 Chron. xvii. 6; xix. 3). He held communication from time to time with two prophets of Jehovah, Jehu the son of Hanani, and Eliezer the son of Dodavah; and though these persons did not in all respects approve of his conduct or his policy, yet they lent him, especially the former, a certain general approval (2 Chron. xix. 3), and probably advised him with respect to the practical reforms which he laboured to introduce. He found an extreme ignorance of God's law prevalent in many parts of the land; and he therefore " in his third year" (ibid. xvii. 7) devised a scheme for remedying this evil by the appointment of competent persons to give instruction all over the country in more precise knowledge of religion and of the legislation of Moses. Five of the most respected of the laity,[1] together with nine Levites and two priests, were formed into a sort of roving Commission, which had orders to visit every place in the kingdom, not omitting the smallest, and to spread abroad among the people generally those blessings of religious knowledge which were apt to die out in remote places, and in troublous times scarcely to be preserved in real purity anywhere except in Jerusalem. They had with them "the Book of the Law of the Lord"[2] (ibid. ver. 9), and "went about throughout all the cities of Judah, and taught the people" (ibid.) out of it.

Jehoshaphat further established an entirely new system for the administration of justice. In every city he appointed a judge or judges—laymen apparently—to try causes of all kinds in the first instance, while at Jerusalem he set up a Final Court of Appeal, to which those who were dissatisfied with the local decision might remove their causes. This Court consisted, like the roving Commission, of three elements, Priests, Levites, and " the chief of the fathers," or laymen of mature age and high position, who might be trusted to administer justice without fear or favour, and especially to be above accepting bribes. It had two presidents. In cases ecclesiastical, where the interests of religion or of the clerical order were concerned, the High Priest of the time was to preside and deliver judgment; while in ordinary civil or criminal causes, a layman of great authority, "the ruler of the house of Judah," was to take his

---

[1] Chron. xvii. 7, with Ewald's comment ("History of Israel," iv. 53).
[2] This is important in its bearing on the question of the preservation of the Book of the Law between the times of Solomon and Josiah.

place.¹ Hitherto the king himself had been, it would seem, the sole official to whom appeal could be made; this must have been found very inconvenient both for king and people, and an alteration of the practice must have been greatly needed. Jehoshaphat's arrangement was based upon sound principles, and seems to have given general satisfaction. It secured the swift and impartial administration of justice, and neither subjected the temporalty to the spiritualty, nor the spiritualty to the temporalty.

There can be no doubt that, on the whole, Judæa was extremely prosperous under Jehoshaphat's rule. He was certainly the ablest and most energetic king that had reigned over Judah since the time of Solomon. While it cannot be denied that the one fatal mistake which he made in joining affinity with Ahab had, in course of time, the most terribly disastrous consequences, leading as it did to the desecration of the Temple, the complete apostasy of the State during the space of six years, and the almost entire destruction of the seed of David, yet the immediate results were, in a worldly point of view, advantageous, and a most flourishing condition of affairs seems to have been temporarily established. Commerce revived; Jehoshaphat's relations with the Edomites enabled him to resume possession of the port of Ezion-geber upon the shores of the Red Sea; and, although on one occasion the fleet which he had prepared to sail to Ophir for gold was destroyed by a storm almost before it was well out of harbour (2 Kings xxii. 48), yet there is reason to believe that the trade was, at any rate to some extent, restored, and that in Jehoshaphat's reign Jewish fleets were once more seen upon the Red Sea and in the Indian Ocean, pursuing the peaceful occupations of traffic and commerce. Jehoshaphat built commercial cities as well as fortresses, and everywhere promoted a vigorous commercial policy.² The riches which flowed in upon him (2 Chron. xvii. 5; xviii. 1) were the natural result of this course of action, though no doubt his resources received large accessions from various other quarters (ibid. xvii. 5, 11; xx. 25).

Jehoshaphat died at the age of sixty,³ leaving behind him seven sons of full age, the eldest of whom, Jehoram, he had designated as his successor (2 Chron. xxi. 2, 3).

---

¹ 2 Chron. xix. 5-11.   ² Ewald, "History of Israel," vol. iv. p. 57.
³ 1 Kings xxii. 42.

CHAPTER XII.

AHAZIAH OF ISRAEL.

Ahaziah of Israel, a shadowy personage—Shortness of his reign—He "does very wickedly"—His commercial alliance with Judah—His unfortunate war with Moab—His accidental fall from a window, and consultation of the god of Ekron—Fire called down from heaven by Elijah on his messengers—His death predicted—His character.

AHAZIAH, the eldest son and successor of Ahab, is one of the most shadowy of the Israelite kings. The duration of his reign is stated at no more than two years (1 Kings xxii. 31); and there is reason to believe that the actual length did not greatly, if at all, exceed a year. (Comp. 1 Kings xxii. 31 with 2 Kings iii. 1.) He lay, moreover, during the greater part of this time, a helpless cripple on a sick-bed, and was incapable of giving any new direction to the policy of the State, which simply drifted on in the line that had been chosen for it by Ahab. He is said by one historian to have "done evil in the sight of the Lord, and to have walked in the way of his father, and in the way of his mother (Jezebel) ; and in the way of Jeroboam the son of Nebat, who made Israel to sin" (1 Kings xxii. 52); by another to have "*done very wickedly*" (2 Chron. xx. 35). It is clear that he maintained both the calf-worship of Jeroboam and the Baal-worship of his father and mother (1 Kings xxii. 53), in one respect even going beyond his father, who had never, so far as we are told, resorted to the foreign shrines of foreign gods for prophetic intimations concerning the future. Ahaziah seemingly recognized no prophetic inspiration as belonging to any of the prophets of Israel, but, although Elijah, Elisha, and probably Micaiah, were still living, did not

care to consult them, but sent his envoys afield, to learn the
future from an oracular shrine in Philistia !

Nothing is related concerning him but what is unfortunate.
He renewed the close alliance with Judah, which had been
made by his father (1 Kings xxii. 44 ; 1 Chron. xx. 36), uniting
with Jehoshaphat in the maritime enterprise on which he was
bent, and engaging in the construction of the joint fleet which
was intended to make voyages to Ophir for gold. The ships
were constructed in the port of Ezion-geber on the Red Sea at
the head of the Gulf of Akabah, and were manned (apparently)
by Jewish sailors only. A disaster followed. Scarcely had
the fleet set sail, when it was driven back to port by a violent
tempest, which greatly damaged most of the vessels. Ahaziah
ascribed the calamity to the unskilfulness of the Jewish
mariners, and proposed that in any future voyage the ships
should be manned by mixed crews from the two nations
(2 Kings xxii. 49), but Jehoshaphat was too proud to accept
such a proposal, and a coolness must have followed in the
relations between the allies, though there seems to have been
no actual rupture.

With the Moabites on the south-eastern frontier of Israel the
case was different. There Ahab's death produced an immediate
rupture of peaceful relations (2 Kings i. 1 ; iii. 5) ; and a war
followed (whereof we have the Moabite account on the "Stone
of Mesha") which seems to have consisted of little more than a
series of Israelite reverses. Mesha recovered in succession
Medeba, Baal-meon, Kirjathaim, Ataroth, Nebo, and Jahaz,[1]
which had all been occupied by the Israelites. In Nebo alone
he slew no fewer than seven thousand men.[2] The entire
country was recovered, and a number of ruined cities rebuilt
and strongly fortified with walls, and towers, and gates, and
moats.[3] The entire tribute which Moab had previously paid
(2 Kings iii. 4) was lost, and a powerful kingdom was set up on
the eastern shore of the Dead Sea, which threatened both
Israel and Judah. It would seem that the Israelites made no
active efforts to meet and defeat the foe in the field, but
contented themselves with resisting behind walls, which in no
instance proved strong enough to protect them against the fury
of the Moabite attack. A single year sufficed for the capture

[1] See the "Records of the Past," vol xi. pp. 166, 167.
[2] Ibid. p. 166, line 16.   [3] Ibid. p. 167, lines 21-30.

or massacre of all the Israelite garrisons, and for the complete establishment of the Moabites as an independent nation in the country which they claimed as their own.

It was probably while this war was in progress, and Israel suffering defeat after defeat, that the accident befell Ahaziah to which we have already alluded.   He had the misfortune to "fall down through the lattice," which closed the window of an upper chamber wherein he was sitting, in his palace at Samaria (2 Kings i. 2).   The lattice opened outwards,[1] and was either weak or insufficiently fastened, so that, when he leant against it, the whole gave way, and he was precipitated to the ground. The fall must have been from a considerable height, and though not fatal at once it yet caused severe injuries.   It was then that Ahaziah showed his want of faith, not only in the Jehovistic prophets of his country, but in those of the new religion equally, and without making any application to the priests or prophets of Baal or Ashtoreth, with which Samaria swarmed, dispatched a sacred embassy to the Philistine city of Ekron, to inquire of the Baal worshipped there whether he was to live or die.   This god was known as Baal-zebul, "Baal, the lord of flies," the god, *i.e.*, who could send on a country a plague of flies or avert it.[2] He was perhaps considered to possess a special healing power, or else to deliver oracles on which complete dependence might be placed.   Ahaziah's messengers started; but ere they had proceeded very far, they were met by a figure which was unmistakable.   Elijah the Tishbite, with his long flowing locks and abundant beard, and general profusion of hair, stood before them, clad in his leathern girdle and his shaggy cloak of undressed sheepskin.   Undoubtedly, they recognized him ; and when he commanded them, in a tone of authority (2 Kings i. 6), to cease their useless journey and return to their master with his answer to Ahaziah's question, instead of the Ekronite god's answer, they obeyed unhesitatingly. The answer was, that the king's sickness was to death—never should he rise from the couch on which he lay in Samaria, but should "surely die" (ibid. ver. 4).   The messengers returned to Ahaziah with the prophet's message, and made it clear to the king who was their interlocutor.   The king at once, with the

---

[1] Like modern "Venetian blinds." This is the case in the East to the present day.

[2] Comp. the Ζεὺς ἀπόμυιος of the Greek.

besotted folly and presumption of his race, sent to seize the prophet's person, as if physical force could avail against one who was divinely commissioned and upheld. Fifty soldiers under a captain were sent to arrest and bring into his presence the king's enemy, with the issue that all know. Elijah commanded fire to come down from heaven, and the fire fell and consumed the captain with his fifty (ibid. ver. 10). The terrible result was reported to Ahaziah, but in no way shook his purpose; a second captain and a second band of fifty were sent upon the same errand, and experienced the same fate. Still the king did not blench. He required a third captain to undertake the perilous duty, and exposed a third band of fifty to the danger which had already cost the lives of two previous bands. Fortunately, the third captain was a man on whom warnings were not lost. He knew the fate which had befallen his predecessors, and determined on a course wholly different from theirs, whereby he hoped to move the prophet to compassion. Instead of commanding, he entreated. "O man of God," he said, kneeling upon his knees, "I pray thee, let my life, and the life of these fifty thy servants, be precious in thy sight" (ibid. ver. 13). He did not even ask Elijah to "come down" and accompany him. But the prophet, having sufficiently vindicated God's honour, was directed so to do, and, descending from the eminence on which he had stood, went to Samaria, entered the royal palace, and standing by the sick-bed of the king, declared to him God's will—"Forasmuch as thou hast sent messengers to inquire of Baal-zebub the god of Ekron, is it not because there is no God in Israel to inquire of his word? Therefore thou shalt not come down from the bed whither thou hast gone up, but shalt surely die" (ibid. ver. 16). The injuries received were not necessarily fatal, but Ahaziah's conduct had rendered them fatal; as a punishment for the insult which he had offered to Jehovah, the Divine fiat had gone forth that he should die. Ahaziah died in the eighteenth year of Jehoshaphat (2 Kings iii. 1), having succeeded his father in Jehoshaphat's seventeenth year (1 Kings xxii. 51), having thus reigned less than two years—possibly not much more than one. He was a weak and incapable prince, obstinate, perverse, and foolish. His death probably saved the kingdom from sinking lower, both religiously and politically.

CHAPTER XIII.

JEHORAM OF ISRAEL.

Ahaziah of Israel succeeded by Jehoram, his brother—Jehoram's pseudo-reformation—His expedition against Moab, and its poor result—His war with Syria—Frustration of his plans through Elisha's foreknowledge—Attempt to seize Elisha's person fails—Brief cessation of hostilities—Renewed attack and siege of Samaria—Siege raised—Jehoram recovers Ramoth-Gilead, but is wounded—Jehu, anointed to succeed him by the command of Elisha, hastens to Samaria, and, taking him by surprise, slays him.

AHAZIAH left no son to succeed him upon the throne (2 Kings i. 17), which consequently fell to his brother, Jehoram or Joram, who was (like Ahaziah) the issue of Ahab by Jezebel. Jehoram began his reign by religious changes, which seemed to promise a complete revolution—the abolition of the Baal-worship introduced into Israel by Ahab at the instigation of his Phœnician consort, and the restoration of the religious system established by Jeroboam.[1] He "put away the image of Baal that his father had made" (2 Kings iii. 2) —removed it, that is, from the temple of Baal in Samaria, or at any rate from the position in which it had been set up for public worship there. According to Ewald, this was a "lofty column with an image of Baal standing in front of it,"[2] which was regarded with extreme veneration by the Baal-worshippers, and was ultimately destroyed by Jehu (2 Kings x. 27). Such a proceeding on the part of the king might have been expected to lead on to further stringent measures, as the destruction of the image, or the shutting up or pulling down of the temple which contained it, and the formal abolition of the worship throughout the country. But Jehoram appears to have been

---

[1] See 2 Kings iii. 3.　　　[2] "History of Israel," vol. iv. p. 78.

half-hearted in his religious changes. He must have personally disapproved of the sensuous Phœnician religion ; but he either shrank from carrying out his views to the full for fear of popular disturbances, or he was so far under the influence of the Queen-mother, Jezebel, that he submitted to a compromise, and while publicly condemning the Baal-worship, privately connived at its continuance. Elisha's angry words (in verse 13)—" Get thee to the prophets of thy father and to the prophets of thy mother " — sufficiently indicate his dissatisfaction with the king's half-measures ; and the history of Jehu's reformation (2 Kings x. 21–28) shows that the Baal temple, image, and worship, all continued to the end of Jehoram's reign, and were not removed until the reign of his successor.

From religious reforms Jehoram turned his attention to matters political. The revolt of Moab in the reign of his predecessor, and the complete recovery by the Moabites of their independence through a series of successes unchequered by a reverse, constituted a new source of danger to the State, which could not afford the lowering of its prestige consequent upon the brilliant campaign conducted by Mesha. An effort was necessary, if not to recover Moab, at any rate to repair the loss of honour involved in the successful rebellion ;[1] and Jehoram, seemingly in his first year, conceived the design of forming a powerful confederation against the triumphant rebels, which should at the least severely chastise them for their audacity. In the first instance he applied to Jehoshaphat, king of Judah, who had shown himself well-disposed both towards Ahab (1 Kings xxii. 4, 29) and towards Ahaziah (ibid. ver. 44–49), and solicited his aid, which was willingly granted (2 Kings iii. 7) ; after which negotiations were entered into with the king of Edom, a semi-independent monarch,[2] and he also was induced to join the league. Edom was at this time growing in power, and probably entertained a covert jealousy of Moab, which was its near neighbour and might be a formidable enemy. The king therefore accepted the third position in the confederacy, and even gave the armies of Israel and Judah passage through his territory, that so they might have the better chance of taking the Moabites by

[1] Ewald, "History of Israel," vol. iv. p. 88.
[2] Comp. 1 Kings xxii. 47 with 2 Kings iii. 9.

surprise. After traversing the waterless tract west and south
of the Dead Sea, the frontier of Moab was approached at a
point where a deep torrent bed[1] separated between Moab and
Edom. Here it seems to have been supposed that water would
be found ;[2] but the bed of the stream proved wholly dry, and
Jehoram gave way to despair. He was, however, persuaded by
Jehoshaphat to make an appeal for aid to the prophet, Elisha,
who had accompanied the host *proprio motu;* and Elisha,
after some contemptuous expressions and a half-refusal, was
induced to exert his supernatural powers in order to save the
army. The details have been already given in our account of
the life of Jehoshaphat,[3] and need not be here repeated. The host,
refreshed in the night by a rush of water down the gully caused
by some heavy rain at a distance, was set upon in the morning
by the Moabites, who, seeing the ruddy sunrise reflected the
pools which the flood had left, imagined that the red liquid was
blood, and that the allies had fallen out and fought each other.
Their error was fatal to them. Rushing, half-armed probably,
and in a disorderly crowd, against the Israelite camp, they were
met by an enemy who was expecting their onset, repulsed, and
routed. A hurried flight followed, and a hot pursuit; great
numbers of the Moabites were slain; even the cities afforded
little protection, and the land was devastated and ruined. At
last the king of Moab stood at bay n Kir-Haraseth, the
strongest of his fortresses. Then occurred that horrible scene,
which has been already described[4]—the king openly offering
his son as a burnt offering upon the wall. Shocked and
dismayed at the sight, the besiegers broke up their camp,
and returned to their respective countries.

A modern historian remarks, that " had there been a Joab or
a David then alive in Israel, such an issue of the campaign
would not have been tolerated; but already a worm of inward
weakness had begun to gnaw at the national heart and at its
confidence in Jehovah. From that day, however, Moab remained independent; and long ages after, every time that other
causes had enfeebled the kingdom of the Ten Tribes, the

---

[1] Probably the modern " Wady Kurahy," or " Wady el Ahsy."

[2] The Wady el Ahsy is now regarded as perennial (Robinson, " Biblical
Researches," vol. ii. p. 488), but it would only require a succession of two
or three dry seasons to render it waterless.   [3] See above, p. 82.

[4] Supra, p. 83.

relations between the two states were inverted, and roving bands from Moab marched across the Jordan on plundering incursions"[1] (2 Kings xiii. 20 ; xxiv. 2 ; Jer. xlviii. 27).

The only other war which Jehoram waged was with Syria. Incursions, on the one side and on the other, were of constant occurrence during almost the whole period of the monarchy. "The Syrians went out by companies, and brought away captives out of the land of Israel" (2 Kings v. 2), and the Israelites no doubt retaliated, and from time to time sent their plundering expeditions into Syria, and took booty and prisoners. But, before Jehoram had been on the throne many years, a more threatening system of attack was organized by the second Benhadad, and attempts were for a second time made to push the war to extremities, and to effect the subjection of Samaria to the Syrian yoke. The enterprising Aramæan monarch led a series of expeditions into the Israelite territory with the hope of surprising and cutting off detachments, or of otherwise gaining some considerable advantage ; but his expectations were frustrated after a manner for which he found it hard to account —his designs seemed to be penetrated, his intentions known, and his best strokes counterplotted and made ignominious failures. Suspecting treachery among his officers, he entreated them to unmask the traitor, when he was met by the assurance that his suspicion was an entire mistake—the Syrian ranks harboured no traitor—but Elisha, by his supernatural powers, was able to penetrate and expose all his plans (2 Kings vi. 8–12). Naturally, he became anxious, under these circumstances, to obtain possession of Elisha's person ; and, having learnt that the prophet was residing in a small Israelite town called Dothan, he sent an army thither to take him. Elisha, though angelic hosts surrounded him (ibid. ver. 17), was instructed to yield, and obeyed. He persuaded his captors, however, that he was not the man they sought, and induced them to accompany him to Samaria, under a strange species of illusion ; after which he delivered them over to Jehoram, whose first impulse was to put them to death. This impulse Elisha checked (ibid. ver. 22). The king, he said, should rather entertain his prisoners hospitably, and release them freely, and let them return to their own country. The advice was followed ; and Benhadad appears to have been so far

[1] Ewald, "History of Israel," vol. iv. p. 90.

touched by the generous treatment of his soldiers, that for some considerable space he refrained from further hostilities against the Israelites. During this interval "the bands of Syria came no more into the land of Israel" (ibid. ver. 23).

But in his heart Benhadad had not laid aside his ambitious projects. It cannot have been many years later that, suddenly and without further provocation, he "gathered all his host," invaded Israel, and, carrying all before him, advanced into the heart of the country, and laid siege to the capital (ver. 24). His troops blocked the city in on every side, and reduced the inhabitants to such straits that "an ass's head was sold for fourscore pieces of silver, and the fourth part of a cab of dove's dung for five pieces of silver" (ver. 25). The famine within the place was intense. Tender and delicate women were driven to devour their own children ; and the king became cognizant of the fact, as he was going the round of the wall, inspecting the garrison (vers. 26–30). Thereupon he threatened to take the life of Elisha, whom he regarded as responsible, since he supposed that, by miracle, the prophet could at any time give deliverance, if he chose. Elisha saved himself by a prophecy—within four and twenty hours, he declared, should wheaten flour be sold in Samaria at the rate of a shekel (half a crown) for a peck and a half, and barley at the rate of a shekel for three pecks (2 Kings vii. 1). Incredible as the prophecy appeared, it produced a certain effect, and procured the prophet a short respite. The general inclination was to wait and see what would be the result, and the king gave way to the popular voice. The morrow was anxiously expected, but ere the morrow's dawn broke, sure intelligence reached Jehoram that the siege was raised. At nightfall the Syrians had heard sounds, which they interpreted as signifying the approach of a vast host— Egyptians, they supposed, or Hittites, summoned to assist them by the Samaritans (ver. 6) :—unprepared to face a new enemy, they fled with all speed "in the twilight," leaving their tents standing, with the baggage animals tethered, and only en- deavouring to put a broad space between themselves and their foes. A little knot of deserters—lepers—learnt the facts during the night, and reported them ere morning came to the king. With the first dawn of day, the famished multitude of Samaria quitted the shelter of their walls and poured into the Syrian camp. It was almost as when the Grecian army at Platæa assaulted and took the fortified camp of the Persians.[1] Costly vessels, gold, and precious raiment lay about on all sides (ver. 8), and became the prey of the conquerors. Such an abundance of provisions was found in the camp that Elisha's prediction received its accomplishment in the letter. Ere evening fell, " a measure of fine (wheaten) flour was sold for a shekel " in the gate of Samaria, and " two measures of barley " for the same money (ver. 16)—scarcity was replaced by plenty, extreme peril by complete safety, despair by triumph and jubilation. A ghastly circumstance impressed the occurrence with extreme force upon the mind of the people. When Elisha delivered his prophecy, the great lord on whose hand the king of Israel leant had openly declared himself incredulous (ver. 2); Elisha had thereupon warned him, that, though he should witness the accomplishment of the prediction, it should be of no personal advantage to him. Now it happened that this identical lord was selected by Jehoram to preside over the gate of Samaria which lay opposite the Syrian camp, and through which crowds of persons were continually passing and repassing in haste to reach the camp or returning from it with their booty. The crush and throng were such, that in the course of the day, the lord, while striving to preserve order, was himself thrown to the ground by the eager people and unfortunately trampled to death (vers. 17–20).

The further course of the Syrian war is not given in Scripture with any detail ; but it appears that Jehoram, shortly after this panic flight of the enemy, took the offensive, and, in conjunction with his nephew and ally, Ahaziah king of Judah, invaded the Syrian possessions in northern Peræa, and recovered the important city of Ramoth-Gilead, which Ahab and Jehoshaphat had failed to take (1 Kings xxii. 29–36 ; 2 Kings viii. 28, ix. 1, 14). He received, however, severe wounds in the course of the siege, and in consequence withdrew to Jezreel for medical aid, leaving his army in Ramoth-Gilead under the command of Jehu, one of the captains of the host, to watch over the place (2 Kings ix. 14) and defend it, should the Syrians attempt its re-capture.

It was while matters were in this position, that Elisha, regarding the fitting time as at last arrived, proceeded to carry out the commission, which had been entrusted to Elijah many

---

[1] Herod. ix. 80.

years previously (1 Kings xix. 16), of anointing a new king to
the throne of Israel in the place of Jehoram, whose sins had
forfeited his crown.   One of the "sons of the prophets" was
sent by him to the Israelite army at Ramoth-Gilead, with instructions to seek out Jehu, the son of Nimshi, and, having
obtained a private audience, to anoint him king of Israel with
the holy oil of the sanctuary, a portion of which the prophet
put into his hands (2 Kings ix. 1).   The mission was carried
out.   The young man hastened to Ramoth-Gilead, and "found
Jehu in the midst of his brother-officers, who were probably
holding a council of war."   He led him apart to a "chamber
within a chamber, i.e., to the innermost room of the house,
hastily explained to him his commission from Elisha," anointed
him with the holy oil, and "disappeared, as if fleeing from
the sight of men."[1]   Jehu went back to his brother-officers,
and when asked what the "wild fellow" had come about, taxed
them with being in complicity with him and knowing his errand.
This they denied (ver. 12), but when Jehu explained that the
man had come to "anoint him king over Israel," they readily
threw in their lot with his, acclaimed him monarch, and
enthroned him after a rude fashion, on the head of the outer
staircase which led down from the room wherein they were sitting
to the court.[2]   Having exhorted them to keep the matter secret,
and let no one leave the town to carry the news to Jehoram,
Jehu mounted his chariot, and, accompanied by a strong escort,
drove in haste to Jezreel.   There, as he approached, he was
espied from a watch-tower, and the king was informed of the
unusual occurrence.   After sending two horsemen to inquire
whether all was well whom Jehu detained, Jehoram himself,
accompanied by Ahaziah king of Judah, who happened to be
with him on a visit, went forth from the gate of Jezreel in his
chariot, Ahaziah following in another, to meet the new comers.
Jehu had been recognized by the warder in the watch-tower,
and the kings probably went out to learn what had brought
him in such hot haste from his post of duty at Ramoth-Gilead
to the royal residence.   Had his army suffered a defeat?   Were
the Syrians on their way to renew the siege of Samaria?   "Is
all well?" Jehoram asked him, as he drew near.   The reply

[1] Ewald, "History of Israel," vol. iv. p. 97, Eng. tr.
[2] See the note on 2 Kings ix. 13 in the "Speaker's Commentary,"
vol. iii. § 45.

revealed the fact that Jehu was a rebel and an enemy. "How can all be well, so long as the whoredoms of thy mother Jezebel, and her many witchcrafts, continue?" Jehoram understood the situation in a single moment, and turned and fled, shouting a warning to his brother monarch (ver. 23). But the movement and the warning were alike too late. Jehu seized his bow, and shot Jehoram in the back immediately between the shoulders, with such force that the arrow pierced to the heart, and the king sank down in his chariot and died. The scene of the fatal deed was close by "the plat of Naboth"; and Jehu, re-membering the prophecy of Elijah (1 Kings xxi. 21), ordered Jehoram's body to be cast into the plat and left to the dogs and vultures. Ahaziah was also pursued by Jehu's orders, and wounded so that he died.

Thus perished Jehoram, the last monarch of the house of Omri, which had reigned for three generations and had given four kings to Israel. He was a less irreligious ruler than either his father or his brother, and submitted himself in a certain measure to the guidance of the prophet Elisha (2 Kings vi. 21–23); but his character, on the whole, was weak and unsatis-factory; he had no stability of principle, no strong religious convictions. The influence of his mother dominated him; and he was himself subject to sudden impulses, which, if they had not met with external restraint, might have led him to the commission of great crimes (ibid. ver. 31). As a military com-mander his talents were respectable, but not first-rate. He somewhat raised the position of Israel among the nations which surrounded her; but he was unable to assume any great or commanding position. In the eye of the general historian, the leading figures of the time are rather Benhadad and Hazael, than Ahaziah or Jehoram. The reign of Jehoram lasted twelve years.

CHAPTER XIV.

JEHORAM OF JUDAH.

Date of Jehoram's accession—Probably associated in the kingdom by his father—His sole reign—Unsuccessful war with Edom—Revolt of Libnah—Jerusalem plundered by the Philistines and Arabs—Baal-worship introduced into Judah through the influence of Athaliah—Character of Jehoram—Warning reaches him from Elijah—His sickness and death.

THE successor of Jehoshaphat on the throne of Judah was his son Jehoram (1 Kings xxii. 50). There is some doubt about the time of his accession. In 2 Kings i. 17, his reign is made to precede by a year that of Jehoram of Israel; but in 2 Kings viii. 16 the order is reversed, and the Judæan Jehoram only becomes king in the fifth year of his Israelite namesake. The accounts are reconciled by the not improbable supposition that Jehoshaphat associated his son, Jehoram, with him in the kingdom in his sixteenth year, when he was about to join Ahab in his attack upon Ramoth-Gilead, and that the two reigned conjointly till Jehoshaphat's death in his twenty-fifth year, when Jehoram became sole king. He then had a reign of eight years, which was signalized by a series of disasters. First, the Edomites rose up in rebellion against him (2 Kings viii. 20), and, though Jehoram invaded their country, penetrating as far as Mount Seir,[1] and defeated their forces by a night attack, when they had surrounded him and brought him into peril (2 Kings viii. 21), yet he found it impossible to re-subjugate the people, and was compelled after a time to withdraw, and acknowledge their independence. About the same time, probably while the war was in progress within the territory of Idumæa, and the

---

[1] The "Zair" of 2 Kings viii. 21, from which it differs only in the sibilant, which is צ instead of ז.

military force of Judah thus engaged at a distance, the little town of Libnah on the Philistine frontier, which had been Jewish for centuries (Josh. xv. 42), broke out into revolt, and probably attached itself to the Philistine confederacy (2 Kings viii. 22). Finally, the Philistines on the south-west, and the Arabian populations on the south and south-east, attacked Judæa, apparently in combination, with such success that they actually stormed and took Jerusalem, plundered the royal palace of its valuables, and carried off as prisoners a number of the king's wives, and all his sons, except the youngest, Ahaziah or Jehoahaz (2 Chron. xxi. 16, 17). Judæa was thus degraded and disgraced in the eyes of all the surrounding nations, while the house of David was threatened with extinction.

It is the distinct statement of the sacred historians, that these calamities came upon Jehoram and upon his people as Divine judgments upon them for their irreligion (2 Kings viii. 18–22 ; 2 Chron. xxi. 10). Jehoshaphat, his father, had been so unwise as to cement his alliance with the kingdom of Israel by marrying Jehoram to Athaliah, the daughter of Ahab and Jezebel.[1] This ill-starred union introduced the Baal-worship into Judah. Jehoram fell completely under his wife's influence. Not only did he encourage the High-Place worship—"making high places in the mountains of Judah, and causing the inhabitants of Jerusalem to commit fornication,[2] and compelling Judah thereto" (2 Chron. xxi. 11); but he also "walked in the way of the kings of Israel, and made Judah and the inhabitants of Jerusalem to go a whoring, *like to the whoredoms of the house of Ahab*" (ibid. ver. 13). It was probably in his reign and with his sanction that there was built in Jerusalem a temple of Baal after the pattern of the temple erected by Ahab in Samaria (1 Kings xvi. 32), adorned with altars and images of Baal himself and his fellow-gods, the same which was afterwards destroyed by Jehoiada the High Priest in the reign of Joash (2 Kings xi. 18). Large numbers of the Jews were attracted by this novel worship with its wild gaiety and its licentious orgies ; the worship of Jehovah was discredited and almost discontinued, and the way was paved for those further changes, which his widow, Athaliah, introduced after his death.

Nor did Jehoram even bear a good character, apart from his idolatries. He was avaricious, cruel, and bloodthirsty. Soon

[1] 2 Chron. xviii. 1.   [2] *I.e.*, "give way to idolatry."

after his accession he murdered his six younger brothers, whom Jehoshaphat had greatly enriched, and had made commandants of the garrisons in the chief of the fortified cities of Judah (2 Chron. xxi. 2–4), the only assignable motive being his desire to seize their possessions.[1] At the same time he also put to death a number of the chief nobles, or "princes" (ibid.), of Judah, on what accusation is uncertain. After a time a Divine judgment of great severity was passed upon him on account of his wickedness. "There came a writing to him from Elijah the prophet," who, it would seem, was not yet translated, warning him that, as he had not " walked in the ways of Jehoshaphat his father, or in the ways of Asa king of Judah, but had walked in the way of the kings of Israel . . . *and had also slain his brethren* of his father's house, which were better than himself, the Lord would smite his people with a great stroke, and his children, and his wives, and all his goods"; and he himself should " have great sickness by disease of his bowels, until his bowels should fall out by reason of his sickness day by day" (2 Chron. xxi. 12–15). The former part of the prophecy had its fulfilment at the time of the Philistine and Arab invasion (ibid. ver. 17) ; and later on, after he had reigned six years and reached the age of thirty-eight (ibid. ver. 19), " the Lord smote him in his bowels with an incurable disease," and for two years he suffered grievously, dying at the age of forty (2 Kings viii. 7), and " departing without being desired" (2 Chron. xxi. 20). He "was buried with his fathers in the city of David" (1 Kings viii. 24) ; but, according to the writer of Chronicles (*l. s. c.*), " not in the sepulchres of the kings." The usual honour of a public funeral was also denied him—" his people made no burning for him, like the burning of his fathers " (ibid. ver. 19). Altogether his reign was one of the darkest and most unfortunate in the entire course of Judæan history, marked by disaster abroad, irreligion at home, and a combination of weakness and wickedness in the monarch.

[1] Ewald, "History of Israel," vol. iv. p. 94.

CHAPTER XV.

AHAZIAH OF JUDAH.

Ahaziah's age at his accession—Influence exercised over him by Athaliah—
Results of this influence—Ahaziah joins Jehoram of Judah in his
expedition against Ramoth-Gilead—Visits Jehoram at Jezreel, and is
involved in his fate—His body conveyed to Jerusalem.

THE captivity and death (2 Chron. xxii. 1) of all his elder
brothers gave the throne of Judah to Ahaziah, the youngest of the
sons of Jehoram, who by some accident had escaped the danger
of the Arab incursion. His age at his accession was no more
than twenty-two. Naturally, he fell, even more completely
than his father, under the influence of the imperious Athaliah,
in whom the spirit of her mother, Jezebel, seemed to live again,
and who, as Queen-Mother, held a most important position at
the Jewish court. "His mother," we are expressly told (ibid.
ver. 3), "was his counsellor to do wickedly." The Baal-
worship, begun under Jehoram, was, by Athaliah's influence,
extended and advanced in honour ; the temple worship was
suppressed, the temple itself treated with violence (2 Chron.
xxiv. 7), and precious ornaments and offerings, once dedicated
to Jehovah, and placed reverently within the temple limits,
were torn rudely from the sacred building, and transferred to
the sanctuary of Baal, where the court worshipped, prostrating
themselves before the images of the Baalim. The sanctuary
was committed to the care of its own high-priest, Mattan,
who probably took the place of the Aaronic high-priest in the
court ceremonial and the national ceremonies. How far the
degradation went, we cannot say. There are no prophetical
writings belonging to the time to furnish us with any amount of
detail, not even any spoken denunciations of prophets, from
which we might gather some idea of the actual amount of moral

evil which the Phœnician idolatry brought in its train. All is vague and obscure ; but there can be no reasonable doubt, that in the fifteen years between the death of Jehoshaphat and the accession of Joash, religion and morality in Judæa reached their lowest ebb, unless it were in the still more miserable time between Hezekiah and Josiah.

In political affairs, Ahaziah allowed his uncle, Jehoram of Israel, his mother's brother, to guide his conduct. At the request of Jehoram, he accompanied him in his expedition against Ramoth-Gilead, and shared in the glory gained by the Israelite arms, when the city was at last captured and re-occupied. From Ramoth-Gilead he returned to his capital ; but subsequently, on the return of Jehoram to Jezreel to be healed of his wounds, Ahaziah made the journey from Jerusalem to Jezreel for the purpose of visiting and cheering his sick relative. It happened that he had prolonged his visit to the time when Jehu, freshly anointed by Elisha's messenger, brought the news of his own rebellion to the Israelite court, and, taking Jehoram unawares, slew him with his own hand (2 Kings ix. 24). Ahaziah had just time to turn and fly ; but he was pursued by Jehu's orders, overtaken, and wounded to the death. His servants conveyed the dead body to Jerusalem, where it was laid with all due honours in the sepulchre of the kings (ibid. ver. 28).[1]

[1] It is scarcely possible to reconcile the two accounts of Ahaziah's death which we find in Chronicles (2 Chron. xxii. 9) and in Kings. The authority of Kings, where it differs from Chronicles, is to be preferred as the older ; and in this case the narrative is the more probable.

CHAPTER XVI.

JEHU.

Jehu's the most important of the Israelite dynasties—His early life—His rise to the high position of "Captain of the host"—Elisha has him anointed as king—His acceptance by the army—His rapid march to Jezreel and murder of Jehoram—His other bloody deeds—Murder of Jezebel — Of Ahaziah of Judah — Of Ahab's seventy sons — Of his partisans in Jezreel—Of forty-two princes of Judah—Of the Baal-worshippers in Samaria—His destruction of the Baal-worship—His character—His internal government—His relations with foreign powers —Tribute paid by him to Assyria—His death and burial.

WITH Jehu begins the most powerful, the most important, and the longest-lived of all the Israelite dynasties. The descendants of Jehu kept the throne "to the fourth generation" (2 Kings x. 30). Five kings in succession, furnished from a single house, showed that, under certain circumstances, God would allow, even to the northern kingdom, a certain prosperity and stability. The five reigns filled the space of above a century, and in the course of this period Israel attained the highest point of her greatness. Under Jeroboam the Second there was a near approach to a restoration of the Davidic kingdom, not, however, in the Davidic line, but in a line which aspired to supersede it.

The circumstances under which Jehu obtained the throne have been already touched upon.[1] His position, when he first comes under our notice, was simply that of a courtier, a member of the royal bodyguard, and an attendant on the king's person. The names of his father and grandfather are placed on record (2 Kings ix. 2), but no facts are recorded of them, nor is it explained why his grandfather's name superseded that of his father in the ordinary designation—"Jehu, the son of Nimshi" —by which he was known to his countrymen (1 Kings xix. 16 ;

[1] See above, p. 97.

2 Kings ix. 20 ; 2 Chron. xxii. 7). It appears that under Ahab Jehu attained to so much favour as to be selected to ride with his royal master in the royal chariot (2 Kings ix. 25). On one such occasion he was an ear-witness of the stern rebuke addressed to Ahab by the prophet Elijah, with respect to Ahab's conduct towards Naboth—"Surely I have seen yesterday the blood of Naboth, and the blood of his sons, saith the Lord ; and I will requite thee in this plat, saith the Lord" (2 Kings ix. 26). Respect for his royal master can scarcely have much out-lived this stern rebuke, and the denunciation following it—a denunciation, in the carrying out of which Jehu, though he sus-pected it not as yet, was to bear his part.

The young guardsman remained, however, in the royal service, and rose by degrees to a very lofty position in it. The thoroughness and earnest zeal wherewith he accomplished what-ever he took in hand (2 Kings ix. 20), carried him ere long to the highest post under the crown, the captainship of the host of Israel. It was in this position that he was left by Jehoram at Ramoth-Gilead, when, for the effectual cure of his own wounds, that monarch returned from the newly-captured city to his capital (2 Kings viii. 29). There is no indication of his having hitherto cherished any specially ambitious projects. He was seated with the other generals in the court of a house, perhaps in council with them, perhaps merely in social converse, when the current of his life was changed. A wild-looking youth, bearing a small flask in his hand, burst suddenly into the presence of the assembled chiefs, with the exclamation : " I have an errand unto thee, O captain " ; and when asked to which of the captains, singled out Jehu. The youth was Elisha's messenger, and having conducted Jehu into the most secret recess of the house, he carried out Elisha's instructions by anointing him king over Israel. He then quitted the house as suddenly as he had entered it, rushed away, and disappeared (2 Kings ix. 10).

The impression made upon Jehu's mind by the strange and unexpected occurrence seems to have been that it was a comedy arranged by the other captains, who, having determined to revolt against the wicked house of Ahab, and to change the dynasty, had selected him to be their leader, and had then contrived the striking scene, which had just been enacted, as the fitting inauguration of the new reign. Accordingly, when, on his reappearance before them, they asked him eagerly, " Is all well? Wherefore came this crack-brained fellow to thee?" he replied, "Ye know the man, and his communication." But the captains had no such knowledge—they were as much taken by surprise as Jehu himself—and they therefore rejoined : " It is false : tell us now." Jehu had now, on the spur of the moment, to determine his course. Should he lock the whole matter up in his own bosom, and continue to act as if nothing had happened, leaving it to God to bring about His purposes— if his own elevation to the crown was among those purposes— in His own good time and in His own good way ; or should he reveal to the captains what had been said and done to him, so in all probability lighting up the flame of a revolt? Jehu decided to take this latter course. "He broke his reserve, and revealed the secret interview."[1] He declared himself a divinely-anointed king—designated by God, consecrated with the Holy Oil of the sanctuary—prophetically summoned to go forth, "the anointed of the Lord," to exterminate the house of Ahab. Then burst out, without a moment's pause, the smouldering discontent. The popularity of the dynasty was gone. If the captains had not plotted a revolt, they were fully ready for one. With one accord, with neither hesitation nor delay, they proclaimed Jehu king, and, as it were, enthroned him. Shouts went up—"Jehu reigns ! Jehu reigns !"—the dynasty of Omri is fallen—Israel has a new king, and one selected for his office by Jehovah.

It would have seemed most natural—and it would certainly have been following the usual course of military revolts—had Jehu at once put his army in motion, and marched in full force on Jezreel, where the court was known to be at the time. But the slow march of a large army would have given an opportunity for preparation and defence, with the not improbable result of a long and bloody civil war. Jehu thought this result might be escaped by means of a surprise. He therefore gave orders that the utmost secrecy should be observed—no one should quit the town under any pretence whatever before himself—he would start, accompanied only by a moderate escort, and make a forced marched upon Jezreel, arriving probably before news of his intention had transpired, and so taking Jehoram unawares. In this way he hoped to gain important advan-

[1] Stanley, "Lectures on the Jewish Church," vol. ii. p. 283.

tage, though he can hardly have looked for so successful an issue as actually arrived. Jehoram's rash exit from the city unattended, and exposure of his person within bowshot of his foe, was an event scarcely to be anticipated. Jehu promptly seized his opportunity, and, by destroying his rival, made civil war, if not impossible, at any rate an improbable contingency.

The destruction of Jehoram was followed by a series of bloody deeds, which, unless we regard them as Divine sentences, whereof Jehu was the mere executioner, must be condemned as going beyond even the usage of the time in barbarity and atrocity.   First in the wretched catalogue came the fearful murder of the Queen-Mother, Jezebel. This miserable woman, having witnessed from a window of the palace her son's death, and his slayer's rapid approach to the town-gate, "tired her head," and smeared her eyelids with antimony, either, as some think, with a view of captivating by her aged charms the new king, or more probably with the design of making herself ready for the death, which she suspected to be impending ; and then, as Jehu drew nigh, leant forward out of the window, and exclaimed, loud enough for him to hear—" Had Zimri peace, who slew his master ? " The taunt was barbed ; but men generally decline to war upon women ; and the triumphant pretender might well have suffered the reproach to pass. But either it infuriated him, or he had previously resolved upon the Queen-Mother's death. Casting his eyes upwards to the harem windows, he called out, " Who is on my side, who ? " and when two or three eunuchs, those pests of an Eastern palace, answered the appeal, and "looked out" to him, " Dash her down," he exclaimed ; and, being obeyed, he urged his horses forward, and trampled the corpse under their feet. The blood spirted up upon the horses and upon the palace-wall, while the woman-slayer, entering within the gateway, calmly sat down to a feast. Not till the feast was over did he show the least sign of a softer feeling. Then, at length, bethinking himself of Jezebel's royal origin, and perhaps afraid of provoking Phœnician attack, he bade his servants see to the queen's burial. But the order was given too late. The half-wild dogs, which serve as scavengers to Eastern cities—"prowling then *as now* round the walls"[1]— had found the body, and had done their work—of the great princess, who had once made Elijah tremble (1 Kings xix. 2, 3),

[1] Stanley, "Lectures on the Jewish Church," vol. ii. p. 286.

and who had been the ruling spirit in Israel during three reigns
(1 Kings xxi. 25; xxii. 52; 2 Kings iii. 13; ix. 22), nothing remained but the hard extremities, the skull, the palms of the
hands, and the soles of the feet. In the portion of Jezreel, on
the very ground that had been "the plat of Naboth," the dogs
had eaten the flesh of Jezebel.

Another tragedy was at the same time in progress. When
Jehoram drove forth from the gate of Jezreel in his impatience
to learn what the approach of Jehu meant, he was accompanied
in a separate chariot by Ahaziah, his nephew, the son of his
sister, Athaliah. With this foreign potentate, king of the neighbouring Judæa, Jehu could have no legitimate quarrel. Yet he
at once gave orders that he should be slain. These orders were
carried out. Ahaziah fled southward, but was pursued and
wounded; whereupon he deflected his course, and reached
Megiddo, where he remained for a time in hiding. Thence,
according to one account (2 Chron. xxii. 9), he made good his
escape to Samaria, where again he concealed himself; but, his
hiding-place being detected, he was ere long dragged out, and
killed in cold blood. The alliance between Judæa and Israel,
which had lasted for two generations, was thus broken up; and
the old hostile attitude of the two states, which had lately been
confederate against Syria, was resumed.

The next of the bloody deeds of Jehu was on a larger scale.
The polygamy, which prevailed in Israel no less than in Judah,
caused royal families to increase and multiply at a rapid rate;
and Ahab's descendants in Samaria now numbered no fewer
than seventy males, who were all recognized as princes of the
blood royal, and were living in the capital under the charge of
influential persons who directed their education. The destruction of these noble youths seemed to the usurper necessary for
his own safety; he shrank, however, from the odium which
he would naturally provoke if he openly sent his guards to
massacre them. An indirect course, leading to the same result,
suggested itself; and this he determined to pursue. First, with
a grim humour, suggesting to the local authorities of Samaria
that they should select from among the princes whichever of
them was "best and meetest" (2 Kings x. 3), and set him up
as king, he next, when they declined this responsibility, and
declared themselves his faithful lieges, proposed to them that
they should give proof of their fidelity by themselves executing

the princes and bringing their heads to Jezreel. The authorities fell into the trap. They put the youths to death, and
sent their heads to the court; whereupon Jehu, disclaiming all
responsibility for the action, proceeded to justify his own
murder of Jehoram by the wholesale destruction of the tainted
race which the authorities of Samaria had deemed necessary.
"There was indeed," he urged, "no blame to be attached
either to him or them—all had been done in accordance with
the Divine will: God's judgments, as pronounced by His
prophet, Elijah, had been executed, most justly and righteously,
upon an accursed house" (2 Kings x. 9, 10). "Nothing should
fall to the ground of all that Elijah had predicted."

As the people acquiesced in this view, Jehu now proceeded a
step further. From destroying the kindred of Ahab, he passed
to the destruction of his partisans. Before quitting Jezreel, he
made a clean sweep of all the adherents of the fallen dynasty
in that city, slaying "all that remained of Ahab's house"
(2 Kings x. 11), together with his "great men," his "acquaintance," and his "priests." Thus was Jezreel, the special
seat of the grove-worship, the favourite abode of Jezebel,
detached from the old and bound to the fortunes of the new
dynasty.

It remained to occupy and purge the capital; but on his way
thither the unscrupulous king added another to the frightful
catalogue of his murderous deeds. At Beth-Eked, half-way
between Jezreel and Samaria, he fell in with a remarkable
cortège—a body of forty-two young travellers of good position,
with their attendants, who turned out to be princes of the royal
house of Judah, on their way to visit the court of Jehoram,
their near relative. Apparently they had left Jerusalem, and
had reached thus far upon their journey, in complete ignorance
of the revolution which had taken place at Jezreel, and were
travelling through the Israelite kingdom without the slightest
suspicion of danger. Jehu had no other ground of quarrel with
them, than they were the friends of his enemies, but this ground
was enough for him. His escort by his orders arrested the
the whole *cortège*, and slew them one by one in cold blood,
casting the dead bodies into the well of the place, as though
ashamed of leaving them to be seen (2 Kings x. 12-14).

Before Samaria was reached, an incident occurred of a more
peaceful and pleasing character. Jehu met in the way a noted

ascetic of the time, Jehonadab the son of Rechab, the originator of the sect of the Rechabites, who was already well known to him as a worshipper of the true God.[1] Jehonadab was "an Arab chief of the Kenite tribe, who was the founder or second founder of one of those Nazarite communities which had grown up in the kingdom of Israel, and which in this instance combined a kind of monastic discipline with the manners of the Bedouin race from whom they were descended."[2] Jehonadab was pursuing his way on foot. Jehu, seated in his chariot, recognized him, and, drawing rein, inquired—"Is thy heart right with mine, as my heart is with thy heart?"—i.e., "Art thou of the same mind with me, anxious to extirpate the Baal-worship and re-establish in Israel the religion of Jehovah?" Assured by an answer in the affirmative ("It is—it is"), Jehu stretched forth his hand, and lifting the ascetic from the ground, placed him by his side in the chariot. Together, the remarkable pair entered the town—"the warrior in his coat of mail, the ascetic in his haircloth"[3]—on the right, the stern, fierce, unscrupulous man of war, on the left the austere hermit-like man of peace—while the multitude looked on, impressed by the combination, and half inclined to extend to the rude soldier the veneration wherewith they had long regarded the Prince of the Ascetics.

The entrance of Jehu into the capital was the signal for fresh bloodshed. Ahab, it appears, had still descendants, or avowed partisans, among the inhabitants, and Jehu's first care, on finding his authority acknowledged, was to effect their destruction (2 Kings x. 17). Again, as at Jezreel, a clean sweep was made—Jehu "slew all that remained unto Ahab in Samaria, till he had destroyed him." He then rested for a while, and the revolution seemed perhaps to be at an end. As yet no declaration had been made with respect to religion; no hint had been given, unless it were privately to Jehonadab (ver. 16), of any intention to alter the State-worship, much less of any design to extirpate Baal by extirpating his followers. The temple of Ashtoreth had, apparently, been left standing at Jezreel; that of Baal still showed itself in all its grandeur and magnificence above the roofs of the houses in Samaria. Jehu's religious leanings were generally unknown to his subjects, and

[1] Joseph. "Ant. Jud.," ix. 6, § 6.
[2] Stanley, "Lectures on the Jewish Church," vol. ii. p. 287.
[3] Pusey, "Minor Prophets"—Commen: on Amos, p. 176.

it was probably without surprise that they heard the proclamation, which shortly went forth—"Ahab served Baal a little, but Jehu shall serve him much. Gather together all the prophets of Baal, all his servants, and all his priests; let none be wanting; for I have a great sacrifice to do to Baal; whosoever shall be wanting, he shall not live" (2 Kings x. 18, 19). Once more "subtilty" was called in to serve the monarch's purposes, and the danger of a "war of religion" was avoided by deceit, subterfuge, and lies. A splendid festival was announced, to be held in honour of Baal on a given day in his temple at Samaria; a royal edict required *all* who honoured Baal to be present; an enormous crowd was collected together; sacrificial feasts were prepared; sacred vestments were brought forth from the royal robe-chamber [1] for all who needed them; the profane were bidden to withdraw, and the worshippers to see that no one of another religion was left among them; the Baalistic priests and prophets led the way, to preside over the ceremonies; even the king himself, keeping up the deception to the last, entered the sacred precincts, and advancing to the altar, presented victims, and witnessed their sacrifice, retiring when it was completed, to make way for others. The rites continued, but on the king's departure the scene suddenly changed. By his orders the temple had been secretly surrounded by the soldiers of his body-guard; and now, at his command, these fierce warriors, eighty in number, entered in, and, first blocking the exits, proceeded to slaughter indiscriminately priests, prophets, and ordinary worshippers, till the temple was strewn with corpses, and not one out of the many thousands who had entered was left alive. Then the edifice itself, and the images which adorned it, were attacked. The soldiers rushed into the inner sanctuary, which rose like a lofty fortress above the rest of the building, and tore down the wooden image of Baal, together with those of his contemplar deities, which were seated around him, dragged them out of the temple, and burned them. The great stone image or *stélé* of Baal, which had formerly stood in front of the building, but which Jehoram had removed from its place (2 Kings iii. 2), was thrown down and broken to pieces. The whole temple was then razed to the ground, and its site made a depositary for all the refuse and filth of the city.

Such was the mode in which Jehu showed his "zeal for the

[1] So Thenius, "Comment. on 2 Kings," x. 22.

Lord." We must give him credit for a real detestation of the
enervating and debasing religion which Ahab had introduced
into Israel, and for a desire to resort to a more manly and
better creed. We must also, perhaps, to some extent excuse
the greater numbers of his murderous acts, as justified in his
own view and in that of his contemporaries by the belief that
he was but executing the Divine commands. Still, we cannot
recognize in him anything but one of those selfish and evil men,
whom God from time to time makes his instruments for accom-
plishing great and salutary changes, and whom He prospers
to a certain extent, without commending or approving. His
character is, as Dean Stanley notes, "altogether unlovely."[1]
He is cold, stern, remorseless, wholly without scruple; and he
is false, treacherous, and cunning. Even his orthodoxy is not
unimpeachable, for, though he puts down the Baal-worship, he
maintains the worship of the calves (2 Kings x. 29, 31), and in
no way "departs from the sins of Jeroboam the son of Nebat,
which made Israel to sin."

We have no account of the internal government of his king
dom by Jehu after he had accomplished the religious revolution
wherewith he inaugurated his reign. He held the throne for
the unusually long period of twenty-eight years,[2] and left his
dynasty well established, as appears by the fact that it maintained its hold upon a state, more than ordinarily fickle and
capricious, for the space of five generations and the long term
of a hundred and fifteen years. His relations with Elisha are
obscure; but the prophet who had in a certain sense placed the
new dynasty on the throne was certainly not indifferent to its
prosperity; and, if he was not in Jehu's reign (as Ewald imagines)
"the most trustworthy adviser and the firmest support of both
king and people,"[3] at any rate watched over the successive
monarchs to the third generation (2 Kings xiii. 14–19), and lent
them all the assistance in his power.

In his external relations with foreign states, Jehu, though from
time to time exhibiting that military prowess which had distinguished him before he was king (2 Kings x. 34), and had led

[1] "Lectures on the Jewish Church," vol. ii. p. 289. An unfavourable
view of Jehu's character is also taken by Dr. Pusey in his comment on
Hosea i. 4 ("Minor Prophets," p. 9).
[2] Of all the kings of Israel only Jeroboam II. exceeded this term.
[3] "History of Israel," vol. iv. p. 121.

to his elevation, was yet, upon the whole, unsuccessful and unfortunate. He lived at a time when the great Assyrian Empire was threatening continually more and more the complete subjugation of Western Asia ;[1] while at the same time Syria, under a young and energetic monarch, was rousing herself to unwonted efforts, and seeking to become the head of a great confederacy which might successfully resist and defy the Assyrian power. Jehu's immediate danger seemed to him to be from Syria. Hazael, who had murdered the aged Benhadad, and succeeded him (2 Kings viii. 7–15), was a bold and enterprising prince, who, though more than once defeated by the Assyrians, resolutely made head against them, and in all the pauses of the Assyrian war sought to compensate himself for his ill-success in his struggle with them by victories and conquests on the side of Palestine. Jehu and he had many desperate encounters, no doubt with varied results, but the upshot of the conflict was, that Israel proved weaker than Syria, and "went to the wall"—Hazael "smote the Israelites in all their coasts" (2 Kings x. 32)—the entire Trans-Jordanic territory, the inheritance of Gad and Reuben and Manasseh, the lands of Gilead and Bashan, was seized and held by the Syrians (ibid. ver. 33)—the territory of Israel was contracted to little more than half its former extent—and its whole eastern flank was laid open to attack from the powerful kingdom which had its headquarters at Damascus. It may have been fear of further Syrian aggression and the desire of extraneous support, or it may have been simple inability to resist a demand accompanied with threats, that induced Jehu towards the close of his reign[2] to consent to pay tribute to Assyria. The Black Obelisk of Shalmaneser II., now in the British Museum, records this fact, and gives a representation[3] of the Israelite envoys, bearded and with turbaned heads, wearing shoes turned up at the toe, and long fringed robes reaching from the neck to the feet, while they carry in their hands, or upon their shoulders, the rich gifts which they are about to lay at the feet of the Great King. According to the legend which accompanies the representation, the gifts consist of " silver, gold, bowls of gold, bottles of gold,

[1] See the "Introduction," p. ix.

[2] The later years of Jehu alone synchronize with any part of the reign of Shalmaneser II.

[3] Compare "Ancient Monarchies," vol. ii. p. 105, 2nd ed.

vessels of gold, maces, royal utensils, and planks of precious woods."[1]   Curiously enough, Jehu is called in the inscription, not " the son of Nimshi," but " the son of Omri."

After a reign of twenty-eight years, when he must have been well-nigh seventy years of age, Jehu died a natural death, probably in Samaria, and was buried there.   His eldest son, Jehoahaz succeeded him (2 Kings x. 35, 36).

[1] G. Smith, " Eponym Canon," p. 114.

CHAPTER XVII.

ATHALIAH

Athaliah destroys the seed royal, and seizes the throne—Pushes the Baal-worship to the front, and builds a temple to Baal in Jerusalem—Joash, preserved by Jehosheba, and brought up secretly by Jehoiada—Made king in his seventh year—Death of Athaliah.

WHEN the news of Ahaziah's murder by Jehu reached Jerusalem, the city was thrown into consternation. A combination of circumstances had reduced the once flourishing house of David to a small and scanty remnant. First, the suspicions or avarice of Jehoram, son of Jehoshaphat, had thinned its abundant branches (2 Chron. xxi. 2–4), then the Arabs and Philistines in combination had cut off a number of the most promising boughs (ibid. xxi. 16, 17 ; xxii. 1) ; finally, Jehu's murderous acts had still further curtailed the dwindled stock (2 Kings ix. 27 ; x. 14), till now a few children, sons of Ahaziah, seem to have been all that was left of it. A regency would, in any case, have been inevitable ; for, as Ahaziah was but twenty-two or twenty-three at his death (2 Kings viii. 26), he could not have left behind him any child of greater age than six or seven, and princes in Judah did not attain their majority until eighteen or twenty.[1] The position would have been critical, had nothing further occurred to complicate it ; its difficulties were, however, greatly aggravated by the audacious action suddenly and without warning taken by the Queen-Mother. Athaliah, daughter of Ahab and Jezebel, wife of Jehoram of Judah, and mother of Ahaziah, had no sooner heard of her son's death at the hand of Jehu, than "she arose and destroyed all the seed royal"

[1] See the "Speaker's Commentary," vol. iii. p. 372 (note on 2 Chron. xxxiv. 3).

(2 Kings xi. 1 ; 2 Chron. xxii. 10), seized the crown, and established her sway over the land (2 Kings xi. 3). The reign of a
woman was contrary to all precedent ; the reign of a foreigner,
not of the seed of David, half-Israelite, half-Phœnician, was
abhorrent to all Jewish notions ; the nation must have been
shocked and grieved, but it was also terrified. Athaliah's
daring cowed the boldest spirits. No one ventured to say her
nay. For six years she held complete dominion over the land
and ruled it at her pleasure.

It is needless to say that her main efforts were directed, during
this space of time, to the establishment and propagation of the
debasing worship introduced by her mother into the sister kingdom of Israel and by herself first brought into Judæa. During
the reign of her husband, Jehoram, and, still more, during that
of her son Ahaziah, she had exercised considerable influence in
the Judæan state, and had used it to advance, as much as she
could, the Baal and Astarte worship, and to depress, as much as
she could, the worship of Jehovah. But now her powers for
evil were much increased. Though she did not venture to put
down the ancient religion altogether, nor even to shut up the
ancient Temple or hinder its rites, and though she abstained
from all persecution of the Jehovah-worshippers, whether people
or priests, yet, apart from the use of such methods, she did all
that was possible to push her own religion to the front, and
make it the religion of the nation. In Jerusalem itself, perhaps
within the Temple precincts,[1] a rival fane rose up, dedicated to
the Phœnician god, adorned with altars and images (2 Kings
xi. 18), and continually enriched with spoils from the neighbouring edifice—nay, in part built of stones, transferred by the
Queen's orders from the old sanctuary to the new (2 Chron.
xxiv. 7). The temple of Solomon was left to decay and ruin ;
that of Baal constantly increased in size and magnificence.
Its services were conducted by a high-priest of Baal,[2] the
counterpart of the Aaronic high-priest, who still maintained,
albeit with shorn splendour, the rites of the Levitical worship in
the old edifice.

The Aaronic high-priest of the time was a certain Jehoiada,
who held a more exalted position than belonged to most high-
priests under the monarchy, in consequence of his close con-

---

[1] So Stanley, "Jewish Church," vol. ii. p. 339.
[2] See 2 Kings xi. 18 ; 2 Chron. xxiii. 17.

nection with the royal house. He was married to Jehosheba, a sister—probably a half-sister only [1]—of Ahaziah, who in virtue of her near relationship had free access to the royal palace, and was there when Athaliah made her attempt to destroy the entire seed royal. Powerless to thwart openly the will of the Queen-Mother, Jehosheba nevertheless contrived to prevent its full accomplishment by snatching from the massacre and secreting one of the children of the late king, an infant boy who had received the name of Joash (2 Kings xi. 2). At first she hid him, with his nurse, in the storeroom of mattresses in the royal palace, whence, later on, she transferred him to a securer hiding-place in one of the chambers attached to the Temple. Her husband was, of course, privy to her actions; and it was with his approval that the child remained concealed in the sacred edifice for six entire years, without the Queen having the slightest suspicion of his existence. Athaliah reigned in fancied security during this space, while all the time she was sitting on a mine, which might at any moment explode. Jehoiada could whenever he pleased have initiated a revolution by revealing the fact that a scion of the house of David existed ; but he thought it best and safest to bide his time, to wait till he could produce before the people, not a mere infant, but an interesting and intelligent boy, while he might also, during the interval, gradually prepare the most important sections of the people for the coming discovery. He seems to have acted with great prudence. "Every step was taken in accordance with the usages which had been gradually gaining head during the previous reigns, and all the means which his office placed at his disposal were freely employed." [2] The soldiery were sounded, and found well disposed towards a revolution and a restoration of the Davidic monarchy. The Levites could, of course, be counted upon. It was not till the seventh year (2 Kings xi. 4), that the high-priest regarded the fitting time as come, and exploded the mine which he had been so long preparing.

On a certain Sabbath-day, Jehoiada, having first made an arrangement with the captains of the royal body-guard, whom he secretly introduced into the Temple, showed the young prince, and bound by oath to espouse his cause, brought to the Temple a strong body of Levites (2 Chron. xxiii. 1–8), and at

---

[1] So Josephus (" Ant. Jud." ix. 7, § 2).

[2] Stanley, " Jewish Church," vol. ii. p. 340.

the same time concentrated on the spot four out of the five divisions of the body-guard, one only being left to guard the palace (2 Kings xi. 5). Of the four divisions, two were to take position at the northern and southern gates of the Temple—the "gate of Sur," as it was called, or "of the foundation" (2 Chron. xxiii. 5), and the "gate of the guard," or "of the runners"[1]— while the other two were to enter the Temple court, and to place themselves on the right and left hand of the young king, in order to protect his person, and prevent any one from approaching near to him. A stand or platform was prepared, on which the king was to take his place, so that he might be visible to all; and the soldiers, to whom Jehoiada distributed arms that had belonged to David out of the Temple armoury, were ordered to kill any one who attempted to penetrate their ranks. Everything being prepared, the high-priest, amid general expectation, " brought forth the king's son" (2 Kings xi. 12), placed him on his pedestal, and then solemnly put upon his head "the crown and the Testimony." The crown, or diadem, was probably a gold band studded with jewels; the Testimony must have been a "Book of the Law"—probably that which was kept ordinarily in the Ark of the Covenant (Deut. xxxi. 26). Finally, the holy oil was brought out, and the young prince anointed with it by Jehoiada and his sons, who at the same time raised the cry— "Long live the king"—which was taken up by the bystanders, guards, Levites, and people, and swelled into a shout that rent the air and was heard afar. Meantime the trumpets blared, the cymbals clashed, the singers raised hymns of praise;[2] the entire multitude that filled the Temple courts joined in the celebration, and with loud acclaim hailed the Davidic king. Suddenly, in the midst of the deafening roar, Athaliah entered. She had heard the first loud shout, and, suspecting its nature, had hurried across from the palace to the Temple, unattended, as it would seem, "with the same high spirit that had marked the last days of her mother."[3] At a glance she saw that all was lost, and rending her robes, she cried out, "Conspiracy! conspiracy!" and turned away. Jehoiada bade the soldiers let her retire, but follow her up, and, as soon as she was outside the Temple, put her to death. His orders were executed, and Athaliah, escorted

---

[1] So called because they commonly ran, to keep up with the king as he drove in his chariot.   [2] See 2 Chron. xxiii. 13.

[3] Stanley, "Jewish Church," vol. ii. p. 341.

by the body-guard through the long array of armed Levites and exulting multitudes untouched and unharmed, passed out by the "horse gate" into the Tyropœon valley,[1] and there met her death.

Thus perished Athaliah, the last survivor of the house of Omri, so far as we know—a bold, bad woman, but one whose unblenching courage compels our respect.

[1] Josephus says "the Kedron valley" ("Ant. Jud." ix. 7, § 4), but this is very improbable.

CHAPTER XVIII.

JOASH OF JUDAH.

Coronation of Joash followed by solemn renewal of the Covenant — Destruction of the temple of Baal and abolition of Baalism — Re-establishment in proper form of the Temple services by Jehoiada, and renovation of the Temple itself by Joash — Supposed "malversation" of the Levites not borne out by the narrative — Death and funeral of Jehoiada — Partial restoration of idolatry — Murder of Zechariah — Legend with respect to his blood — Judæa invaded by Hazael — Gath taken — Jerusalem purchases its safety — Illness of Joash — His murder by some of his household — His burial.

THE coronation of Joash, described in the last section, was followed by two scenes of striking interest. Jehoiada, whose position seems to have given him the regency without any need of formal appointment, took the opportunity of the great gathering in the Temple, and the general exaltation of feeling produced by the events of the day, to bind the people afresh to God by a solemn league and covenant, so that "the joyous festival of homage to the young king became on this occasion identical with that of renewed allegiance to Jehovah."[1] Such a solemn covenant had been first made by the nation at Sinai (Exod. xxiv. 3–8); but there had been a repetition of it in the fifteenth year of Asa (2 Chron. xv. 9–15) after the half-apostasy of Rehoboam and Abijam ; and Jehoiada now, either following this example, or moved by his own feeling of what was right and fitting, caused the nation for the third time to renew the sacred engagement. Later in the history, Hezekiah (2 Chron. xxix. 10) and Josiah (ibid. xxxiv. 41) did the same, regarding such solemn renewal of obligations as necessary, or at any rate appropriate, whenever the nation generally had fallen away from God and lapsed into idolatry.

[1] Ewald, "History of Israel," vol. iv. p. 136.

The other incident of importance was the fierce assault made upon Baalism. From the inner court of the Temple, which was the scene of the coronation, the multitudes, beyond all doubt encouraged by Jehoiada, streamed forth to the neighbouring seat of idol-worship, bent upon its complete demolition. "The people of the land went into the house of Baal, and brake it down" (2 Kings xi. 18). It was a popular outburst. A multitude is always ready to destroy, and few kinds of destruction are so agreeable to the mob, whether Eastern or Western, as those which come under the designation of iconoclasm. Baal's sanctuary was soon torn down, the altars and images which adorned it broken to pieces, and Mattan the high-priest slain as he officiated. Baal-worship was thus for a time completely rooted out of Judah, and the old religion resumed its place.

But much required to be done, before the destruction wrought by Athaliah could be repaired and obliterated. The venerable fabric of the Temple had suffered considerably at the hands of the wicked queen and those who are called "her sons" (2 Chron. xxiv. 7). Breaches had been broken in it (2 Kings xii. 5); its stones had been removed to be used elsewhere; and nothing had been done to check or hinder the progress of natural decay. As some understand an important passage of Chronicles,[1] its very foundations had suffered and required to be renewed. Its treasures had also been plundered, its "dedicated things" carried off, and its vessels employed in the service of Baal. The porters had been removed from the gates, and unclean persons allowed to enter in (2 Chron. xxiii. 19)—probably unclean things also, as will always happen when a place is uncared for. As the king was so young, the work of renovation and restoration fell to Jehoiada. His first care was to renew the personal staff on the old scale—the scale appointed by David; for which purpose he re-established the courses of the priests and Levites, set in order the sacrificial and the musical services (ibid. ver. 18), and once more placed porters in all the gates. To the fabric he appears to have paid less regard; and it was not until the young king was so far grown up as to be allowed a voice in the management of affairs, that the repair and renewal of the building was seriously taken in hand. Then, however, a great effort was made. A large portion of the offerings given by the

[1] 2 Chron. xxiv. 7. Comp. Stanley, "Lectures on the Jewish Church," vol. ii. p. 343.

faithful year by year for the service of the Temple and the support of the priests was, it was agreed, to be set aside and devoted wholly to the repairs, which would (it was thought) in this way be speedily completed (2 Kings xii. 4, 5 ; 2 Chron. xxiv. 4, 5). A delay, however, occurred, which is unexplained ; and it required another impulse from the king for the matter to be placed on a sound footing, and the work begun and in a short time finished. The " repairs" seem to have amounted to an almost complete renovation of the edifice by carpenters, masons, and builders, who with "timber and hewn stone " (2 Kings xii. 12), and "iron and brass" (2 Chron. xxiv. 12), "mended " the house of the Lord, and " set it in its state and strengthened it " (ibid. ver. 13). When the repairs were completed, the overplus of the money subscribed was utilized for the holy vessels required in the various services, for " vessels to minister, and to offer withal, and spoons, and vessels of gold and silver " (ibid. ver. 14)—probably for " bowls of silver, snuffers, basons, trumpets" (2 Kings xii. 13), and the like—in fact, for replacing all those " dedicated things" of which the house of Jehovah had been plundered, and which had been irremediably desecrated by employment in the worship of Baal.

It has been supposed that, in the course of the proceedings with respect to the repairs, a suspicion of malversation on the part of the priests and Levites arose in the king's mind, who "gently but decidedly rebuked" the sacerdotal order for conduct which verged upon dishonesty, and made arrangements the object of which was to check and foil their rapacity for the future.[1] But the accounts which have come down to us in Kings and Chronicles fail to justify any such "unpleasant" supposition, being incompatible with a belief in the dishonesty of the priests, if not expressly denying it.[2] All that the priests and Levites are fairly taxable with, is a want of business-like capacity, which the king's arrangements remedied, and thus there was no " rupture," open or secret, between the monarch and the sacerdotal order, so long as Jehoiada was alive. Jehoiada enjoyed the king's full confidence till the day of his death, which was at any rate later than the twenty-third year of his reign (2 Kings xii. 6, 7), probably several years later. Joash was guided by Jehoiada's " instructions " (ibid. ver. 2), took wives at his suggestion (2 Chron. xxiv. 3), and must have been a consenting

[1] Stanley, pp. 343, 344.   [2] See 2 Kings xii. 15.

party to the extraordinary honours which were paid him at his decease. As preserver of the royal dynasty, and as restorer of the Lord's house, the great high-priest was granted a distinction never allowed to any other subject during the whole period of the monarchy—he was buried in state within the walls of the city of David, in the sepulchres of the kings (2 Chron. xxiv. 16).

It was subsequently to this event that troubles arose in the state in connection with religion, and the priestly order was alienated from the king by his apostasy from Jehovah. Accustomed from his childhood to lean upon some external support, Joash, on losing the adviser of his youth and middle age, accepted for guides and counsellors "the princes of Judah" or the heads of the Jewish aristocracy. These persons, though they had joined in the revolt against Athaliah (2 Chron. xxiii. 2), were now, five and twenty or thirty years later, ill-disposed towards the Jehovistic worship, and anxious for a toleration, at any rate, of the licentious and seductive rites connected with Baalism. They approached the king with soft speech, offering him obsequious homage (ibid. xxiv. 17), and obtained his consent to the re-introduction of "grove-worship" and other forms of idolatry. At once a fierce opposition was roused. The priests and the prophetical order raised their voices against the defection. A multitude of fierce denunciations—"burdens," in the language of the time (2 Kings ix. 25 ; 2 Chron. xxiv. 27)—were uttered, and perhaps written and circulated,[1] by persons possessed with the spirit of prophecy, who predicted national calamities as the sure result of the national sin (2 Chron. xxiv. 19). Among these prophets of evil there was one conspicuous above all the rest. Jehoiada had been succeeded in the high-priesthood by his son Zechariah ; and Zechariah was bound by the nature of his office to lead the opposition. Moreover, there fell upon him suddenly, as he stood raised above the rest of the people in the Temple court, the prophetic spirit, and he shouted out : "Thus saith God—Why transgress ye the commandment of the Lord, so that ye cannot prosper? Because ye have forsaken the Lord, He hath also forsaken you" (2 Chron. xxiv. 20). The words were reported to the king, and an order obtained from him for Zechariah's execution (ibid. ver. 21), which was at once carried into effect. In the Temple court, right in front

[1] The writer of Chronicles had, apparently, seen the "burdens" (2 Chron. xxiv. 27).

of the holy edifice, and probably not far from the altar,[1] God's high-priest, the son of the man who had placed the king upon the throne, was, by that king's command, ruthlessly stoned to death, for vindicating God's honour and resisting a national apostasy. It has been charitably suggested, that by "the commandment of the king" we should understand some "hasty words" like those of Henry II. which led to the murder of Becket;[2] but the expression will scarcely bear this interpretation. The murder is reckoned by the writer who records it as the sin of Joash (2 Chron. xxiv. 22), and on Joash, he tells us, it was requited (ibid. vers. 24, 25).

After ages declared, that the blood of Zechariah continually bubbled up from the part of the pavement on which he fell.[3] When the Babylonian general, Nebuzaradan, after the capture of Jerusalem, entered the Temple court, he was struck by the phenomenon, and inquired into its cause. The Temple servants strove to persuade him that the blood was that of victims recently offered; but when he confuted them by himself slaying sacrificial animals, whose blood did not bubble, they confessed the truth. The blood was that of a prophet, priest, and judge, who had foretold all the calamities which Jerusalem had just suffered at his hands and at those of Nebuchadnezzar, and who for his plain-speaking had been done to death by his own countrymen upon the spot. On hearing this, the Babylonian general, bent on propitiating the martyr, slew on the place, by thousands, all the rabbis, the school-children, and the young priests, on whom he could lay his hands—but still the blood bubbled on. Then he cried—"O Zechariah, Zechariah; thou hast destroyed the best of thy people; wouldst thou have me destroy all?"—and the blood was quiet, and ceased to bubble.

The last words of Zechariah, as he gave up the ghost, were— "The Lord look upon this, and requite it" (2 Chron. xxiv. 22). Vengeance, he knew, was God's; and to God it belonged to exact a penalty for each act of wickedness. To God consequently he made appeal; and his appeal was heard and answered. Within less than a year, Hazael, the brave and warlike king of

---

[1] See Matt. xxiii. 35. It is doubted whether our Lord referred to this Zechariah; but, on the whole, the arguments on the affirmative side preponderate. [2] Stanley, "Jewish Church," vol. ii. p. 345.
[3] See the Talmud, *Taanith*, quoted by Bishop Lightfoot in his comment on Matt. xxiii. 35.

Syria, not content with the damage which he had inflicted on the northern kingdom (2 Kings x. 32, 33), invaded the south. His main attack was on the Philistine town of Gath (ibid. xii. 17) ; but having been successful there, he suddenly resolved to make a dash upon Jerusalem.   Here plunder, rather than conquest, was his object ; and when Joash, after a battle in which he was severely defeated (2 Chron. xxiv. 24), offered to buy off his hostility by the sacrifice of the Temple and Palace treasures, Hazael readily consented.   All the stores accumulated since Asa bribed Benhadad (1 Kings xv. 18) were made over by the Jewish to the Syrian monarch as the price of peace, were brought to Hazael in his camp, and carried off by him to Damascus. Jerusalem was allowed to escape ; but the wretched king, humiliated and disgraced, fell into a sick condition, and had to take to his bed in the castle of Millo, which he had perhaps made his residence in expectation of a siege.   Here, advantage was taken of his illness by some of his attendants, who formed a conspiracy against him among those of his household, and slew him on his sick-bed.   The chief conspirators were, Jozachar, the son of Shimeath, an Ammonitess; and Jehozabad, the son of Shomer (or Shimrith), a Moabitess (2 Chron. xxiv. 26). The motive for the murder is uncertain.   Some, as Ewald,[1] understand the author of Chronicles to assert that the conspirators "desired to revenge the murder of Zechariah upon the king."   Others question whether he means to assert more than that God thus in fact avenged Zechariah's death, whatever the motives of the conspirators may have been.

The corpse of the murdered king was buried somewhere within the limits of the city of David, but was not—at any rate, at first—consigned to the sepulchres of the kings (2 Chron. xxiv. 25).   It may afterwards have been, in Amaziah's reign transferred to them (2 Kings xii. 21).

[1] "History of the Jewish Church," vol. iv. p. 141, note a, English translation.

CHAPTER XIX.

JEHOAHAZ OF ISRAEL.

Jehoahaz allows idolatry—His reign a series of disasters—Cruel inroads
of Hazael and loss of towns to him—Constant incursions of Ammon
and Moab—Disappearance of Elisha from the history—Repentance of
Jehoahaz unsatisfactory—Relations of the two Hebrew kingdoms at
the time.

JEHOAHAZ, who succeeded his father, Jehu, upon the throne of
Israel, while the Syrian war was still raging under the conduct
of the great Hazael, though a prince not inferior in valour to
his father,[1] had a reign which was little more than one continued series of disasters. He had none of his father's "zeal
for Jehovah" (2 Kings x. 16), and was not only content to
maintain the long established worship of the calves at Dan and
Bethel (ibid. xiii. 2, 6), but even suffered the sacred tree
(ashêrah) which Ahab had set up in Samaria on his marriage
with Jezebel (1 Kings xvi. 33), to stand erect and to receive
once more the adoration of the people. How it happened that
Jehu had not destroyed the idolatrous emblem with the other
abominations belonging to the Baal-worship, we are not told:
perhaps he had thought it sufficient to "put it away," as Jehoram, the son of Ahab, "put away" the image of Baal (2 Kings
iii. 2). But, under Jehoahaz, it appears to have recovered its
place, and, if he did not himself pay it reverence, yet certainly
it would seem, from the connection in which it is mentioned
(ibid. xiii. 6), to have attracted the devotions of many of his
subjects.[2] The result was that "the anger of Jehovah was

[1] Compare 2 Kings xiii. 8 with ch. x. 34.

[2] It cannot be supposed that the ashêrah would have been mentioned in
connection with the sins of the people unless they still sinned in respect
of it.

kindled" against both king and people, and Hazael was made the special scourge to chastise them, and, if possible, bring them to a better mind (2 Kings xii. 3). Now first were the anticipations of Elisha on his introduction to Hazael near Damascus fully realized ; now first did all those evils which his prophetic soul had presaged, come on the unhappy Israelites. Invasions of their land fell upon them year by year, accompanied with all the horrors of the most savage and cruel warfare —"the strongholds were set on fire and burnt to the ground ; the young men were slain with the sword ; the innocent children were seized and dashed to the ground ; the women great with child were ripped up and brutally slaughtered " (2 Kings viii. 12). Ewald thinks that Jehoahaz had in some measure pro voked these severities by attacking Hazael [1] and seeking to recover the Trans-Jordanic territory, whereof that monarch had deprived Jehu (ibid. x. 32, 33) ; but there is no evidence of this attack, and it would rather appear from the narrative, that the Syrian king, not satisfied with his Trans-Jordanic conquests, invaded the territory west of the Jordan year after year, conquering continually fresh cities (ibid. xiii. 25), and subjecting the inhabitants to the above-mentioned outrages. We do not know whether Jehoahaz ventured to fight any battles, but if so it was without success. Year by year he grew weaker ; his warriors were destroyed, his cities taken and sacked ; his territory ravaged ; his resources exhausted. At last he was reduced to such straits that the utmost force which he could bring into the field [2] consisted of ten war-chariots, fifty horsemen, and ten thousand infantry (ibid. ver. 7).

It was not, however, Syria alone which had produced this extraordinary exhaustion. The triumph of Hazael had been the signal for other enemies also to flock in, like vultures upon a carcase, and to bring Israel lower and lower. "The Ammonites, often before in close alliance with the Aramæans, seized the opportunity of spreading themselves more widely in Gilead, and vied with the Aramæans in the barbarity with which they carried on the war (Amos i. 13). Marauding hosts of Moabites moreover, penetrated every year (2 Kings xiii. 20) into the very

[1] "History of Israel," vol. iv. p. 120.

[2] It has been supposed by some that Hazael limited the standing army of Jehoahaz to this number ; but the idea of such limitation does not appear in history until the time of Antiochus the Great (B.C. 190).

heart of the western country,"[1] and slew, and swept off captives, and destroyed the crops, and took vengeance for the injuries which had been done them in the days of Mesha (ibid. iii. 25). It may seem strange that we hear nothing of Elisha during this dark period of depression. He was still alive, as we learn from the history of the next Israelite reign, and he still took an interest in the temporal fortunes of the Israelites (ibid. xiii. 14-19). But during the entire reigns of Jehu and Jehoahaz— a space of forty-five years—he disappears from sight, leaves Israel to itself, and only reappears, in the reign of Jehoash, just as he is at the very point of death. Ewald, indeed, by a new arrangement of the earlier chapters of the Second Book of Kings, is able to assign to the time of Jehoahaz, some of the most striking events of Elisha's ministry;[2] but most other commentators shrink from following him in this erratic course, and allow that Elisha's ministry practically terminated with his anointing of Jehu (ibid. ch. ix. 1-10) and his visit to Damascus (ibid. ch. viii. 7-13). The course of the prophetical activity was, we must remember, determined *for* the prophets, not *by* them ; and Elisha would take no active part in public affairs, unless divinely commissioned so to do.

Some have supposed that he did come forward from his obscurity to perform a public act once at least in the reign of Jehoahaz. Lange suggests that it was Elisha who "induced King Jehoahaz to humble himself and turn to God in prayer."[3] No doubt this may have been so ; but the written record gives us no hint of it. We cannot safely conclude, that he did in fact "take advantage of the distress of the king and the people to direct them to their true weal and their real strength," because he may appear to us the " right man" to have done so.[4]

Altogether, the repentance of Jehoahaz has an unreal air, and is eminently unsatisfactory. He does not "beseech the Lord," until driven to do so by the extreme oppression which he suffers at the hand of Hazael, nor does he after his repentance at all alter the course of his life, or suppress the *ashêrah*, or the calves (2 Kings xiii. 6). And it was doubtless in consequence of the unreality of his repentance that God gave him in his own person no relief. "Hazael, king of Syria, oppressed Israel all

[1] Ewald, "History of Israel," vol. iv. p. 121.   [2] Ibid. pp. 121, 122.
[3] Lange, "Commentary," on 2 Kings, p. 143.
[4] Ewald, "Hist. of Israel," vol. iv. p. 122.

the days of Jehoahaz" (ibid. ver. 22). The "saviour" spoken
of in 2 Kings xiii. 5 was not given until Jehoahaz was dead,
and his son Jehoash had succeeded him on the throne (ibid.
ver. 35).

Jehoahaz reigned seventeen years (incomplete), from the
twenty-first year of Joash, king of Judah,[1] to his thirty-
seventh year (ibid. ver. 10). He left his crown to his son,
Jehoash, or Joash, to whom he had given the same name
as that borne by the contemporary Jewish sovereign. This
act would seem to imply that the friendly relations which
had subsisted between the two kingdoms during the rule
of the House of Omri were now resumed ; and it would
not have been surprising if a close alliance had at this time
been formed between the two countries. To have the same
enemies disposes men towards friendship ;[2] and the Syrians
were, under Hazael, almost an equal danger to both kingdoms.[3] Probably neither would have suffered so much had
they joined hands, and made common cause against their
common foe. But old jealousies were allowed to prevail ; and
the opportunity for alliance being suffered to slip, it was not
long ere the ancient hostility once more showed itself (2 Kings
xiv. 8–14), and came to such a head, that henceforth the two
sister nations continued estranged during the remainder of
their joint existence.

---

[1] So Josephus, "Ant. Jud." ix, 8, § 5.   [2] Aristot. "Rhet." ii. 4.
[3] See 2 Kings xii. 17, 18.

CHAPTER XX.

JEHOASH, OR JOASH, OF ISRAEL.

Partial recovery of Israel under Joash—His character—His visit to Elisha
and the prophecy given him—His three victories over Benhadad and
their result—He is challenged to fight by Amaziah—His reply and
defeat of his antagonist—His early death.

JOASH of Israel, the son of Jehoahaz, and grandson of Jehu,
is a monarch superior to most of those who sat upon the
Israelite throne. Though, like every other king of Israel, he
maintained the system of Jeroboam as originally established,
and thus shares in the universal condemnation—that "he did
evil in the sight of the Lord ; he departed not from all the sins
of Jeroboam the son of Nebat, who made Israel sin, but walked
therein" (2 Kings xiii. 11), yet, apart from this one error of
conduct, his life is almost faultless. Josephus ventures to say
of him openly and boldly [1]—"He was a good man, and in his
disposition entirely unlike his father." When he ascended the
throne, his country was at the lowest point of weakness and
depression. Hazael ravaged it and oppressed it at his pleasure.
Moab and Ammon indulged themselves in frequent kicks at
the dead lion. When he died after an eventful reign of sixteen
years, Samaria was once more independent and respected.
Not only had the advance of Syria been checked, but she had
received defeats, and been deprived of a large portion of her
conquests. The kingdom had to a considerable extent recovered
itself, and the way had been prepared for that fuller, and indeed,
astonishing recovery which makes the reign of Jeroboam the
Second the turning-point of the later Israelite history.

It would seem to have been very shortly after the accession

[1] "Ant. Jud." ix. 8, § 6.

of Joash to the throne that intelligence reached him of Elisha being prostrated by a serious illness. The prophet must by this time have reached a very advanced age. It was sixty-three years since his call, when he can scarcely be supposed to have been less than twenty years old, so that, at the very least, he must now have been eighty-three, and may not improbably have verged upon ninety. Very few Israelites, at this period of the nation's history, attained to so great an age, and it may have been increasing years and increasing infirmities which had caused the prophet's retirement from public life and long-continued seclusion. In his seclusion he had, apparently, been forgotten ; amid the troubles that had befallen Jehu in his later years, and Jehoahaz throughout his entire reign, no recourse had been had to the aged " man of God " for counsel or advice ; no one had thought to ask, " Is there not anywhere in Israel a prophet of the Lord, that we may inquire of the Lord by him ? " But Joash was of a different temper from his father and grand-father. He was more God-fearing, keener-witted, more sensitive. The thought that to his other troubles was to be added the loss of so eminent a subject, so valuable a support, smote him with dismay, and determined him at any rate to pay a last visit to the aged seer, and see if, before he died, any help was to be got from him. Introduced into his presence, the sight of the dying saint completely unmanned him, and he burst into a flood of tears, weeping over Elisha's face, as he bent above his prostrate form, and exclaiming amid his sobs—" O my father, my father "— our best, our one defence—" the chariot of Israel, and the horsemen thereof ! " The sight of the youth's emotion aroused the prophet, awoke his sympathy, called forth his patriotism, nerved him to make one last dying effort for God, for his country, and against Syria. " Take bow and arrows," he said, " open the window eastward, and shoot ! "—and then, when the king had taken the bow, and placed an arrow on the string, the prophet reared himself from his sick couch, and through the window open towards the eastern quarter, whence the hostile armies of Syria came, placing his aged hands on the youth's hands, he caused the king to shoot. Once, twice, thrice the prince shot ; and the seer exclaimed—" an arrow of deliverance wrought by the Lord, and an arrow of deliverance from Syria ; for thou shall smite the Syrians in Aphek, till thou have consumed them." Then suddenly, though he had not exhausted

his store of arrows, the prince stopped. Elisha was angered—
"Thou shouldest," he said, "have smitten (shot) five or six times,
then hadst thou smitten Syria till thou hadst consumed her;
whereas now thou shalt smite Syria but thrice" (2 Kings xiii.
14-19). The lukewarmness and apathy of man stints the out-
pouring of the Divine favour. A little more faith, a little more
zeal, a little more energy, and Joash himself might have accomplished the task, which through his faint-heartedness was
reserved for his son, and have completely broken the power of
Syria and carried the Israelite kingdom to the highest point
of its glory.

As it was, his success was limited. Hazael, after a long reign,
had died, leaving his throne to a son, whom he had named after
his murdered master, Benhadad. Against this prince, whose
military talents had been exhibited during his father's lifetime,
(2 Kings xiii. 3 and 25), Joash proceeded to make war. Thrice,
according to the prophecy of Elisha, at or near Aphek, on the
east of the Sea of Galilee, the scene of the great victory over
Syria won by Ahab (1 Kings xx. 29), he beat the forces of Benhadad, inflicting on his foe defeats, which were not barren of
result, but which gradually drove the Syrians from their conquests to the west of the Jordan, and recovered to Israel all the
cities which Jehoahaz had lost to Benhadad in that region.
Joash was able to feel that he had achieved an important
success, had turned the tables on his foe, and arrested the decline of his country. He did not perhaps at once view himself
as " a cedar in Lebanon," but he acquired the self-respect which
made it natural for him so to describe himself when provocation
came.

Provocation came from an unexpected quarter. Judæa, under
Jehoram, Ahaziah, and Joash, had shown itself almost as weak
as the kingdom of Samaria. It had lost Edom and Libnah
(2 Chron. xxi. 8-10), had been ravaged by the Philistines and
Arabs (ibid. vers. 16, 17), and had had to buy off the hostility of
Hazael (2 Kings xii. 18). Very recently, however, under Amaziah, the tide had turned. That warlike prince had no sooner
ascended the throne than he determined on making a vast effort
to re-subjugate the revolted Edom. Collecting a huge army,
and at first hiring mercenaries also from Israel, he invaded the
Idumæan territory, defeated the Edomites with great slaughter
in the Valley of Salt, took Petra, the capital, and returned

victorious with a large booty (2 Chron. xxv. 9) to Jerusalem.
Then, in the insolence of victory, or perhaps provoked by some
hostile acts on the part of the Israelite mercenaries, whom he
had hired and then dismissed (ibid. vers. 10, 13), the Jewish
king sent a challenge to his Israelite brother, in the curt but
perfectly clear phrase—" Come, let us look one another in the
face " (2 Kings xiv. 8 ; 2 Chron. xxv. 17). Nowise frightened
or abashed, Joash answered the challenger, in true Oriental
fashion, with a parable : " The thistle that was in Lebanon," he
said, " sent to the cedar that was in Lebanon, saying, Give thy
daughter to my son to wife : and there came by a wild beast
that was in Lebanon, and trode down the thistle " (2 Kings xiv.
9) ; or, as Josephus paraphrases,[1] " There were in the range of
Lebanon a cypress of vast size and a thistle. The thistle sent
to the cypress to propose the betrothal of her daughter to the
other's son. But as the offer was being made, there passed by
a wild beast and trod down the thistle." To his parable he
added a few words of advice : " Thou hast indeed smitten
Edom, and thine heart hath lifted thee up : glory of this, and
tarry at home : for why shouldest thou meddle to thy hurt, that
thou shouldest fall, even thou, and Judah with thee ? "

But Amaziah had gone too far to draw back. Instead of
" tarrying at home," he put himself at the head of his army, and
marched out to attack his foe, who was well on the alert, and
met him at Bethshemesh, not far from Jerusalem, where the
two kings " looked one another in the face," and fought a bloody
battle. The host of Judah was discomfited before Israel, and
fled away in confusion ; Amaziah himself being taken prisoner
upon the battlefield. Joash forthwith advanced upon Jerusalem,
which, being quite unable to resist the conqueror, had to submit
upon disgraceful conditions. A space of four hundred cubits
(two hundred yards) in the northern wall was levelled (2 Kings
xiv. 13) ; and, according to Josephus,[2] the victorious Joash,
mounted in his war-chariot, and carrying his royal prisoner with
him, entered the conquered city through the breach. All the
treasures contained in the Temple and in the royal palace,
whether in the shape of bullion or of vessels, were considered
to be forfeited, and were seized and carried off (ibid. ver. 14).

[1] " Ant. Jud." ix. 9, § 2.
[2] Ibid. ix. 9, § 3 :—'Εφ' ἅρματος εἰσήλασε διὰ τῆς διακοπῆς εἰς Ἱεροσό-
λυμα.

Hostages also were demanded and given—a new feature in the warfare of the time ; after which Joash, having released Amaziah and restored him to his throne, returned in triumph, with his victorious army, to Samaria.

It would seem that Joash did not very long survive his great victory. His entire reign lasted only sixteen years (2 Kings xiii. 10), and the earlier part of it must have been occupied with the Syrian war. Amaziah did not, probably, ascend the Jewish throne till Joash's fourth year,[1] and then must have been for some considerable time engaged in his preparations against Edom (2 Chron. xxv. 5-11). The Edomite campaign can scarcely have been fought earlier than his tenth or eleventh year, which was Joash's thirteenth or fourteenth. Even if the battle of Bethshemesh took place in the year following, Joash can have survived it only for a year or two. He appears to have died peacefully in Samaria, and to have been buried there in the sepulchres of the kings (2 Kings xiii. 13).

[1] Our present text (2 Kings xiv. 1) says the "second" year ; but a comparison of 2 Kings xiii. 10 with xii. 1 shows that for "second" should be read "fourth."

CHAPTER XXI.

AMAZIAH.

Amaziah punishes his father's murderers, but spares their sons—His
character—He makes preparations for the conquest of Edom, and
hires Israelite mercenaries—Rebuked by a prophet, he dismisses them
—Their conduct — Amaziah's successful war against Edom — His
challenge to Joash — His defeat and later inaction — His strange
idolatry—Conspiracy formed against him—He flies to Lachish, but is
pursued and killed—His burial.

THE murder of Joash, king of Judah, by two officers of his
court at Jerusalem (2 Kings xii. 20, 21), threw the southern
kingdom into a state of trouble and confusion. The conspirators
had, in all probability, a party at their back ; possibly, it was a
strong party. Though, as the kingdom was understood to be
hereditary, the succession naturally devolved upon Amaziah, the
late king's eldest son, and no one ventured to contest it with
him, yet it was some time before his authority was generally
acknowledged and his rule " established " (ibid. xiv. 5). When,
after a while, disturbance subsided, and he found himself free to
discharge the kingly functions according to his own views of
duty, the first step that he took was to arrest the murderers of
his father, and to punish their crime with death. But, while
thus vindicating law and right, he exhibited also what was regarded as extraordinary clemency, since he punished only the
guilty parties themselves, and did not visit their crime upon
their sons, as was, in spite of the Law of Moses (Deut. xxiv. 16),
the ordinary Jewish custom. Policy might be, and no doubt
was, pleaded for the practice,[1] which in the East, where the
blood feud was an established institution, might seem to be
almost a necessity ; but Amaziah had studied the Law, as all

[1] The old Greek adage—Νήπιος, ὃς πατέρα κτείνας παῖδας καταλείποι
—spoke the general Oriental sentiment on the subject.

faithful Israelites were bound to do, and would not allow ex-
pediency or reasons of state to overrule it. When he came to
the throne, he was undoubtedly a conscientious and pious prince,
attached to the worship of Jehovah, and, if not of a "perfect
heart" (2 Chron. xxv. 2), yet at any rate anxious to maintain
true religion (2 Kings xiv. 3), and observe the Law in his own
person. Like his father Joash, he seems to have fallen away in
later life (2 Chron. xxv. 14-16); and at best he lacked the
earnest zeal of a true religious reformer (2 Kings xiv. 4); but on
the whole he was reckoned among the good Jewish princes, and
even the author of Chronicles allows that "he did that which
was right in the sight of Jehovah" (2 Chron. xxv. 2).

In respect of valour and love of enterprise Amaziah was, as
Ewald notes,[1] a strong contrast to his father. His first great undertaking was the re-conquest of Edom. Edom, since its revolt from
Jehoram, the son of Jehoshaphat (2 Kings viii. 20), had been a
thorn in the side of Judæa, causing perpetual trouble and annoy-
ance. Edom "did pursue his brother with the sword, and did cast
off all pity, and his anger did tear perpetually, and he kept his
wrath for ever" (Amos i. 11). Southern Judæa was subject to
continual ravages. Towns and villages were burnt; crops carried
off or destroyed; trees cut down; good land marred; prisoners
carried into slavery. To subdue Edom, to put an end to these
losses, was well worth a great and sustained effort, an effort
which needed very careful preparation. Amaziah began with
his own subjects. Having numbered the men capable of bearing arms through all Judah and Benjamin, from twenty years
old and upwards, and found them to amount to three hundred
thousand, he proceeded to organize and discipline this vast
host, appointing officers on the decimal system introduced
by Moses (Exod. xviii. 25), captains over thousands, and captains over hundreds, and perhaps over fifties, and tens (2
Chron. xxv. 5). These were armed with spear and shield, and
trained in their use. Amaziah then looked abroad, in search of
foreign assistance. An alliance with Israel may have crossed
his mind; but the relations between the two kingdoms were
scarcely such at the period as to promise success to an attempt
of this character. Instead, therefore, of entering into negotiations with the monarch, Amaziah sent his emissaries among the
people, and succeeded in enlisting in his service a number of

[1] "History of Israel," vol. iv. p. 141, Eng. tr,

mercenaries, who are estimated by the author of Chronicles (2 Chron. xxv. 6) at a hundred thousand. The number is extraordinary, considering the depressed state of the kingdom of Israel very recently (2 Kings xiii. 7), and is perhaps to be reckoned one of the many places in which our present text of Chronicles has suffered corruption. But, as Ewald notes, "the Chronicler must have found an account of this sort in an ancient document," [1] and his outline of facts is worthy of acceptance, even if we a little misdoubt his "colouring." An Israelite con-tingent had been hired, and was on the point of setting out, in company with the Judæan troops, to invade Edom, when a prophet, whose name is not given, interfered, and representing to Amaziah the wickedness of making common cause with an idolatrous people, [2] threatened him with God's anger, and the failure of his enterprise, unless he sent the army of Israel away (ibid. vers. 7, 8). "But what," exclaimed the monarch, "shall we do for the hundred talents"—the amount of their hire—"which I have given to the army of Israel?" How shall I recoup myself for this expenditure? "The man of God answered —The Lord is able to give thee much more than this." Then, we are told, "Amaziah separated them, to wit, the army that was come to him out of Ephraim, to go home again" (2 Chron. xxv. 10); and they returned home, while he went on to the Edomite war without them. Naturally, they were indignant; and on their way back through Judæa to their own country, they vented their wrath in petty plundering of Jewish towns and villages, which was sometimes resisted, with the result that as many as three thousand Jews fell in the tumults and skirmishes (ibid. ver. 13). It was now the turn of the Judæans to feel pro-voked and indignant, and to cherish a grudge, which they would be sure to take the first opportunity of venting.

Meanwhile, Amaziah had pushed forward through south-eastern Judæa towards the Edomite country, and passing the border at the south-western angle of the Dead Sea, found the troops of Edom drawn up to meet him in the "Valley of Salt," or plain of the Sabkah, an open space between the southern shore of the sea, and the high ground that separates between the Jordan depression and the Arabah. [3] Here a decisive battle

---

[1] "History of Israel," vol. iv. p. 142, Eng. tr.

[2] Compare 2 Chron. xix. 2 ; xx. 37.

[3] See the article on the "Valley of Salt," in Dr. Smith's "Dictionary of the Bible," vol. iii. pp. 1097, 1098.

was fought, in which the Edomites suffered complete defeat, losing ten thousand men ; while Amaziah's victorious host pressed upon the flying columns, and chased them to Selah, or Petra, the strange Idumæan capital amid the mountains.[1] Selah was besieged and taken (2 Kings xiv. 7), and its name contemptuously changed to Joktheel, "the subdued of God." Numerous prisoners were made, roughly reckoned at ten thousand (2 Chron. xxv. 12) ; and these unfortunates were dragged to the brink of the cliffs for which Petra is noted, and precipitated from them into the gulf below. Edom was for the time completely cowed and subdued ; while Amaziah was greatly elated at his success, and encouraged by it to turn his thoughts immediately to another and more difficult enterprise.

The behaviour of the Israelite mercenaries, whom he had dismissed, in their passage through his country gave Amaziah reasonable ground for complaint, and, if he chose to make it a *casus belli*, for war. It would seem, however, from the general tenor of the narrative in Chronicles, and still more in Kings, that it was not so much this provocation on their part, as his own pride and self-conceit, which caused him to determine on challenging the king of Israel to a trial of strength. At any rate, whatever may have been his motive, the challenge was sent. "Amaziah, king of Judah, took advice"—doubtless with some kindred spirits, as hot-headed as himself—"and sent to Joash, the son of Jehoahaz, the son of Jehu, saying—Come, let us look one another in the face" (2 Chron. xxv. 17 ; 2 Kings xiv. 8)—"Come," *i.e.*, "and let us contend with our armies in the open field, and see which will be the conqueror." The reply of Joash to this invitation has been given at length in the sketch of his life.[2] Its scoffing tone was little calculated to soothe or pacify an already enraged antagonist. Amaziah therefore flew to arms. Joash was quite as ready for the fray, and even seems to have anticipated his adversary and to have invaded Judæa before Amaziah was ready to invade Israel. The battle, at any rate, was fought at Bethshemesh, to the west of Jerusalem, in Judæan territory. It resulted in the entire defeat of the Jewish army, and the capture of the proud and boastful king. The rout was complete. Jerusalem could make no resistance. There does not seem to have been any siege. The conqueror,

---

[1] Compare Stanley, "Sinai and Palestine," pp. 88–92.
See above, p. 132.

according to Josephus,[1] insisted on entering the city through a great breach which he broke in the northern wall—a breach two hundred yards in length, "from the gate of Ephraim to the gate of the corner" (2 Kings xiv. 13). He then demanded and received the treasures—all that was contained in the Temple treasury, all the gold and silver of the house of God, all that was of value in the royal palace, was swept off, and carried to Samaria. The buildings of the city and Temple were spared—there seems to have been no sack, no massacre, no carrying of prisoners into captivity. Amaziah was released, and re-established upon the throne, but "fallen from his high estate"; Judæa was evacuated, and left to itself. Joash was content to return to his capital without any long train of captives, and without (as it would seem) imposing on the Judæan kingdom any further obligation than that of placing in his hands a certain number of hostages (ibid. ver. 14).

Amaziah continued to occupy the throne for fifteen years after his defeat by Joash. During this space of time he appears to have undertaken no warlike enterprises. He and his subjects, no doubt, distrusted one another. Edom, however, seems to have continued subject (2 Chron. xxvi. 3); and neither Joash, nor his successor Jeroboam, gave further trouble to the Judæan kingdom. There were, perhaps, hostilities on the part of the Philistines and Arabs, which Uzziah afterwards avenged (ibid. vers. 6, 7); but no great impression was made by these chronic enemies, who indulged in raids rather than in attempts at conquest.

In the matter of religion, Amaziah was guilty of one grievous falling away. On his return from his Edomite campaign he brought with him to Jerusalem a number of images of the Idumæan gods (2 Chron. xxv. 14). These, with an infatuation that is astonishing, but not without a parallel (2 Chron. xxvii. 23), he set up as objects of worship in Jerusalem, but in private, perhaps, rather than in public, offering them incense, and bowing himself down before them. Hereupon a prophet was commissioned to rebuke him for his unfaithfulness, and to point out, not only its wickedness, but its folly. To honour gods who had just shown that they could not protect their own votaries, was surely the height of absurdity. Yet this was what Amaziah had done. He had taken for his protectors gods who were utterly

[1] "Ant. Jud." ix. 9, § 3.

without power to do him either good or harm, and had thereby offended the God to whom he owed everything. Could anything be more insensate? Amaziah felt the justice of the reproach, and, greatly nettled by it, retorted with keenest irony —"Art thou made of the king's counsel?" (Art thou, *i.e.*, entitled to offer me advice? Have I made thee one of my counsellors, and forgotten it?) "Forbear; why shouldest thou be smitten?" (If thou art not a counsellor, *i.e.*, forbear; keep thy advice to thyself? Why provoke me to have thee scourged for thy impertinence?) "Then the prophet forbare, and said: I know that God hath counselled to destroy thee, because thou hast done this"—(I am of His counsel, if not of thine), and with this barbed shaft he left the royal presence. We are not told whether his rebuke had any effect, or whether Amaziah persisted in his idolatry in spite of it; but it seems scarcely probable that, if he had maintained the worship, he could have been reckoned as decidedly among the good kings, as he is both by the writer of Kings (2 Kings xv. 3) and by the writer of Chronicles (2 Chron. xxv. 2).

Amaziah never recovered the prestige which he had lost in his war with Joash. His subjects despised him for his ill success, and though they tolerated his rule for the space of at least fifteen years after his defeat, it continued to rankle in their minds, until at last the smothered discontent broke out. A conspiracy was formed against him in Jerusalem, which assumed such dimensions, that he was led to regard resistance as hopeless, and to seek safety in flight. His place of refuge was Lachish, now Um-Lakis, on the south-western border of Judah. This was a city of considerable strength (2 Chron. xi. 9; 2 Kings xix. 8), and had the king been accompanied by even a small body of faithful troops, he would probably have been able to maintain himself against his revolted subjects for months, or even years; but Amaziah had made himself generally unpopular, and seems not to have had even a knot of adherents. When the conspirators "sent after him to Lachish" (2 Kings xiv. 19), he succumbed to them without a struggle. Those who seized his person put him to death, but offered him no further indignity. On the contrary, they placed the corpse in the royal chariot, in which Amaziah had reached Lachish, and so honourably conveyed it to Jerusalem, and buried it in the royal sepulchres. Amaziah had reigned altogether twenty-nine years, and had reached the fifty-fourth year of his age (2 Kings xiv. 2).

CHAPTER XXII.

JEROBOAM THE SECOND.

Significance of Jeroboam's name—His connexion with the prophet Jonah—
His wars—With Syria of Damascus—With Hamath—With Moab and
Ammon—His long reign—Prosperity of Israel under him—Result of
the prosperity, general corruption—Jeroboam's worship of the calves
denounced by Amos—The general wickedness denounced by Hosea—
Results of Jeroboam's reign—His death.

IT is significative of the position taken up by the house of Jehu
in Israel, that its third monarch should have given to his eldest
son the name of "Jeroboam."   The name necessarily recalled the
founder of the kingdom—the crafty inventor of the religion
which was to combine a profession of faithfulness towards
Jehovah with practical idolatry and materialism.   It implied
that the first Jeroboam's system was thoroughly approved, and
would be zealously maintained by the dynasty, which, while
basing its claim to rule on its detestation of foreign superstitions, fostered and cherished such as were not of foreign
but of home growth.   Each successive monarch of the house
had, in fact, protected and encouraged the calf-worship (2 Kings
x. 29-31 ; xiii. 2, 6, 11) ; it remained for the third king, Joash,
openly to proclaim his adherence to it by showing that the name
of its founder was that which he most delighted to honour.

Jeroboam succeeded to the throne "in the fifteenth year of
Amaziah" (2 Kings xiv. 23), very shortly after his father's great
victory over Judah.   The military successes of his father
against Benhadad (ibid. xiii. 25), and against Amaziah (ibid.
xiv. 11-13), naturally led him to raise his thoughts to greater
enterprises than even his father had attempted ; and it appears

to have been not long after his accession [1] that he commenced
that series of wars which covered his name with glory, and
cause modern historians to recognize in him the predestined
"deliverer" of the Israelite nation (ibid. xiii. 5), and to speak
of him as "the greatest of all the kings of Samaria." [2] In
entering upon the series of expeditions which led to these
glorious results, he had, it would seem, the support of a
prophet to whose actions and character attaches a more than
ordinary interest. Jonah, the son of Amittai, of Gath-Hepher
in Galilee (Josh. xix. 13), was to Jeroboam the Second what
Ahijah the Shilonite had been to Jeroboam the First, and what
Elisha had been to Jehu. He may, or may not have been, "the
child of the widow of Zarephath, the boy who attended Elijah
to the wilderness, the youth who anointed Jehu," [3] but he was
certainly the unfortunate cast into the sea by the Phœnician
mariners (Jonah i. 15), the preacher of repentance to Nineveh
(ibid. iii. 4), the man deemed worthy to furnish a type or
"emblem of the deliverance of our Lord Himself from the
jaws of death and the grave" (Matt. xii. 40). Prophecies of
Jonah, the son of Amittai, now lost to us, declared, in the name
of Jehovah, the Lord God of Israel, the great things that
Jeroboam would do for Israel, the extraordinary success which
he would have, and the extent of the dominion which he would
build up (2 Kings xiv. 25). We must view Jeroboam as going
forth to his wars with the words of Jonah's prophecies in his
ears, and as strung by them to the high pitch of daring that
achieved such grand results.

We are not able to lay down, on any historical authority, the
order of Jeroboam's wars. But, taking probability for our guide,
we shall not be likely to stray very far from the truth, if we put
his war with Syria of Damascus first, that for the recovery of
Hamath second, and that with Moab and Ammon in the far
south third. Syria of Damascus still retained at Jeroboam's
accession the whole territory east of the Jordan—"all the land
of Gilead, the Gadites, and the Reubenites, and the Manas-
sites, from Aroer which is by the river Arnon, even Gilead and
Bashan" (2 Kings x. 33)—all the tract conquered by Hazael
from Jehu. Joash had recovered only the cities taken by Ben-

---

[1] See the arguments on Ewald ("History of Israel," vol. iv. p. 125,
Eng. tr.). [2] Stanley, "Lectures on the Jewish Church," vol. ii. p. 299.
[3] Ibid. p. 301.

hadad, the son of Hazael, from Jehoahaz (2 Kings xiii. 25). It would be natural that Jeroboam should seek first to "recover his border." His father had been estopped from further successes against Syria by his faint-heartedness in the death-chamber of Elisha, when he was content to shoot eastward thrice. Jeroboam had been guilty of no such weakness; and, confident in Jonah's promises of victory, would cross the Jordan, and begin the re-conquest of his own proper territory, with a good heart. Rapid and strange success seems to have attended him. Not only was the entire Trans-Jordanic region recovered, but the Damascene kingdom was itself invaded; the troops of Jeroboam carried all before them; and the capital city—the great and ancient "Dammesek"—was taken (ibid. ver. 28). When we consider the great power of Damascus, how under Benhadad and Hazael it had warred, on tolerably even terms, against Assyria,[1] what a strength of chariots it possessed,[2] and how nearly it had, but a little while previously, conquered the kingdom of Israel (2 Kings xiii. 7), the change of fortune does indeed seem remarkable, and the success of Jeroboam extra-ordinary. In view of the wonderful facts, we can but say, with King Asa, "Lord, it is nothing with Thee to help, whether with many, or with them that have no power" (2 Chron. xiv. 11); or, with holy David, "The Lord saveth not with sword and spear; for the battle is the Lord's" (1 Sam. xvii. 47).

Hamath, in the time of Jeroboam, was the capital of a king-dom, quite distinct from that of Damascus, and belonging to an entirely distinct nationality. The Hamathites, according to the Inscriptions of Assyria,[3] were a branch of the nation of the Hittites. They had their own native kings,[4] their own organi-zation, their own language, their own form of writing,[5] their own peculiar ethnic character. They were certainly not Semites. We must regard them as allied to those Scythic or Turanian races, which from time to time disputed with the Semites the mastery of Western Asia, and even for a certain space held

[1] See G. Smith's "Eponym Canon," pp. 108-114, and compare the author's "Ancient Monarchies," vol.ii. pp. 360-364; 1st ed.

[2] Benhadad is said to have brought into the field on one occasion 12,000 chariots ("Eponym Canon," pp. 108, l. 90). Hazael lost in one battle 1,121 (ibid. p. 113, l. 11).   [3] "Eponym Canon," p. 112, l. 87.

[4] Ibid. p. 107, l. 88; p. 108, l. 91; &c.

[5] On the Hamathite writing, see the "Transactions of the Society of Bibl. Archæology," vol. vii. pp. 429-442.

dominion over Egypt.[1] Recently the Hamathites had joined
in the resistance offered to the progress of Assyria by the
Syrians of Damascus under the conduct of Benhadad and
Hazael, and by the cities of the Phœnicians. A strong league
had been formed; great armies had been collected; for the
space of fifteen or twenty years the contest had raged with
doubtful success; and Hamath had borne her fair part in it.
On one occasion she had brought into the field ten thousand
infantry and seven hundred chariots;[2] on another she had had
eighty-nine of her cities captured.[3] The result had been that
the Assyrian advance was stayed; Hamath, and the states in
alliance with her, had beat back their assailant, and though
possibly suffering several severe defeats, succeeded in maintaining their independence. It was probably from her conduct in
these wars, that Hamath obtained the name under which she
was known to Amos, a contemporary of Jeroboam II. (Amos i.
1; vii. 10), of "Hamath the Great" (ibid. vi. 2).

Jeroboam determined on attacking "great Hamath." The
distance from Samaria was considerable—not less than two
hundred miles; but the route was a comparatively easy one.
The proper Israelite territory reached northward as far as the
gorge of the Litany (lat. 33° 30'), and by following the course of
the Litany to its rise near Baalbek, and then descending the
course of the Orontes, Hamath was reached without any
mountainous ground having to be traversed or any difficult
passes to be forced. The entire route lay along the broad and
fertile Cœlesyrian valley, which separates between Lebanon and
Anti-Lebanon, falling gently towards the south in its lower,
and towards the north in its upper portion. Jeroboam's host
would meet with no natural obstacles to check or retard it, and
if it could defeat the Hamathite army in the field, would easily
capture the city, either by assault or by blockade. As we have
no details of the campaign, we can only say that any resistance
which the Hamathites may have offered—and it can scarcely
be doubted that they resisted strenuously—was overcome.
Jeroboam "recovered Hamath to Israel" (2 Kings xiv. 28) after
it had enjoyed independence for the space of a hundred and
fitfy years, regaining thereby the sovereignty over it which had
been lost upon the death of Solomon.

---

[1] See the author's "History of Ancient Egypt," vol. ii. pp. 189-204.
[2] "Eponym Canon," p. 108, l. 91.   [3] Ibid, p. 112, l. 88.

Thus victorious in the north-east and the north, Jeroboam seems to have turned his arms against the south. He did not indeed attack Judah, which was growing in strength under the judicious rule of Uzziah, the son of Amaziah, but in re-establishing his south-eastern border he could not fail to come in contact with the Ammonites and Moabites, and there is reason to believe that he severely chastised both nations, and even conquered them,[1] or at any rate made their kings tributary. Some have thought that Isaiah's striking words belong to this time, being quoted by him from an earlier prophet[2] : " Because in the night Ar of Moab is laid waste, and brought to silence ; because in the night Kir of Moab is laid waste, and brought to silence ; he is gone up to Bajith, and to Dibon, the high places, to weep : Moab shall howl over Nebo, and over Medeba ; on all their heads shall be baldness, and every beard cut off " (Isa. xv. 1, 2).

How long it took Jeroboam to effect his numerous and important conquests is uncertain. He had a reign of very unusual length, extending—according to our present text of Kings —over a space of forty-one years (2 Kings xiv. 23) ; according to the computations of the best critics, over a space of fifty-three years.[3] There is reason, however, to believe that his great victories and successes belong to the earlier, rather than to the later, portion of his reign, and that, after they were completed, the people of Israel enjoyed under Jeroboam's rule a long term of continually increasing material prosperity.[4] Occasional calamities, such as drought, locusts, pestilence, and even earthquake (Amos. i. 1), broke the even tenor of the years, and taught, or should have taught, the people how entirely their material well-being depended upon God ; but, on the whole, these visitations were but temporary and occasional—they did not seriously interfere with the prosperity which was grounded upon causes that were permanent and constantly at work—the enlarged territory, the increased prestige, the respect of surrounding nations, the influx of tribute, and the like. Jeroboam the Second's reign was, to a certain extent, a reproduction of

---

[1] See Ewald, " History of Israel," vol. iv. p. 124 ; Stanley, " Lectures on the Jewish Church," vol. ii. p. 300 ; Pusey, " Minor Prophets," p. 208.

[2] Stanley, " Lectures on the Jewish Church," vol. ii. p. 300.

[3] Ewald, " History of Israel, ' vol. iv. p. 124.   Compare p. 118.

[4] Ibid. p. 125.

Solomon's. Time seemed to have rolled itself backwards. The people "dwelt in their tents" in peace "as in the days of old" (2 Kings xiii. 5), under the shadow of their vines and fig-trees,[1] secure from raids and incursions, able (as a general rule) to gather in year after year the full crops that their fertile and prolific soil produced under skilful and laborious husbandry—crops of corn, and wine, and oil, of figs, of grapes, and of pomegranates. Commerce also flourished. There was free intercourse with the surrounding nations, especially with such as had distinguished themselves by progress in manufactures and in the arts; and precious products were imported from distant lands, which were ultimately bought by the opulent, enriching the various traders through whose hands they passed.

The prosperity exhibited itself in magnificent buildings of various kinds, in a vast number of the most luxurious contrivances for material enjoyment, and in a general expensiveness and softness of living among the upper classes which tended, as time went on, to injure the morals and sap the physical vigour of the nation. "Great houses" were built, "palaces," as they are called in some places (Amos iii. 11; vi. 8), of hewn stone (ibid. v. 11), and liberally adorned with ivory (ibid. iii. 15); some were used as winter, others as summer residences (ibid.); they were richly and luxuriously fitted up with ivory beds (ibid. vi. 4), and soft couches draped with Damascus cloth (ibid. iii. 12); the harp and the viol resounded in them (ibid. vi. 5); and their owners indulged in a continuous round of feasting and revelry. As Ewald says[2]: "The comfortable prosperity of the people passed, in the metropolis of Samaria and in many other parts of the country, into debauchery and excess, and then again into such pampered effeminacy of morals that the austere old Israel could hardly be recognized, and the prophets could not pour out their divine wrath, or the moralists their ridicule, abundantly enough. The clearest sign of the degradation of public morality was furnished then, as at all similar times, by the growing effrontery of women, and the decline of domestic chastity (Hos. iv. 13; Amos ii. 7, iv. 1-8, viii. 13). Such a vehement appetite for debauchery and ostentation created an

[1] See 1 Kings iv. 25.
[2] "History of Israel," vol. iv. pp. 125, 126. Compare Stanley, "Lectures on the Jewish Church," vol. ii. pp. 307-309; and Pusey, "Minor Prophets," pp. 2, 3 and 148.

equally powerful tendency to avarice and all kinds of fraudulent oppression of the most defenceless citizens ; and the opportunities for these perversions of justice increased in proportion as the king came to be regarded simply as the first among a number of similar potentates and military chiefs (Hos. v. 1 ; Amos iii. 9 ; &c.). And now, too, as in the time of Solomon, the freer intercourse of the people with heathen nations, who had either been conquered or were distinguished by commerce and art, together with the general spread of looseness and intemperance of life, caused an extensive introduction of heathen religions ; while it became customary to satisfy the claims of the ancient religion of the land, in the low state to which it had sunk, by rich offerings and drunken orgies, so that it thus actually plunged the people yet deeper in moral apathy."

There is no evidence that Jeroboam himself either took part in the various heathen rites that crept in under his sovereignty, or that he even lent them any encouragement. But he gave the fullest countenance to the calf-worship at Dan and Bethel, which dated from the foundation of the kingdom. "He did that which was evil in the sight of the Lord ; he departed not from all the sins of Jeroboam, the son of Nebat, which made Israel to sin" (2 Kings xiv. 24). The sanctuary at Bethel was during his reign "the king's chapel," and reckoned a portion of "the king's court" (Amos vii. 13). The prophet Amos, who was commissioned by God to raise his voice against all the abominations of the time, made Dan and Bethel—Bethel especially—objects of the severest denunciations. He appeared personally at Bethel, and confronted Amaziah, the high-priest of the Temple there, boldly declaring that "the high places of Isaac should be desolate, and the sanctuaries of Israel laid waste, and that God should rise against the house of Jeroboam with the sword" (ibid. vii. 9). Amaziah understood him to threaten that Jeroboam himself should "die by the sword" (ibid. ver. 11), and accused him of "conspiring against the king" ; but this was putting a gloss upon his words. However, on the strength of this interpretation, which was communicated to Jeroboam, the prophet, who, though of Jewish birth (Amos i. 1), had for some time taken up his abode in the kingdom of Samaria, was formally banished from the land, and bidden to return into Judæa, "and there eat bread, and prophesy there" (ibid. vii. 12)—"the land of Israel was not able to bear his words" (ver. 10). So the preacher of righteousness retired, but in retreating launched a Parthian shaft at his adversary—"Now therefore hear thou," he said to Amaziah, "the word of the Lord. Thou sayest, Prophesy not against Israel, and drop not thy word against the house of Isaac. Therefore thus saith the Lord : Thy wife shall be a harlot in the city, and thy sons and thy daughters shall fall by the sword, and thy land shall be divided by line ; and thou shalt die in a polluted land ; and Israel shall surely go into captivity forth of his land" (ibid. vii. 16, 17).

Another prophet also lent his voice to enforce the warnings of Amos, and to re-echo his denunciations. Hosea was a native of the Samaritan kingdom, and prophesied under Jereboam the Second (Hos. i. 1), when the worst effects of the prosperity had become apparent in the generally prevalent drunkenness, debauchery, idolatry, and cruel oppression. His picture of the general condition of things is even more gloomy than that of Amos. "There is no truth," he says, "nor mercy, nor knowledge of God in the land. By swearing, and lying, and killing, and stealing, and committing adultery, they break out, and blood toucheth blood" (chap. iv. 1, 2). "My people ask counsel at their stocks, and their staff declareth unto them : for the spirit of whoredoms hath caused them to err, and they have gone a whoring from under their God. They sacrifice upon the tops of the mountains, and burn incense upon the hills, under oaks and poplars and elms, because the shadow thereof is good ; therefore your daughters commit whoredom, and your spouses commit adultery" (ibid. vers. 12, 13). "They commit falsehood ; and the thief cometh in ; and the troop of robbers spoileth without. And they consider not in their hearts that I remember all their wickedness : now their own doings have beset them about, they are before My face. They make their king glad with their wickedness, and the princes with their lies. They are all adulterers, as an oven heated by the baker. . . . They are all hot as an oven, and have devoured their judges ; all their kings are fallen ; there is none among them that calleth upon Me" (ibid. vii. 1–7).

Thus the fair promise with which the reign of Jeroboam opened passed away, and was succeeded by a time of general corruption and depravity. The existing dynasty was declared to lie under the Divine displeasure, and was threatened with speedy extinction (Hos. i. 4; Amos vii. 9). The kingdom itself was declared to be approaching its dissolution (Hos. *l. s. c.*; Amos iii. 12, v. 27, vii. 17). Assyria was not obscurely indicated as the world-power by which the destruction would be accomplished (Hos. x. 14). A sad and dismal prospect must have lain before the aged Jeroboam in the later years of his life, when, denounced by the prophets of Jehovah, and at war with one of them (Amos vii. 12), he must have felt that his dynasty approached its term, and that even his kingdom's days were probably numbered. The dark cloud which lay along his eastern and north-eastern horizon cannot but have been well known to him, and have caused him serious apprehension. The internal condition of his kingdom can scarcely have afforded him any counterbalancing satisfaction. At the age of threescore years and ten, or more,[1] he at length "slept with his fathers" (2 Kings xiv. 29), having reigned longer, and probably having lived longer, than any other king of Israel; having also done more than any other king to increase the glory and raise the military *prestige* of his kingdom, but having greatly sapped its strength, and brought it into a condition which would naturally make it an easy prey to the first powerful enemy with which it should be brought into contact. Jeroboam the Second may perhaps be pronounced *felix opportunitate mortis*, since he was "taken away from the evil to come"—allowed to depart before any of those calamities fell upon the land, which its condition under his rule provoked, and which the prophets who witnessed that condition predicted.

[1] If he was even twenty years old at his accession, and if he reigned fifty-three years, as Ewald thinks, he would be seventy-three or seventy-four at his death.

CHAPTER XXIII.

UZZIAH OR AZARIAH.

Uzziah made king by the popular choice—His greatness both in war and peace—His occupation of Elath—His war with the Philistines—His conquest of the Arabs of Gur-Baal and of the Maonites—Submission to him of the Ammonites—His measures for home defence—His patronage of husbandry—General character of his reign—His great sin—His deposition and death.

ON the murder of Amaziah, king of Judah, by conspirators at Lachish, *the people* are stated to have taken Azariah, or Uzziah, one of Amaziah's sons, a youth of sixteen years of age, and made him king in his father's room (2 Kings xiv. 21). It is uncertain whether he was Amaziah's eldest son, and so pointed out for monarch by the law of primogeniture ; or whether he was a younger son, whom the people selected from a belief that he possessed qualities that made him especially fit to rule. There seems to be an indication of his having already won the popular favour, in the expression used by the writer of Chronicles (2 Chron. xxvi. 1), that "*all* the people of Judah took him and made him king." The choice made, if it were really a choice, was amply justified by the result. Azariah, as Ewald says,[1] "was equally great in the arts of peace and in those of war." His reign was, as Dean Stanley remarks,[2] "the most prosperous, excepting that of Jehoshaphat, since the time of Solomon." By his military successes in various quarters he amply compensated for his father's defeat at Beth-shemesh (2 Kings xiv. 13), and by his judicious preparations against

[1] "History of Israel," vol. iv. p. 143, Eng. tr.
[2] "Lectures on the Jewish Church," vol. ii. p. 372.

attack he obtained the respect of all the neighbouring nations. The Chronicler tells us that "his name spread far abroad, even to the entering in of Egypt" (2 Chron. xxvi. 8, 15).

Among his earliest enterprises seems to have been an expedition into Edom, for the purpose of re-establishing the sea-port of Elath, and renewing the navigation of the Red Sea, and the commerce in that quarter, which had been once established by Solomon, and the renewal of which had been subsequently attempted, but without successful result, by Jehoshaphat (1 Kings xxii. 48 ; 2 Chron. xx. 35–37).   If Edom had, as some think, revolted from Amaziah after his misfortune at Beth-shemesh, and recovered its independence, Azariah's expedition must have been on a great scale, and have effected the re-conquest of the country ; but if, as seems more probable, there had been no such rebellion, then it would have been merely a peaceful enterprise, involving no great difficulty, but still of very considerable importance.   The power which held Elath naturally exercised a certain influence over the Sinaitic peninsula with its mines of copper and turquoise, could enter readily into relations with Egypt, and might even aspire to a share in the valuable Red Sea commerce, which gave Solomon his great wealth (1 Kings ix. 26–28 ; x. 11, 14).   It was indicative of much vigour and self-confidence that such an enterprise should have been undertaken at all, especially by a youth of sixteen ; and the actual establishment of Judah upon the southern sea must have much increased her *prestige*, and, as time went on, would be sure to increase her prosperity.

Azariah seems next to have "gone forth and warred against the Philistines" (2 Chron. xxvi. 6).   The Philistines were always unquiet neighbours of the Jews, and required from time to time to be severely chastised, and compelled, as it were, into good behaviour.   Azariah invaded their country in force, and attacked successively Gath, Jabneh, and Ashdod, three of their strongest fortresses.   None of them was able to resist him.   Azariah "smote whole Palestina with a rod" (Isa. xiv. 9); took the places one after another, and "brake down the walls" (2 Chron. xxvi. 6); or, as some think, actually razed the cities to the ground.[1]   Moreover, he occupied the subjugated territory, and

---

[1] So Ewald ("Hist. of Israel," vol. iv. p. 143) and Stanley ("Lectures," vol. ii. p. 372).   Compare Josephus, "Ant. Jud." ix. 10, § 3 :—κατέσκαψεν αὐτῶν τὰ τείχη.

planted it with new towns, in which, no doubt, Philistines and Hebrews would dwell together. This was probably the origin of that mongrel race, whereof we hear later in the history, which could not speak Hebrew properly, but used a jargon partly Hebrew and partly Ashdodite (Neh. xiii. 24 ; Zech. ix. 6).

While thus employed in extending and consolidating his power in the south-east and the south-west, Azariah naturally came into hostile collision with the Arab tribes, which regarded the wild districts of the Negeb as a sort of " happy hunting-ground," over which they were free to wander, and within which they were free to plunder, at their pleasure. " The Arabs of Gur-Baal, and the Mehunim," or Maonites, are especially mentioned (2 Chron. xxvi. 7) ; but under these designations may be included the wild tribes generally which formed the population of the sterile tract intervening between Southern Judæa and the Egyptian frontier. It was necessary to bring these fierce marauders into subjection in order to give tranquillity to his own southern border, to the territory taken from Philistia, and to the subjected country of the Idumæans. Azariah engaged in hostilities against these tribes, and, God helping him (ibid.), brought them under subjection.

The submission of the Ammonites seems to have been effected in a different way. Nothing is said of any campaign against them ; and the probability is that their submission (ibid. ver. 8) was voluntary. Ewald's statement on the subject, if a little too positive, embodies the view, which, under all the circumstances of the case, is best worthy of acceptance. " When, on the fall of the house of Jehu," he says,[1] " the countries beyond Jordan were thrown into great confusion, Ammon, Moab, and the Hebrew districts lying between them, implored the protection of Uzziah (Azariah), and paid him a yearly tribute. This surprising phenomenon, which, however, is historically beyond question, is sufficiently explained by the circumstances of the time. Ammon and Moab had been again subject to the kingdom of the Ten Tribes, even if they retained princes of their own, for half a century. Damascus, itself in a state of dissolution at the time, could guarantee them no protection ; and yet the Assyrians in the distance, and the constantly repeated incursions of the Arab tribes near at hand, might seem so

[1] " History of Israel," vol. iv. pp. 144, 145.

threatening, that they voluntarily sought the protection of the just and powerful monarch who already possessed Edom on their southern boundary, and had subdued the neighbouring Arabs. By this arrangement, moreover, they retained their own princes (2 Chron. xxvii. 5). These relations continued under Uzziah's son Jotham, but led to fresh complications, which will be explained hereafter." The submission of the Ammonites seems to have included, besides the payment of tribute (2 Chron. xxvi. 8), the cession of a right of pasture to Uzziah for his flocks and herds in their country [1] (ibid. ver. 10).

Azariah's successes abroad were accompanied by a policy of wise vigilance and activity at home, which was well calculated to secure his territories from attack on the part of his neighbours. He strengthened the defences of Jerusalem by building towers at its three weakest points—"the corner gate," a gate probably at the north-western angle of the city, where the north wall abutted on the Valley of Hinnom—"the valley gate," midway in the western wall, corresponding to the modern gate of Jaffa—and "the turning of the wall," a weak place in the defences of the eastern city (Neh. iii. 19), perhaps "the southern point of the valley of the Tyropœon." [2] He protected the wild pasture region towards the south-east and south, by building towers (2 Chron. xxvi. 10) in which the population could take refuge in case of a sudden raid, and at the same time improved the productiveness of the tract by cutting cisterns [3] for the storing of the rain-water in many places. He organized, equipped, and disciplined the military force of the country on a new plan. Retaining or recalling David's institution of the *Gibborim*, or "Mighty men of valour," he raised the number from the "Six Hundred" of David's time to two thousand six hundred, thus more than quadrupling this important body of picked troops. The remainder of the fighting force of the country, which amounted to three hundred and seven thousand five hundred men, was organized into bands by his captain of the host, Hananiah, assisted by Jeiel the scribe and Maaseiah the ruler, who made out and kept a register of the entire num-

[1] See the writer's note on 2 Chron. xxvi. 10, in the "Speaker's Commentary," vol. iii. p. 344.

[2] So Ewald ("History of Israel," vol. iv. p. 144).

[3] See the *marginal* translation of 2 Chron. xxvi. 10 in the Authorized Version.

ber ('bid. ver. 11, 13). The arms provided for them consisted of shields, spears, helmets, habergeons, bows and arrows, and slings (ibid. ver. 14). For the defence of Jerusalem in case of attack, Azariah collected a large number of military engines, such as had long been employed by the Assyrians and Egyptians in their sieges;[1] some resembled the Roman *balistæ*, which hurled huge stones against the enemy; others corresponded to the Roman *catapultæ*, which shot forth darts and javelins. These were distributed along the line of the walls and placed in commanding positions upon the towers, ready for instant use in case the siege of the city were attempted.

Moreover, Azariah "loved husbandry." He possessed, himself, numerous flocks and herds, for which he claimed a right of pasturage, both in the high Judæan upland, and in the Shephelah or low country towards the coast, and also in the *midbar*, or rolling downs, east of the Jordan and the Dead Sea (ibid. ver. 10). He had "husbandmen and vine-dressers" in the mountains, and many a vineyard in the "Carmels" or fertile and sheltered regions among the hills.[2] The "towers" and "cisterns" which he constructed were no doubt mainly for his own use, but they must also have been of general advantage to his subjects.

The summary of Azariah's reign, both in Kings (2 Kings xv. 3) and Chronicles (2 Chron. xxvi. 4), declares him to have been a good king—"He did that which was right in the sight of the Lord, according to all that his father Amaziah had done." There is, of course, the usual reservation, that under him "the high places were not removed; the people sacrificed and burnt incense still on the high places" (2 Kings xv. 4); and the writer of Chronicles adds the qualifying statement, that Azariah "sought God *in the days of Zechariah*, who had understanding in the visions of God" (2 Chron. xxvi. 5), by which it would appear that Azariah, like Joash, his grandfather, was in the earlier part of his reign faithful to Jehovah and the national religion under the influence of a Jehovistic prophet, but afterwards, when this influence was removed, probably by the pro-

---

[1] See the author's "Ancient Monarchies," vol. ii. p. 81.

[2] Stanley speaks of "*the* southern Carmel" ("Lectures," vol. ii. p. 373); but no such place is known to us. Any sheltered tract among the hills suited for the growth of fruit trees was a "carmel." (See Isa. xxix. 17, xxxii. 15; Jer. ii. 7; &c.)

phet's death, fell away and became irreligious. Still, no act of sin is recorded against him until nearly the close of his long life. Then, we are told, he became puffed up with pride on account of his continuous and extraordinary prosperity—"his heart was lifted up to his destruction, and he transgressed against the Lord his God " (2 Chron. xxvi. 16). Wantonly and without excuse, he invaded the priestly office, not, like Saul, assuming priestly duties because the priest was absent (1 Sam. xiii. 8–12), but, when there were scores of priests in and about the Temple, and the high-priest himself was within call, Azariah, intent on self-exaltation, entered the sanctuary, advanced towards the Holy of Holies, and proceeded himself to offer incense on the golden altar of incense, which stood directly before the vail that shrouded the inner chamber. The act was a flagrant assumption, not only of the priestly, but of the high-priestly office (Exod. xxx. 7, 8), and, if tamely submitted to, would have practically subordinated the entire priesthood to the monarch, and have gone far to destroy the whole Mosaic system, so carefully handed down hitherto from generation to generation. Azariah, the high-priest of the time, a namesake of the monarch, understood the gravity of the crisis, and was equal to meeting it. With a band of eighty ordinary priests (2 Chron. xxvi. 17) he followed the king into the sacred building, and hastening to the golden altar, there "withstood" his sovereign. " It appertaineth not to thee, Uzziah," he said, " to burn incense unto the Lord, but to the priests, the sons of Aaron, that are consecrated to burn incense : *go out of the sanctuary ;* neither shall it be for thine honour from the Lord God" (ibid. ver 10). The king was in the act of offering ; the censer was "in his hand to burn incense " (ver. 19) ; a fierce passion of rage was kindled in him at the opposition of the priests ; what he would have done in his passion, had he been left to himself, we do not know ; but he was not left to himself : suddenly he was struck with the terrible scourge of leprosy—leprosy of so pronounced a form that it was visible to all—"the leprosy rose up in his forehead before the priests in the house of the Lord. . . . And Azariah the chief priest, and all the priests, looked upon him, and, behold, he was leprous in his forehead, and they thrust him out from thence ; yea, himself hasted also to go out, because the Lord had smitten him " (ibid. vers. 19, 20). The king himself felt and knew what had happened, and dared no longer to resist ; he acknowledged the Divine hand, and yielded ; but the priests would not spare him the indignity of being "thrust out." They drove him from the Temple, and made him take up his abode in a "several house" (2 Kings xv. 5), or "house of separation," where he lived during the remainder of his days. It was impossible for a leper to discharge the kingly office, and the regency was consequently conferred on Azariah's eldest son, Jotham, who lived in the royal palace and exercised the royal functions, while his unhappy father endured a species of living death. Azariah's reign is reckoned to have lasted fifty-two years (2 Kings xv. 2, 27 ; 2 Chron. xxvi. 3) ; so that, as he was sixteen on his accession, he must have died at the age of sixty-eight. We are not told whether during his incarceration he repented of the sin that he had committed ; but we may perhaps assume that he did so, since he certainly left behind him the character of a good, rather than a wicked, king. (See 2 Kings xv. 3, 34 ; 2 Chron. xxvi. 4, xxvii. 2). He was buried in the royal burial-place (2 Kings xv. 7), but apparently in a sepulchre of his own (2 Chron. xxvi. 23).

CHAPTER XXIV.

ZACHARIAH, SHALLUM, AND MENAHEM.

Corruption of Israel under the dynasty of Jehu—Six months' reign of Zachariah, its last prince—Thirty days' reign of Shallum—Accession of Menahem—His expedition against Tiphsach—Its importance—Change in the condition of Assyria—Accession of Tiglath-Pileser, or Pul—His invasion of Palestine—Menahem submits to him—Ransoms Samaria—Becomes an Assyrian tributary—Dies.

THE destruction of his house, wherewith Jeroboam II. had been threatened (Amos vii. 9) during his lifetime, was not very long delayed after his death. The house of Jehu had been tried and found wanting. Its "zeal for Jehovah" (2 Kings x. 16) had proved shortlived. No attempt had been made by the dynasty from first to last to undo the sin of Jeroboam. Moral corruption had been allowed to creep in, and to prevail more and more. What Isaiah said of Judah towards the close of the reign of Azariah was still more true of Israel : "The whole head was sick, and the whole heart faint ; from the sole of the foot even unto the head there was no soundness " in the body politic ; " but wounds, and bruises, and putrifying sores " (Isa. i. 5, 6). It was time to make an end of the experiment. " Israel was an empty vine " (Hos. x. 1), " a backsliding heifer" (ibid. iv. 16) ; there was no longer any hope of her recovery, at any rate under the dynasty of Jehu. Moreover, the fated time prophesied to the founder of the dynasty (2 Kings x. 30), probably by Elisha, had arrived—with the accession of Zachariah the fourth generation of Jehu's descendants sat upon the throne of Israel—the promise of continuance was fulfilled—a change was to be expected. Six months only after Zachariah's coronation a rebellion broke out against his authority, unprovoked, so far as appears, by any special misconduct on the part of the prince, who had simply followed in the steps of his father, maintaining the worship of the calves in the two sanctuaries of Dan and Bethel (2 Kings xv. 9), but not otherwise guilty of any offence either towards God or towards the people. The adventurer who headed the movement was a certain Shallum, the son of Jabesh, a man otherwise unknown to us, but successful in his bold undertaking. Shallum "conspired against Zachariah, and smote him before the people" (ibid. ver. 10)—*i.e.*, not secretly, but openly—"and slew him, and reigned in his stead." But he held the crown for no more than a month. Menahem, the son of Gadi, a native of the old capital, Tirzah (1 Kings xiv. 17 ; xvi. 6, 9, 23), rose up against Shallum, and marching at the head of an army [1] upon Samaria, where Shallum had established himself, took the city, and put the usurper to death on the scene of his crime (2 Kings xv. 14). He then naturally became king, and is said to have reigned for ten years (ibid. ver. 17) with a certain amount of military glory. He undertook an expedition against a city called Tiphsach, which some suppose to have been in Palestine,[2] but which *may* have been the famous city of "Thapsacus" on the Euphrates. The inhabitants resisted his attack, whereupon he laid siege to the place, took it by assault, and treated it with a severity which was, even according to the ideas of the time, barbarous—"Menahem smote Tiphsach, *and all that were therein* ; because they opened not unto him, therefore he smote it ; and *all the women therein that were with child he ripped up*" (ibid. ver. 16). If the Tiphsach intended was really the Euphratean city, the expedition must have been one of extreme importance, transcending even that of Jeroboam II. against Hamath (2 Kings xiv. 28). It must have constituted a defiance to Assyria, which claimed sovereignty over all the upper and middle Euphrates valley, and it must have required an effort such as no previous king of Israel had ever put forth. Thapsacus must have been reached either by way of Tadmor, or by way of Aleppo, a march from Tirzah, in either case, of above three hundred miles.[3] It is difficult to

[1] Josephus represents him as Captain of the host, and as being with the army at Tirzah when he heard of Zachariah's death ("Ant. Jud." ix. 11, § 1).

[2] So Ewald ("History of Israel," vol. iv. p. 154, note 4).

[3] By way of Aleppo the march could not have fallen much short of *four* hundred miles.

imagine that the Israelite kingdom could have been equal, in
the time of Menahem, to such an undertaking, and could have
carried it through successfully. On the other hand, the bold
aggression would account for the expedition of Pul, which so
soon followed, since Assyria would feel bound to resent and
revenge the indignity offered her.

The power of Assyria, which had been great in the time of
Ahab and Jehu, and which had then seemed to threaten seriously
the independence of the Palestinian kingdoms,[1] had soon afterwards began to decline, and for nearly a century the pressure
of the mighty inland empire on the states situated towards
the coast had relaxed, and, except on rare occasions, was
scarcely felt. Either the kings had been unenterprising, or
internal troubles had occupied them, or the nations of the north
and east had been aggressive, and the armed force of the empire
had had to be employed in keeping them in check. The western
states had been left to themselves; and it was probably the
known decline of Assyria which had encouraged Jeroboam II.,
and which now encouraged Menahem, to make their expeditions.
Assyria seems to have reached her lowest point of weakness
about the time that Menahem made himself king; but very
soon afterwards a reaction took place; instead of the *fainéants*
who had occupied the throne for the preceding twenty or thirty
years,[2] an energetic prince was raised to power; the period of
internal trouble and external inaction came to an end; foreign
expeditions were resumed; aggressors were chastised; and
Assyria once more entered upon a course of conquest, and
absorption of her neighbours. For an entire century—from
B.C. 745 to B.C. 645—her policy was directed by ambitious and
warlike monarchs, who carried her arms into regions never
before even threatened, and greatly enlarged her dominions in
every direction. The *acmé* of Assyrian glory is reached during
these hundred years, towards the close of which her influence
extended from the highlands of Armenia to the furthest limits of
Egypt, and from the Persian desert to the shores of the Egean.

The monarch who effected the change, and inaugurated the
most brilliant period of Assyria's history, bore the two names
of Tiglath-Pileser and Pul. Properly, Tiglath-pileser (Tiglathi-

[1] See "Ancient Monarchies," vol. ii. pp. 360–364.
[2] As Shalmaneser III., Asshur-dayan, and Asshur-nirari—especially the
two latter.

pal*z*ira), was the throne-name which he bore in Assyria, as monarch of that country, and Pul (Pulu) was the throne-name which he bore in Babylonia, as king of Babylon. The double nomenclature was not readily understood by foreigners ; and it may be doubted whether the compilers of either Kings or Chronicles [1] were aware of the fact that it was the same monarch who bore the two appellations. We are indebted for the identification to a cuneiform document.[2]

It was probably soon after Tiglath-Pileser had acquired the sovereignty (B.C. 745), that he made his first expedition into Syria, to advance his interests there, and especially to punish the audacity of Menahem. Apparently, he led his expedition in person. Now for the first time did the well-armed and highly disciplined troops of Assyria, inured to warfare, tread the soil of the Holy Land, and threaten the northern portion of it with subjugation. Isaiah's prophecy received a first fulfilment :—" Jehovah shall lift up to the nations an ensign from far, and shall hiss unto them from the end of the earth : and behold they shall come with speed swiftly : none shall be weary nor stumble among them ; none shall slumber nor sleep ; neither shall the girdle of their loins be loosed, nor the latchet of their shoes be broken : whose arrows are sharp, and all their bows bent, their horses' hoofs shall be counted like flint, and their wheels like a whirlwind : their roaring shall be like a lion, they shall roar like young lions : yea, they shall roar, and lay hold of the prey, and shall carry it away safe, and none shall deliver it " (Isa. v. 26–29). It was felt that resistance was hopeless—that in submission lay the only chance of escape from entire destruction. Accordingly, Menahem sent an embassy, and made request that the Great King would be pleased to accept his submission, and to confirm the authority which he had ventured to assume under peculiar circumstances, but which he would henceforth be content to hold as an Assyrian feudatory (2 Kings xv. 19 ; Hos. v. 13). The request was granted. Menahem was allowed to purge his past misconduct by the payment of a thousand talents of silver (nearly a quarter of a million of our money), and the promise—as appears from the Assyrian Inscriptions [3]—of a further annual tribute. He

[1] See 1 Chron. v. 26.
[2] See " Transactions of the Society of Bibl. Archæology " for 1884, p. 75.   [3] " Eponym Canon," p. 120, l. 29.

wǎs then left in peace, the Assyrian monarch withdrawing into his own country (2 Kings xv. 20).

Shortly afterwards Menahem died—apparently, a natural death—and was buried in Samaria, leaving his crown to his son, Pekahiah, the last Israelite monarch who could boast that he was not a usurper

CHAPTER XXV.

PEKAHIAH AND PEKAH.

Accession of Pekahiah—His murder by Pekah—Pekah's ability—He crushes his domestic foes—Designs a confederacy to resist Assyria—Joins with Rezin in an attack on Ahaz—Called in by Ahaz, Tiglath-Pileser conquers Damascus, and brings the reign of Pekah to an end—Pekah murdered by Hoshea.

PEKAHIAH held the throne for no longer a space than two years (2 Kings xv. 23 ; comp. ver. 27). Nothing is recorded of him except that he maintained the calf-worship, like his predecessors, doing " that which was evil in the sight of the Lord, by not departing from the sins of Jeroboam, the son of Nebat, who made Israel to sin " (ibid. ver. 24), and that he was barbarously murdered by one of his captains—Pekah, the son of Remaliah. The scene of his slaughter was the royal palace in Samaria, where he was attacked by Pekah at the head of a band of fifty Gileadite desperadoes, who slew him in his harem, with the two attendants who alone were faithful to him, Argob and Arieh. Pekahiah probably deserved his fate. At any rate, he was unfit for his position, which required a man of vigour and energy. Pekah was far more suited for the situation ; and, if Israel had been so circumstanced as to make her preservation as a kingdom possible, it might have been expected that Pekah would have accomplished the task. He was, as Ewald says,[1] " so far as warlike prowess combined with skill in diplomacy could qualify any one, the one man of the day best fitted to ward off for a little while longer the ruin of the decaying kingdom." Internal

[1] " History of Israel," vol. iv. p. 157.

troubles are what every usurper must expect to encounter.
Pekah met and crushed those which gathered around him in
the earlier years of his reign with a determination and a force
that at once terrified his domestic foes, and secured him the
respect of his foreign neighbours. He is thought to be the
"shepherd" described by a prophet, as "eating the flesh of the
fat and tearing their hoofs in pieces, with the sword ever upon
his arm and upon his right eye," who slays, instead of gently
chastising, the people.[1] Certainly, he seems to have succeeded,
very soon after his accession, in so far securing tranquility and
obedience at home, that he was able to turn all his attention to
the dangers which threatened him from abroad, and to devise
means whereby he hoped to bid defiance to the impending
perils, and to preserve to his country a continuance of independence.

The expedition of Pul, or Tiglath-Pileser, into Samaria in the
reign of Menahem, and the success which had attended it, far
from contenting that ambitious prince, had only whetted his
appetite for more. It must have been tolerably early in the
reign of Pekah that he a second time took the field, and
marched into Palestine, with the determination to conquer at
least a part of the Samaritan kingdom. His attack fell especially upon the north, where he took "Ijon, and Abel-beth-Maa
chah, and Janoah, and Kedesh, and Hazor, and Gilead (perhaps
Gaulanitis), and Galilee—all the land of Naphtali—and carried
them captive to Assyria" (2 Kings xv. 29)—thus commencing
the "Captivity" which had been so long and often threatened.[2]
A foreign population was probably settled in the tract conquered,
to take the place of the deported Israelites, and the whole of
it was formally added to the territories of Assyria, Assyrian
governors being placed over it.[3] It was then that Pekah took
alarm. He saw that, unless a powerful confederation could be
formed in the Palestinian region, Assyria would to a certainty,
little by little, absorb the entire country, enslave or deport its
people, put down its kings, and extend its own hated sway from
Nineveh to the borders of Egypt. He therefore set himself to
work to induce the principal Palestinian states to join together
and form a confederacy, or league, whereby the Assyrian arms

[1] See Zech. xi. 16, and Ewald. *l. s. c.*
[2] Hos. ix. 3, xi. 5 ; Amos v. 27, vi. 7, vii. 17 ; &c.
[3] "Eponym Canon," p. 123, lines 6-8.

might be resisted, and the subjugation of the country prevented, or at any rate deferred. According to the ordinary ideas which govern human policy, it was a wise and prudent thought. A century earlier the advance of Assyria had been checked by the league between Damascus, Phœnicia, and Hamath. Why might it not be again checked, or even rolled back, by a union of Damascus, Samaria, and Judah? Pekah would no doubt have created a more effectual barrier, could he have reformed his people, turned them from their idolatries, and so restored them to the Divine favour and the Divine protection; but perhaps corruption had progressed too far for this to be possible. Acting according to his lights, he did perhaps what was best under the circumstances. He entered into close alliance with Rezin, king of Damascus (2 Kings xv. 37, xvi. 5; Isa. vii. 1), who was even more exposed to the attacks of the Assyrians than himself; and the two agreed to fall upon Judah conjointly, and either force it to join the league under its existing king, who appears to have been Ahaz, or dethrone him, and set up in his stead a creature of their own, who would be ready to do their bidding. The individual selected was a certain Ben-Tabeal, who is thought to have been a Syrian.[1] Pekah and Rezin, after failing to take Jerusalem, seem to have fallen upon Ahaz separately (2 Chron. xxviii. 5, 6), both of them gaining victories, and carrying off large bodies of captives[2] (ibid. vers. 5, 8). Hereupon, Ahaz, greatly alarmed, sent an embassy to Nineveh, with rich gifts in gold and silver, offering to become an Assyrian feudatory (ibid. vers. 7, 8), and beseeching Tiglath-Pileser to come to his aid, and "save him out of the hand of the king of Syria, and out of the hand of the king of Israel, who were risen up against him." To this call it was impossible for the Assyrian monarch to turn a deaf ear, so deeply was he interested in frustrating Pekah's schemes, and preventing the formation of the triple confederacy designed by him. He therefore at once took the field, and marching against Damascus, as the nearest of the hostile powers, engaged in a war with Rezin, which seems to have lasted for some years and of which he gives the following account :—[3]

[1] Ewald, "History of Israel," vol. iv. p. 158.
[2] The Israelite captives were, however, allowed to return to their homes (2 Chron. xxviii. 15). [3] See "Eponym Canon," p. 121, lines 1–15.

" Rezin's warriors I captured, and with the sword I destroyed [his
    people] :
Of his charioteers and [his horsemen] the arms I broke :
Their warriors bearing bows, [their footmen] armed with spear and
    shield,
With my hand I captured them, and those who fought in their line of
    battle :
He, to save his life, fled away alone ;
Like a deer [he ran], and entered into the great gate of his city.
His generals, whom I had taken alive, on crosses I hung ;
His country I subdued. . . .
Damascus, his city, I besieged ; and, like a caged bird, I enclosed him :
The trees of his forests, which were without number, I cut down ; I left
    not one.
Hadara, the palace of the father of Rezin of Syria [I burnt] ;
The city of Samalla I besieged, I captured ; eight hundred of its people
    and children [I took] ;
Their oxen and their sheep I carried away captive.
Seven hundred and fifty women of the city of Kuruzza,
. . . hundred of the city Armai, five hundred and fifty of the city Mituna
I bore off as prisoners ; I took five hundred and ninety-one cities ;
Over sixteen districts of Syria, like a flood, I swept."

According to the writer of Kings, the captives from Damascus were carried away and settled in Kir (2 Kings xvi. 9), the
country from which they had traditionally sprung (Amos ix. 7) ;
while Rezin himself was either slain in the siege, or put to
death by the conqueror.[1]

Having reduced Damascus, Tiglath-Pileser proceeded against
Samaria, where Pekah offered but a feeble resistance.   Internal
treachery weakened his power within the capital, while the host
of Assyria threatened it from without.   His territories were
rapidly overrun, plundered,[2] and in part stripped of their inhabitants (1 Chron. v. 26).   With the connivance of the Assyrians, a pretender rose up against him, in the person of
Hoshea the son of Elah, within the walls of Samaria itself ;
and this adventurer, having got the king into his power and
lain him (2 Kings xv. 30), was accepted by Tiglath-Pileser as
his feudatory.[3]   The length of Pekah's reign, according to the

---

[1] See 2 Kings xvi. 9.   The Assyrian inscriptions are illegible exactly
where Pekah's fate would seem to have been mentioned.   (See " Eponym
Canon," p. 123, l. 17 ; p. 124, l. 18.)

[2] " Eponym Canon," p. 123, lines 16, 17.

[3] Ibid. l. 17, and p. 124, l. 18.

present text of the Second Book of Kings (chap. xv. 27) was twenty years; but the Assyrian inscriptions throw a doubt upon the number, and render it probable that the space covered was not nearly so long. Pekah must be regarded as a daring and unscrupulous prince, not altogether wanting in worldly wisdom, but placed in such difficult circumstances that his plans, however well laid, could scarcely succeed. He played a bold game, and lost it. We cannot commiserate the murdered usurper, who did but suffer the fate which he had himself inflicted upon his predecessor; but we must feel a certain respect for the ability with which, under circumstances that were well-nigh desperate, something of a struggle was made, and the complete absorption of the kingdom of Samaria into Assyria delayed for twenty or thirty years.

CHAPTER XXVI.

JOTHAM.

Jotham, regent for his father, Uzziah, succeeds him as king of Judah—Doubts concerning the length of his reign—He maintains Uzziah's policy—Fortifies Jerusalem and builds fortresses—Crushes the revolt of Ammon—Suffers attack from Pekah and Rezin—Advance of corruption in Judæa during his reign—His death.

JOTHAM, who became regent when his father, Azariah or Uzziah, was stricken with leprosy, is said to have held the throne of Judah for sixteen years (2 Kings xv. 33) ; but it is questionable whether his sole reign lasted so long, or whether the space mentioned does not also include the period of his regency. He is reckoned a good prince—one who "did right in the sight of the Lord, according to all that his father Uzziah had done" (ibid. ver. 34), but who avoided Uzziah's sin—" howbeit he entered not into the temple of the Lord" (2 Chron. xxvii. 2). In his general policy, he simply trod in the footsteps of his father. First of all, he further improved the defences of the country. He " built the high gate of the house of the Lord" (ibid. ver. 3), *i.e.*, fortified strongly the principal entrance to the Temple area—probably the gate which looked towards the north, whence it was almost certain that any attack upon Jerusalem must be made. Secondly, " on the wall of Ophel he built much"—*i.e.*, he added greatly to the defences of that long southern swelling, or promontory, from the Temple hill, which alone seemed to furnish a means of approaching its walls by a gradual and gentle ascent. He also " built cities "—*i.e.*, fortresses, "in the mountains of Judah, and in the forests he built castles and towers " (ibid. vers. 3, 4) ; in other words, " on the barren plateaus of the mountains in the south of Judah he founded new cities, the land round which was taken into cultivation; and in the forests—probably on the other side of the Jordan especially—he erected castles and towers for the observation of the enemy."[1] He had one only important war. The Ammonite nation, subdued by his father (2 Chron. xxvi. 8), rebelled against him, and refused to pay him tribute, where upon Jotham invaded their country, defeated the Ammonite monarch, re-imposed the tribute, and increased it for the first three years, as a punishment. For this space of time a hundred talents of silver (£24,000) annually, ten thousand measures of wheat, and the same quantity of barley, were required (2 Chron. xxvii. 5), after which it would seem that the nominal rate was restored. Towards the close of his reign he had to sustain attacks on the part of Pekah and Rezin, who had already formed their alliance;[2] but these attacks do not seem to have become formidable until the reign of his son (2 Kings xv. 37; xvi. 5).

The internal condition of Judah did not improve under Jotham. Notwithstanding his own faithfulness to the Jehovistic worship, "the people did yet corruptly" (2 Chron. xxvii. 2). The high-place worship, as a matter of course, still continued (2 Kings xv. 35); and with it were joined a number of base and degrading foreign superstitions. The opening chapters of Isaiah depict the Judæa of Jotham's time. "The whole head was sick, and the whole heart faint" (Isa. i. 5). The rulers were no better than "the rulers of Sodom"; the people were like the "people of Gomorrah" (ibid. ver. 9). A "form of godliness, without the power," prevailed. Sacrifices were offered; incense was burnt; new moons and sabbaths were carefully observed; the appointed feasts were kept; assemblies were called; solemn meetings were held; hands were spread forth; "many prayers" were even put up (ibid. vers. 11–15). But all this was a mere show of religion, worthless—nay, abominable—in the sight of God. The hands held up in prayer were "full of blood" (ibid. ver. 15). The "princes were rebellious and companions of thieves" (ibid. ver. 23); the judges gave false judgments, following after reward; the once "faithful city" had "become an harlot; righteousness had formerly dwelt in it; but now murderers" (ibid. ver. 21). In manners there was that extreme corruption, which prosperity

[1] Ewald, "History of Israel," vol. iv. p. 166, Eng. tr.
[2] See above, p. 165.

so often breeds. "Men rose up early in the morning, that they might follow strong drink, and continued until night, till the wine inflamed them. The harp and the viol, the tabret and pipe, and wine were in their feasts" (chap. v. 11, 12); they boasted of being "mighty to drink wine, and men of strength to mingle strong drink" (ibid. ver. 22). The women were as bad as the men, or worse. "The daughters of Zion were haughty, and walked with stretched forth necks and wanton eyes, walking and mincing as they went, and making a tinkling with their feet" (chap. iii. 18). The love of dress and of the toilet had become a mania. No woman was happy unless she could vie with her neighbours in "the bravery of tinkling ornaments for her feet, in cauls, and round tires like the moon, and chains, and bracelets, and mufflers, and bonnets, and orna- ments for the legs, and headbands, and tablets, and earrings, and rings, and nose jewels, in changeable suits of apparel, and mantels, and wimples, and crisping pins, and glasses, and fine linen, and hoods, and vails" (ibid. vers. 18–23). Besides all this extreme luxury and worldliness, there were some who gave themselves up to unlawful arts, as soothsaying and magic (chap. ii. 6), while others indulged in idolatry (ibid. ver. 10), and in those licentious rites which were connected with the worship maintained in groves and gardens (ibid. chap. i. 29).

Jotham died at the age of thirty-one, in Jerusalem, apparently a natural death, and was buried with his fathers in the city of David (2 Kings xv. 38 ; 2 Chron. xxvii. 29).

CHAPTER XXVII.

AHAZ.

Accession of Ahaz—His character—Difficult circumstances under which he came to the throne—His war with Pekah and Rezin—Attacks made on him by Edom and Philistia—He invokes the aid of Assyria, and becomes an Assyrian feudatory — Visits Tiglath-Pileser's court at Damascus—His numerous idolatries, and desecration of the Temple and its vessels—His persistency in wickedness, and his early death.

AHAZ, who succeeded his father, Jotham, upon the throne of Judah at the age of twenty (2 Kings xvi. 2 ; 2 Chron. xxviii. 1), has left behind him the reputation of being among the worst, if not actually the very worst, of all the princes of the house of David. He had neither courage, nor patriotism, nor energy, nor prudence, nor piety, nor even a decent regard for the traditions of his house and nation. No doubt he succeeded to the throne under difficult circumstances. He found the nation far advanced in corruption[1]—the nobles, and even the members of his own family, attached generally to the heathenizing party[2]—his kingdom menaced by a combination of two powerful states, which threatened its destruction, or at least his own deposition (Isa. vii. 6)—and his only hope of efficient support the interposition and protection of some powerful heathen sovereign. It was hard for him to hit upon a course which should be at once safe and patriotic, at once honourable and conducive to his own advantage. And he had scant time for consideration. His two deadly enemies, Pekah and Rezin, who had commenced the war in the lifetime of his father (2 Kings xv. 37), were

[1] See above, pp. 167, 168.
[2] See Ewald's "History of Israel," vol. iv. p. 168, who quotes Isaiah vii. 13, and Micah vi. 16.

encouraged and inspirited by the accession of a mere youth, and thought by a rapid attack to carry everything before them. Having combined their forces, they came up together against Jerusalem, and laid siege to it (2 Kings xvi. 5 ; Isa. vii. 1). A horrible fear fell upon both king and people—"The heart of Ahaz was moved, and the heart of his people, as the trees of the wood are moved with the wind" (Isa. vii. 2). Nevertheless, encouraged by Isaiah, who scoffed at his assailants and bid him feel no dread of such mere "tails of smoking firebrands" (ibid. ver. 4), Ahaz resisted, and after a while forced his antagonists to raise the siege, and attempt the subjugation of Judæa by a different method. Rezin drew off his troops, and proceeding southwards, fell upon the southern Judæan territory, overran the whole of it, and pushed his conquests to the shore of the Red Sea, where he "drave the Jews from Elath" (2 Kings xvi. 6), and restored to the Idumæans[1] the the city and adjacent territory. Pekah also gave up the siege, and set to work to ravage the territory, where he slew, we are told (2 Chron. xxviii. 6), a hundred and twenty thousand men,[2] and took two hundred thousand women and children prisoners (ibid. vers. 7, 8). In this deep affliction of the Jewish nation her old foes, moreover, rose up against her. The Edomites on the south-east, and the Philistines on the south-west, poured in their troops upon the devoted land, and added to its calamities. Edom was content, apparently, with a single desolating raid, in which numerous captives were carried off (ibid. ver. 17) ; but the Philistines were bolder in their aggression, and more bitter in their hostility. They "invaded the cities of the low country, and of the south of Judah, and took Beth-shemesh, and Ajalon, and Gederoth, and Shocho with the villages thereof, and Timnah with the villages thereof, Gimzo also and the villages thereof; *and they dwelt there*" (ibid. ver. 18). Instead of ravaging, that is, they took permanent possession of the territory which they had overrun, occupying it, and adding it to their dominion. Judah was indeed "brought low, and made naked' (2 Chron. xxviii. 18). Her "country was desolate, her

---

[1] For "Syria" and "Syrians" in 2 Kings xvi. 6, it seems right that we should read "Edom" and "Edomites." The change is very slight in the Hebrew.

[2] The text adds "in one day," which is no doubt possible, but scarcely probable. Perhaps we should read 12,000 or 20,000 for 120,000.

cities burned with fire : her land, strangers devoured it in her presence ; it was desolate, as overthrown by strangers " (Isa. i. 7). The territory that remained to her was truly but " a very small remnant " (ibid. ver. 9), and even this was threatened. Pekah and Rezin might be expected at any moment to resume their attacks. It is not surprising that, under these circumstances, Ahaz thought himself entitled to call in foreign aid, and judged that the power from which he was most likely to obtain effectual aid was Assyria.

Effectual foreign protection was at no time to be looked for by Judæa, excepting from one of two quarters. She must either " call to Egypt," or " go to Assyria " (Hos. vii. 11). At this particular juncture, Egyptian aid was out of the question. Egypt, after a long period of depression under feeble native sovereigns, was now in the throes of a conflict, which ended in her falling under a foreign sway, and becoming a dependency of Ethiopia.[1] She was split up, divided against herself, and in no condition to spare any of her troops for a hazardous campaign in Asia. With Assyria the case was wholly different. She had reached well-nigh the zenith of her power. She was under the strong rule of a single energetic and warlike prince.[2] No enemy of any importance threatened her. She had a large disciplined army ready for any service ; and just at this time it was her special desire to extend her influence towards the south-west, and round off her dominion in that quarter, by absorbing into it the Palestinian region. Ahaz, therefore, having determined on calling in foreign aid, could not hesitate as to the power whereto he should make appeal ; but, having collected all the treasure on which he could lay his hand, sent a humble embassy, with the rich gift, to the court of Tiglath-Pileser (2 Kings xvi. 7 ; 2 Chron. xxviii. 16).

We have seen already Tiglath-Pileser's response to this appeal.[3] His sudden march against Damascus, his devastation of its territory, his siege and capture of the city, his cruelties to its chief men, his deportation of its inhabitants to Kir, have been related. Rezin lost his life in the encounter, and Damascus its separate existence. Then the conqueror advanced against Samaria, and finding a party friendly to him

[1] See the author's " History of Ancient Egypt," vol. ii. pp. 433-450.
[2] The mention of "Kings of Assyria " in 2 Chron. xxviii. 16, if a correct reading, is probably a mere vague plural. [3] See above, p. 163.

within the walls, who undertook to remove Pekah, negotiated with them, and appointed their chief, Hoshea, to be tributary king. Ahaz was thus effectually relieved from the enemies whose attack he had feared ; but to obtain this relief he had been forced to sacrifice the independence of his country. As Ewald says—" The price paid for the Assyrian aid was much more than the treasures of the temple and of his palace (2 Kings xvi. 8) ; it was the independence and honour of the realm itself."[1]   Ahaz became, by his compact with Tiglath-Pileser, a mere subject—almost a mere nominal—king ; his position was no better than that of Hoshea.

Subjection to Assyria involved not only the continual payment of tribute year by year (see chap. xvii. 4), and the occasional sending to the monarch of rich presents besides, but appearance before him, to do him homage, whenever he was in the neighbourhood.   Ahaz, we are told, humbly paid his court to Tiglath-Pileser at Damascus, before that monarch returned to Nineveh (ibid. chap. xvi. 10).   This is probably the occasion, of which Tiglath-Pileser has left an account, when he says that tribute was brought him by twenty-two kings, among whom we find those of Ammon, Moab, Edom, Askelon, Gaza, and also " Jehoahaz of Judah."[2]   Ahaz had either, like Jehoiakim (2 Kings xxiii. 34) and Zedekiah (ibid. xxiv. 17), taken a new name on becoming an Assyrian feudatory, or else, his true name having always been Jehoahaz, he had been called Ahaz by his subjects, to mark their disapproval of his idolatrous practices.[3]

In such practices he seems to have gone beyond almost any other Jewish king. He " walked in the way of the kings of Israel, according to the abominations of the heathen," even offering one of his own sons to Moloch (2 Kings xvi. 3).   He " sacrificed and burnt incense in the high places, and upon the hills, and under every green tree" (ibid. ver. 4).   He was himself the centre of all the superstitious practices which prevailed in his reign.   " Not only did he employ to the utmost all the existing sanctuaries, but he introduced new ones in every direction.

[1] Ewald, "History of Israel," vol. iv. p. 171, Eng. tr.

[2] "Eponym Canon," p. 124, lines 57–62.

[3] Compare the changes of Jeconiah into Coniah (Jer. xxii. 24), of Beth-el into Beth-aven (Hos. x. 5), and of Esh-baal (1 Chron. viii. 33) into Ish-bosheth (2 Sam. ii. 8).

The worship of Moloch, the savage god of Ammon, was now established, not only on the heights of Olivet, but in the valley of Hinnom, on a spot known by the name of Tophet, close under the walls of Jerusalem. There the brazen statue of the god was erected, with the furnace within or at his feet, into which the children were thrown. . . . Superstitions appeared in every part of the country. Gold and silver statues glittered throughout Judæa. Soothsayers came from the East; wizards, familiar spirits, ghosts, were consulted, even by the most outwardly religious (Isa. ii. 6, 8, 20; viii. 19). Altars were planted in the corners of the streets. . . . Oriental influences penetrated to the Temple itself, and even materially affected the structure and appearance of the building. On its roof were erected little altars, apparently for the worship of the heavenly bodies of the Zodiac (2 Kings xxiii. 5, 12). At the entrance of its court were kept chariots dedicated to the Sun, with their sacred white horses, as in Persia, ready to be harnessed on great occasions" (ibid. ver. 11). [1] Even the interior of the Temple was invaded. When Ahaz visited Tiglath-Pileser at Damascus, he saw an altar there of a pattern unknown to the Jews, which he determined to make the model of a new altar, to take the place of the old altar of Solomon, in the Great Court of the Temple, directly before the porch. The erection was probably Assyrian, rather than Syrian; and it may be suspected that it was either in compliment to his suzerain, or at his express command, that the new arrangement was resolved upon. Assyrian kings in their expeditions carried altars with them, and in the countries which they conquered generally " set up the laws of Asshur, and altars to the Great Gods." [2] What is most remarkable in the action of Ahaz is his introduction of his new altar into the Temple of Jehovah, and his substitution of it for the altar of Solomon. For this purpose it was requisite that the old altar should be removed, taken away from the conspicuous place which it had hitherto occupied, and relegated to a comparatively obscure position. It is surprising that the high priest, Urijah, the friend of Isaiah (Isa. viii. 2), lent himself to this desecration (2 Kings xvi. 11–16). But worse was to follow. The sacred furniture of the Temple, and its vessels, were despoiled and mutilated. Ahaz " cut off the borders of the bases "

[1] Stanley, "Lectures on the Jewish Church," vol. ii. p. 393.
[2] "Ancient Monarchies," vol. ii. p. 531.

from the ten brazen lavers that Hiram had made for Solomon, and took down the " molten sea," or great laver of all, from off the brazen oxen, twelve in number, that had been made to support it, depositing the "sea" itself upon "a pavement of stone" (ibid. vers. 17).   Moreover, he removed the brazen canopy from the royal seat within the court of the Temple, and the passage by which the king ordinarily entered the sacred edifice, to eke out his presents to his royal master (ibid. ver. 18). Finally, towards the close of his reign, he shut up the great doors of the Temple (2 Chron. xxviii. 24), caused the lamps to be no longer lighted (ibid. xxix. 7), discontinued the offering of incense and the morning and evening sacrifice (ibid.), and left the whole interior to decay, neglect, and untidiness (ibid. xxix. 5, 16).

Thus was true religion almost wholly extinguished under this wicked king.   In vain did Isaiah warn him, rebuke him, offer him signs, threaten him, urge him to rely on Jehovah ;[1] he doggedly pursued his own course, sought help in every quarter but the right one, put his trust in arms of flesh, or in the gods of the nations—Assyrian, Syrian (2 Chron. xxviii. 23), Phœnician (ibid. ver. 2), Ammonite (2 Kings xvi. 3)—cared not how he degraded his country or disgraced his noble lineage, persisted in evil, ever trespassed more and more (2 Chron. xxviii. 22), till, at the age of thirty-six (2 Kings xvi. 2), when he was in the very prime of life, God cut him off, called him to his account, and so stopped the further degradation of His people. Ahaz seems to have died in the same year with His patron, Tiglath-Pileser, B.C. 727.   He was buried, like his fathers, in the city of David (ibid. ver. 20) ; but, according to the writer of Chronicles (2 Chron. xxviii. 27), " not in the sepulchres of the kings."

[1] See Isa. vii. 4-17 ; viii. 1-4 ; &c.

CHAPTER XXVIII.

HOSHEA.

WITH Hoshea's reign the closing scene of the southern kingdom opens upon us. He is not greatly responsible for his
country's ruin, since the predisposing causes had long been at
work, and nothing less than extraordinary ability, joined with
extraordinary good fortune, could have warded off the evil day
for any considerable period. Hoshea himself occupied the
ambiguous position of subject-monarch, half dependent, half
independent. He had no natural claim to the crown, but,
like so many of the later kings, was a mere usurper. Difficulties would be sure to beset him on all sides, and only very
consummate skill and prudence could have steered him safely
through them. He was less positively irreligious than his predecessors (2 Kings xvii. 2), but still is stated to have " done
evil in the sight of the Lord," by which we may gather that he,
at any rate, maintained the calf-worship, if he did not also
encourage foreign idolatries. But he was so far a patriotic
Israelite that his subjugation galled him, and from a very early
date in his reign he began to cast about for a means of escaping
from it. Tiglath-Pileser, the great conqueror, who had resus-
citated the Assyrian power so wonderfully in the space of

seventeen years,[1] died very soon after he had established
Hoshea upon the Samaritan throne; and on his death, as so
usually happened in Assyria, his empire was shaken to its
centre. Revolts broke out on all sides; Phœnicia especially
declared itself independent,[2] and Hoshea thought the time was
come when he might safely follow the example thus set. But
he considered it necessary to secure a protector in the first
instance. Egypt had now passed through the phase of disorganization and weakness above noticed,[3] and had become
once more united under a single head. The Ethiopians had
prevailed, and a powerful monarch of Cushite blood—by
name, Sabaco [4]—sat upon the throne of the Pharaohs, and
ruled over the entire Nile valley from Napata and Meroe to the
Mediterranean. With this prince Hoshea entered into negotiations (2 Kings xvii. 4; comp. Hos. vi. 11, xii. 1), which were
so far successful, that he was encouraged by them to declare
himself openly; and, about the year B.C. 725, he withheld the
tribute, which he had hitherto paid to Shalmaneser as his
suzerain (2 Kings xvii. 3, 4), and assumed an attitude of independence. Shalmaneser was engaged at this time in his war
with Phœnicia,[5] and especially in an attempt to reduce the
Island Tyre, which had for some years defied his arms; but
the challenge thrown down to him by the petty Israelite king,
which might easily tempt other subject-monarchs to follow the
same course, together with the danger of a new enemy appear-
ing upon the scene, seemed to require his immediate and principal attention. Accordingly, in B.C. 724, he descended in force
upon the country, succeeded, probably by treachery,[6] in seizing
Hoshea's person (2 Kings xvii. 4; Hos. x. 7), and then poured
his troops in upon the unhappy kingdom, left without a head,
and in a short time overcame all the resistance that the Israelites could offer in the field. A bloody scene was enacted
" in the deep glen of Beth-Arbel,"[7] where a part of the population had taken refuge in the caves and precipitous cliffs, mothers
and children being ruthlessly dashed from the top of the rocks

[1] "Eponym Canon," pp. 64, 65. Tiglath-Pileser ascended the th-one
in B.C. 745, and was succeeded by Shalmaneser in B.C. 727.
[2] "Ancient Monarchies," vol. ii. p. 137.   [3] Supra, p. 171.
[4] Herod. ii. 137; Manetho, Fr. 64, 65; Diod. Sic. i. 65, § 2.
[5] Joseph. "Ant. Jud." ix. 14, § 2.
[6] See Ewald, "History of Israel," vol. iv. p. 164, Eng. tr.
[7] Stanley, "Lectures on the Jewish Church," vol. ii. p. 316.

down to the valley beneath (Hos. x. 14); other strongholds and fortresses were also taken and spoiled (ibid.); a single battle was perhaps fought in the plain of Esdraelon—the great battle-field of Palestine—where "the bow of Israel" was utterly and finally "broken" (ibid. i. 5); and then the victorious monarch, mounting from the low plain into the Samaritan upland, with-out meeting further resistance, massed his troops around the capital. Within walls the Hebrew race has often shown itself capable of a prolonged and desperate defence. Samaria now withstood the whole might of Assyria for well-nigh three years. She was besieged probably in the early spring of B.C. 724; she was not taken until near the end of B.C. 722 (2 Kings xviii. 9, 10). Her population must by that time have been utterly worn out through fatigue and privations. Perhaps they were sus-tained by a hope that their newly acquired ally, the great Shabak, would for very shame, if they made a gallant fight, come to their aid. But the "bruised reed" was never to be depended on. Shabak, so far as appears, made no movement, rendered no help at all to the unfortunates whose rebellion he had encouraged. They were left wholly to themselves, while the siege was continually more and more closely pressed. Then famine and pestilence did their work. At length despair set in, and while some bemoaned their fate (Hos. xiii. 9–14), others betook themselves to wild orgies and frantic revellings (Isa. xxviii. 1–4). Finally, the besiegers prevailed; the city was stormed and taken. There was the usual massacre, in which neither age nor sex were spared (Hos. xiii. 16); but twenty-seven thousand two hundred of the inhabitants were made prisoners and carried into captivity by the conqueror.[1] Samaria was not destroyed; much less razed to the ground.[2] She con-tinued to be an important provincial city; and is sometimes found taking part in a rebellion,[3] but generally remains tranquil under Assyrian governors.[4] The kingdom of Jeroboam, how-ever, was brought to an end, after an existence of about two centuries and a half.

The fate of Hoshea is unknown to us. Shalmaneser probably had him imprisoned at Nineveh; but whether he languished long in close confinement, like the unhappy Jehoiachin (2 Kings

[1] "Eponym Canon," p. 125, l. 24.
[2] As Dean Stanley seems to have supposed ("Lectures," vol. ii. p. 316).
[3] "Eponym Canon," p. 125, l. 38; p. 127, l. 20.   [4] Ibid. p. 70.

xxv. 27), or whether, like so many rebel monarchs, he was ulti-mately executed by his offended suzerain, is uncertain.   With his imprisonment he vanishes from our sight, "like the foam upon the face of the earth" (Hos. x. 7).   His reign lasted less than nine years.

CHAPTER XXIX.

HEZEKIAH.

Pre-eminence of Hezekiah among the kings of Judah—His subject position under Assyria—His reformation of religion at Jerusalem—His Passover attended both by Jews and Israelites—His destruction of the High Places—His iconoclastic raid into the kingdom of Samaria—His great temporal prosperity—War with Philistia—Relations with Sargon— Relations with Sennacherib—First invasion of Sennacherib and submission of Hezekiah—Alliance made with Egypt—Second invasion of Sennacherib—Embassy of Rabshakeh—Sennacherib's threatening letter—Miraculous destruction of Sennacherib's host—Private life of Hezekiah—His lack of children—His dangerous illness and recovery— Embassy of Merodach-Baladan—Hezekiah rebuked by Isaiah—His soft reply—A son born to him—His final greatness and prosperity— His death.

OF all the monarchs who ruled over the kingdom of Judah after its separation from Israel, Hezekiah is the most remarkable, and the interest which attaches to the history of the separate kingdom culminates in him. He was a statesman, a warrior, a poet, an antiquarian, an engineer, and the leader of a most important religious movement. Judæa in his day seemed to be at the point of dissolution ; it was to him that she owed a recovery, which gave her a fresh lease of life, and enabled her to outlive her sister kingdom by nearly a century and a half.

Hezekiah's political position when he ascended the throne was that of a tributary to Assyria. His father's voluntary compact with Tiglath-Pileser (2 Kings xvi. 7) involved his own subjection ; and nothing could set him free from this obligation, or restore his country to independence, but an open and avowed revolt. To this height of audacity he does not seem to have lifted himself at once. It rather appears that he paid his tribute, as it became due, regularly, both to Shalmaneser and to Sargon, deferring his open rebellion, which he had probably contem-plated from the first, to the time of Sennacherib, Sargon's son and successor.

Meanwhile, all the energies of his powerful and active mind

were devoted to the internal condition of his country, and especially to the removal of those impious innovations which his father, Ahaz, had introduced into the arrangements of the Temple, and into the religious ceremonial generally, to the rooting out of idolatry, and to the re-establishment of the religion of Jehovah in its pristine purity and splendour. It was in the very first year of his reign (2 Chron. xxix. 3), within a few months of his accession, that he commenced his reformation of religion by re-opening the Temple doors, and repairing them, after which he proceeded to clean and purify the sacred edifice, and make it fit for the worship of Jehovah, by clearing it from all that accumulation of dust, and dirt, and rubbish, which had been caused by the neglect and contempt of Ahaz during the later years of his life (ibid. vers. 5, 16, 18). The new-fangled altar of Ahaz, made after a pattern seen in Damascus (2 Kings xvi. 10), was no doubt removed, and probably broken up, while the old altar of Solomon was restored to its place in front of the porch ; the "molten sea" was probably replaced upon the twelve bronze oxen, and the other lavers repaired or restored. The lamps were re-lighted, the shew-bread tables placed in order, the sacred vessels recovered or replaced by new ones, and the entire building, and its appurtenances, brought into a condition of order, cleanliness, and decency. It took sixteen days to accomplish this necessary work (2 Chron. xxix. 17), and it was not till the close of the sixteenth day that the priests and Levites employed in the task were able to "go in" to Hezekiah, and say to him, "We have cleansed all the house of the Lord, and the altar of burnt offering, with all the vessels thereof, and the shew-bread table, with all the vessels thereof : moreover all the vessels, which king Ahaz in his reign did cast away in his transgression, have we prepared and sanctified, and, behold, they are before the altar of the Lord" (ibid. vers. 18, 19).

The purification of the Temple was followed by the inauguration of the restored worship, which was effected by means of a solemn sacrifice upon a large scale. The king, the princes, and "all the congregation" (ver. 28), went up, probably in a long procession, to the house of the Lord, where the priests and Levites were already gathered together, prepared to take their several parts in the offering. Hezekiah brought with him, as "a sin offering for the kingdom, and for the sanctuary, and for Judah," seven bullocks, seven rams, seven lambs, and seven he-goats ; and the priests, at his command (ver. 21), sacrificed them. The Levites were set in their places, with cymbals, and with psalteries, and with harps, and a body of priests stood near, carrying trumpets (vers. 25, 26). " When the burnt offering began, the song of the Lord began also with the trumpets, and with the instruments of David. . . . And all the congregation worshipped, and the singers sang, and the trumpeters sounded : and all this continued until the burnt offering was finished " (vers. 27, 28). After this a further song of praise was sung (ver. 30), and the congregation were given leave to bring in their offerings, which amounted to seventy bullocks, six hundred oxen, a hundred rams, two hundred lambs, and three thousand sheep (vers. 32, 33). The priests appear to have looked a little coldly on the reforming zeal of the good king, which is not surprising, since Urijah the high priest had taken part in the impieties of Ahaz (2 Kings xvi. 10–16), and had probably carried many of the ordinary priests with him ; but the Levites lent themselves heartily to the work (2 Chron. xxix. 34), and the people generally seem to have sided with the king, notwithstanding the " suddenness " of his proceedings. " God," we are told, " had prepared them " (ibid. ver. 36). The earnest preaching and pleading of Isaiah, and the other prophets of the day, had had, we may presume, a wholesome effect upon the hearts of numbers, causing them to repent of their weak dalliance with the idolatries and other superstitions of Ahaz, and disposing them to welcome a reformation. Hezekiah seems certainly to have carried the popular favour with him, even when he proceeded to more stringent measures of repression than those which he employed at first, and in these early endeavours he had the cordial support both of the people and the princes.

Hezekiah's re-establishment of the ordinary Temple worship seemed to him incomplete unless he could replace the great festivals in their primitive position, and once more gather to them, not the Two Tribes only, but the Ten. The condition of the kingdom of Samaria appeared to him to be favourable to such an enterprise. Hoshea, already threatened by Shalmaneser, had but a weak hold upon the country, whereof he was the nominal sovereign. All the bonds which unite a healthy state together were relaxed ; the extremities were no longer content to yield an unquestioning obedience to the orders issued from the head ; they were inclined to think for themselves, and had

perhaps been shaken in their allegiance to the established system
of religion by the bold and passionate invectives which their
own native prophets had recently launched against it (Hos. iv.
15-19; viii. 5-8; x. 1-15, &c.). Hezekiah determined to "send
letters unto *all Israel*" (2 Chron. xxx. 1)—not to Judah only,
but to "Ephraim and Manasseh" (ibid.) and to "Zebulun and
Asher" (ibid. ver. 11)—*i.e.*, to the furthest extremities of the
Israelite kingdom—and to invite "all Israel, from Beersheba
even to Dan" (ver. 5), to "come and keep the passover to the
Lord God of Israel at Jerusalem." The strictly legal time for
the holding of the festival was indeed gone by ; but the Mosaic
Law provided a second Passover—on the fourteenth day of the
second month (Numb. ix. 10, 11)—for such as, from whatever
cause, should be unable to participate in the first. Hezekiah
seized on this provision (2 Chron. xxx. 2), and made proclamation that all Israel should gather themselves together to Jerusalem to "keep the passover in the second month." "So the
posts went with the letters from the king and his princes
throughout all Israel and Judah, according to the commandment of the king" (ibid. ver. 6).

The response made to this appeal was not very hearty, nor
very general ; but still the appeal succeeded to a certain extent.
As Hezekiah's messengers "passed from city to city through
the country of Ephraim and Manasseh even unto Zebulun,"
they were for the most part treated with derision—the people
"laughed them to scorn, and mocked them" (ibid. ver. 10) :
but, nevertheless, there were "divers of Asher and of Manasseh
and of Zebulun" (ver. 11), and likewise of "Ephraim and
Issachar" (ver. 18)—amounting altogether to "a great multitude" (ibid.), who "humbled themselves," and accepted the
royal invitation, and "came to Jerusalem" (ver. 11). In Judah,
all were of "one heart to do the commandment of the king
and of the princes," and there "assembled much people to
keep the feast . . . a very great congregation" (vers. 12, 13).
First of all, however, it was thought necessary to cleanse the
Holy city, as Hezekiah had cleansed the Holy edifice, and to
put away all those scandalous pollutions which Ahaz had
introduced, or encouraged, as altars to strange gods "in every
corner of Jerusalem" (2 Chron. xxviii. 24) and "high places to
burn incense on" (ibid. ver. 25) : so the people "arose, and
took away the altars that were in Jerusalem, and all the altars

for incense took they away," and probably ground them to powder (comp. 2 Kings xxiii. 6), "and cast them into the brook Kidron" (2 Chron. xxx. 14). Then the Passover feast was held. " The children of Israel that were present at Jerusalem kept the feast of unleavened bread with great gladness; and the Levites and the priests praised the Lord day by day, singing with loud instruments unto the Lord. And Hezekiah spake comfortably unto all the Levites that taught the good knowledge of the Lord, and they did eat throughout the feast seven days, offering peace offerings, and making confession unto the Lord God of their fathers. And the whole assembly took counsel to keep other seven days; and they kept other seven days with gladness. For Hezekiah king of Judah did give to the congregation a thousand bullocks and seven thousand sheep; and the princes gave to the congregation a thousand bullocks and ten thousand sheep; and a great number of priests sanctified themselves. And all the congregation of Judah, with the priests and the Levites, and all the congregation that came out of Israel, and the strangers that came out of the land of Israel, and that dwelt in Judah, rejoiced. So there was great joy in Jerusalem; for since the time of Solomon, the son of David, king of Israel, there was not the like in Jerusalem " (ibid. vers. 21-26).

The great Passover was followed by a tumultuary proceeding of a remarkable character. Hezekiah, having stirred the spirit of his people, and, in part, of their northern neighbours, to an unwonted pitch of enthusiasm, determined to take advantage of the occasion for the removal, not merely of recent religious innovations, but of all that tended to cherish an idolatrous spirit among his subjects. "Beside the Temple worship in Jeru-salem, had descended to his times what may be called the rural worship of the 'high places'—at Bethel (2 Kings xxiii. 15), at Beersheba (Amos viii. 14), at Moriah (?), on the mountains of Gilead (Hos. xii. 11), at Ophrah, on the hills of Dan, at Mizpeh and Ramah, on the top of Olivet (2 Kings xxiii. 13), on Mount Carmel (1 Kings xviii. 30), at Gibeon (ibid. iii. 4). They had been sanctioned by the Patriarchs, by Samuel, by David, by Solomon, by Elijah, by Asa and Jehoshaphat, by Joash and the High Priest Jehoiada, by the first four books of the Pentateuch, if not expressly, at least by implication (?). The 'high place, properly so called, though doubtless originally deriving its name from the eminence on which it stood, was a pillar of stone, covered, like Mussulman tombs, or like the sacred house of the Kaaba, with rich carpets, robes, and shawls (Ezek. xvi. 16). An altar stood in front, on which, upon ordinary occasions, oils, honey, flour, and incense were offered, and, on solemn occasions, slain animals, as in the Temple. Round about usually stood a sacred hedge or grove of trees. Such a grove, as we have seen, was allowed to stand even within the Temple precincts. There was a charm in the leafy shade of the oak, the poplar, and the terebinth, peculiarly attractive to the Israelite and Phœnician devotion. With these was joined, within the walls of Jerusalem itself, the time-honoured worship of the Brazen Serpent. It had been brought from Gibeon with the Tabernacle; and before it, from early times, incense was offered up, as it would seem, by the northern as well as by the southern kingdom." [1]   Hezekiah resolved to sweep all these things away. He regarded them as obstacles to true religion, as inconsistent with the strict unity and purity of the Mosaic worship, and as having a tendency to lead men on to the dark polytheism of the neighbouring nations. God might have " winked at them " in former times; but he lived in an age of greater enlightenment. He had Isaiah, "the evangelical prophet," to be his guide and instructor. He therefore determined on making a clean sweep. For once, he would let loose the passions of the crowd, and allow popular fury to accomplish in a few days, or a few weeks, what authority might have striven vainly to effect in a long course of years. [2]   By his permission, " all Israel that was present " at the great Passover " went out to the cities of Judah, and brake the images in pieces, and cut down the groves, and threw down the high places and the altars out of all Judah and Benjamin . . . until they had utterly destroyed them all " (2 Chron. xxxi. 1). At the same time (2 Kings xviii. 4) the sacred Serpent, "the symbol of the Divine Presence " [3]—the type of the Redeemer who was to be lifted up in the latter days (John iii. 14)—sacred to religious hearts for its spiritual significance, dear to the entire nation as a precious historical memorial—was broken in pieces by the king's command, who saw no other way of preventing his

---

[1] Stanley, "Lectures on the Jewish Church," vol. ii. p. 400.
[2] Compare 2 Chron. xiv. 3-5 with xv. 17 and xvii. 6 with xx. 33.
[3] Stanley, "Lectures on the Jewish Church," vol. ii. p. 401.

misguided subjects from offering incense to a "piece of brass." [1]

But Hezekiah's efforts for the suppression of idolatry were not confined within the limits of his own kingdom. The same tumultuary mob, which, with his sanction, had visited the cities of Judah, to destroy the high places, the images, the altars, and the groves, not content with the successes thus achieved, proceeded to invade the sister kingdom also, and passing through the territory of Ephraim and Manasseh, wrought there a similar devastation (2 Chron. xxxi. 1). The reformation was, however, necessarily incomplete. Samaria, where Hoshea held his court, was unassailable, and many other cities may have defied attack; the remoter districts of the north seem also to have escaped: but over much of the Samaritan territory an enthusiastic crowd swept, bent upon iconoclasm, and on all sides the idols were abolished. Hoshea was too weak to resent this invasion of his dominions, and seems to have passively submitted to it. He was reduced to such straits that war with his southern neighbour seemed impossible. All his troops were needed to oppose his great enemy upon the north : and thus the inroad from Judah was unresisted. How it would have been, had Hezekiah claimed the temporal allegiance of Israel, in addition to the spiritual, we do not know ; but at any rate Hoshea did not care to meet with carnal weapons the spiritual assault made upon his people.

A period of great temporal prosperity appears to have followed on Hezekiah's restoration of the religion of Jehovah. "The Lord was with him," says the writer of Kings, "and he prospered whithersoever he went forth" (2 Kings xviii. 7). "Hezekiah," adds the author of Chronicles, "had exceeding much riches and honour : and he made himself treasuries of gold, and for precious stones, and for spices, and for shields, and for all manner of precious vessels ; storehouses also for the increase of corn, and wine, and oil ; and stalls for all manner of beasts, and cotes for flocks. Moreover he provided him cities, and possessions of flocks and herds in abundance ; for God had given him substance very much" (2 Chron. xxxii. 27–29). God's blessing was upon the land, and it brought forth its increase of corn and wine and oil in unusual plenty, and like-

---

[1] This seems to be the meaning of "Nehushtan," which is from נְחֹשֶׁת, "brass," not from נָחָשׁ, "a serpent."

wise its increase of cattle. We see in the very first year a sign of this abundance in the vast gifts which were brought into the Temple as first-fruits and tithes (ibid. chap. xxxi. 5–9)—a "great store" (ver. 10), "heaps upon heaps" (ver. 6). Store-chambers had to be prepared within the Temple precincts for the superabundant offerings (vers. 11, 12) of the faithful, while the king's own lands (comp. 2 Chron. xxxvi. 10) produced so much, that he had to enlarge the number of his own granaries and repositories (ibid. xxxii. 28). Agriculture, encouraged by his personal interest in it, flourished throughout the land ; while commerce also received its due meed of attention. " Gold," and "silver," and "spices"—all of them foreign products— flowed into the treasury (ver. 27). " Ships of Tarshish " brought their merchandise (Isa. ii. 16). By the fourteenth year of Hezekiah's reign, the "house of his precious things" was so full of treasure in gold and silver, in spices, and in precious ointment, that he was tempted thereby into the great sin of his life—the ostentatious display of his vast riches to the ambassadors of a heathen king (2 Kings xx. 12–15).

Meanwhile he also prospered in at least one war which he undertook. "He smote the Philistines, even unto Gaza, and the borders thereof, from the tower of the watchman even unto the fenced city " (2 Kings xviii. 8). Gaza, it must be remembered, was the last town of Philistia towards Egypt, and the Jewish king who "smote the Philistines even unto Gaza," must have subdued, or at any rate overrun, the whole country. Philistia was at this time becoming, owing to its position, a highly important power. Its cities were of great strength, and commanded the line of march between Assyria and Egypt. Assyrian monarchs had long been looking towards Philistia with a covetous eye ; and now that Sargon was king of Assyria, and at war with Sabatok or Sevechus of Egypt, he had a great desire to add Philistia to his empire. About the year B.C. 720, he overthrew Hanun, king of Gaza, in a great battle near Raphia, notwithstanding that he had the help of an Egyptian contingent.[1] Philistia, upon this, became disorganized ; and it was probably before she could recover herself, that Hezekiah made his expedition. The Assyrians would certainly have regarded such a proceeding on his part with jealousy ; and it

[1] "Eponym Canon," p. 126. Hanun was captured, and either put to death, or carried off to Assyria.

may be questioned whether Hezekiah would have ventured upon it, unless he was prepared to cast off the Assyrian yoke and declare himself independent. This he appears to have done about B.C. 711, when Sargon reckons Judah [1] among the nations that were conspiring against him. This time Ashdod was the city which took the lead in resisting Assyrian encroachment, and which bore the brunt of Sargon's attack. Twice it rebelled, and twice was taken and punished, on the last occasion with extreme severity. [2] Whether Hezekiah was engaged personally in this war or not is uncertain. We have no clear evidence that he ever came into direct contact with the forces of Sargon. Sargon does not mention him in his inscriptions; and, on the whole, it seems most probable, that there was no actual conflict between Assyria and Judæa until after the accession of Sennacherib. [3]

The Assyrian annals place the accession of Sennacherib in the seventeenth year after the capture of Samaria by Sargon, [4] which was the twenty-third year of Hezekiah. He was the eldest son of Sargon, and succeeded his father without interregnum or difficulty, in the summer of B.C. 705. Born in the purple, and bred up as Crown Prince, his primary characteristic was an overweening pride and arrogance which shows itself in all his inscriptions. He calls himself "the great king, the powerful king, the king of the Assyrians, of the nations, of the four regions, the diligent ruler, the favourite of the Great Gods, the observer of sworn faith, the guardian of law, the establisher of monuments, the noble hero, the strong warrior, the first of kings, the punisher of unbelievers, the destroyer of wicked men." [5] He was mighty both in war and peace. His warlike glories are attested by Herodotus, by Polyhistor, by Abydenus, by Demetrius, and by his own annals. His peaceful triumphs are witnessed to by the great palace which he erected at Nineveh and the magnificent series of sculptured slabs with which he adorned it, by his canals and aqueducts, his gate-towers and embankments, his Bavian sculpture, and his *stelé*

---

[1] "Eponym Canon," p. 130, ll. 32–35:—"The people of Philistia, Judah, Edom, and Moab . . . were speaking treason."

[2] See "Eponym Canon," pp. 129–131. Compare Isa. xx. 1.

[3] Sargon is said in one place to speak of himself as having conquered Judæa (Cheyne's "Isaiah," vol. i. p. 69), but he has left no account of the expedition.   [4] "Eponym Canon," pp. 66, 67.

[5] 'Ancient Monarchies,' vol. ii. p. 178, note 10.

at the Nahr-el-Kelb. He was a worthy successor of his
father Sargon, and of the second Tiglath-Pileser, active in his
military enterprises, indefatigable, persevering, full of resource.
No more energetic soldier ever found himself at the head of a
huge army eager for battle ; no more vigorous administrator
ever commanded the resources of a vast empire.

Sennacherib, on mounting the throne, found the condition
of affairs in Babylonia more critical, and more requiring his
immediate presence, than those of any other portion of his
dominions. Merodach-Baladan, who had been driven from
Babylon by Sargon, had returned thither as soon as Sargon
was dead, and had succeeded in establishing himself as king
for a second time. Sennacherib was engaged for some years
in recovering Babylonia to the Assyrian Empire,[1] and it was not
till his fourth year, B.C. 701, that he was able to turn his attention to the western provinces, and set himself to the task of
placing matters there on a satisfactory footing. He found that
on all sides intrigues were afoot to organize a powerful combination against Assyrian influence in south-western Asia.
Phœnicia under Elulæus, king of Sidon, Judæa under Hezekiah, Philistia under Zidqa, king of Ascalon, and Egypt under
Tirhakah, who held his court at Meroë, were banded together,
and bent on checking Assyrian progress by all the means in
their power. One mode adopted was to dethrone such princes
as were faithful and stedfast to Assyria in these parts, and to
replace them by the advocates of an opposite policy. In this
way a seeming unanimity was produced ; but in most of the
states there appear to have been divided counsels, two parties,
one for submission, the other for resistance, one leaning on
Egypt, the other anxious to make the best terms possible with
Assyria. Unwisdom and unreadiness, as was natural, showed
themselves. No general union of the confederates took place.
Sennacherib was allowed to fall upon his adversaries separately,
and crush them one by one. In the spring of B.C. 701 he
marched his troops into Syria, and directing his attack upon
Phœnicia first of all, proceeded to take " Great Sidon, the
lesser Sidon, Sarepta, Hosah, Ecdippa, Accho," and other
towns,[2] forcing Elulæus to flee before him, and establishing in
his place another king. Thence he marched southward, along
the coast, to Ascalon, taking Beth-Dagon, Joppa, Bene-berak,

[1] " Ancient Monarchies," vol. ii. pp. 156, 157.   [2] " Eponym Canon," p. 132.

and Azor upon his way, and compelled Ascalon to submit, and receive another monarch instead of Zidqa.[1] Tirhakah had by this time sent an army to assist his confederates. This force Sennacherib fell in with at Eltekon, and completely defeated, or (as he says) "accomplished its overthrow."[2] He next reduced Ekron;[3] and having thus carried all before him, and left Hezekiah without an ally, he, last of all, turned upon Judæa. With an army of, probably, at least two hundred thousand men, he swept over the land, especially on the west and on the south, ravaging the territory, besieging and taking the fortified places, and gathering spoil and captives at every step.   His own account of his invasion is the following :—"Because Hezekiah, king of Judah, would not submit to my yoke, I came up against him, and by force of arms and by the might of my power I took forty-six of his strong-fenced cities ; and of the smaller towns which were scattered about, with the marching of a host and surrounding of a multitude, with attack of ranks, and force of battering-rams, and mining and missiles, I besieged and captured a countless number.   From these places I took and carried off 200,150 persons, old and young, male and female, together with horses and mules, asses and camels, oxen and sheep, a countless multitude.   And Hezekiah himself I shut up in Jerusalem, his capital city, like a bird in a cage, building towers round the city to hem him in, and raising banks of earth against the gates, so as to prevent escape. . . . Then upon this Hezekiah there fell the fear of the power of my arms, and he sent out to me the chiefs and the elders of Jerusalem, with thirty talents of gold, and eight hundred talents of silver, and divers treasures, a rich and immense booty. . . . All these things were brought to me at Nineveh, the city of my dominion, Hezekiah having sent them by way of tribute, and as a token of his submission to my power."[4]

The author of Kings compresses this history into four short verses : "Now, in the fourteenth (?) year of king Hezekiah," he says, "did Sennacherib king of Assyria come up against all the fenced cities of Judah, and took them.   And Hezekiah king of Judah sent to the king of Assyria to Lachish, saying, I have

---

[1] "Eponym Canon," p. 133.   [2] Ibid. l. 55.   [3] Ibid. p. 134.
[4] See "Ancient Monarchies," vol. ii. pp. 161, 162, and compare G. Smith, "Eponym Canon," from whose translation a few phrases have been taken (pp. 134, 135).

offended ; return from me : that which thou puttest upon me
will I bear.   And the king of Assyria appointed unto Hezekiah
king of Judah three hundred talents of silver and thirty talents
of gold.   And Hezekiah gave him all the silver that was found
in the house of the Lord, and in the treasures of the king's
house.   At that time did Hezekiah cut off the gold from the
doors of the temple of the Lord, and from the pillars which
Hezekiah king of Judah had overlaid, and gave it to the king
of Assyria" (2 Kings xviii. 13–16).   We learn, however, from
certain other of the sacred writers something concerning the
feelings with which the approach of the great Assyrian monarch
was popularly regarded, and concerning the precautions which
were taken against him on the part of Hezekiah.   Isaiah describes the state of feeling in Jerusalem, when it found itself
invested.   "What aileth thee now," he says, "that thou art
wholly gone up to the housetops—thou that art full of stirs, a
tumultuous city, a joyous city ?   Thy slain men are not slain
with the sword, nor dead in battle   All thy rulers are fled together, they are bound by the archers : all that are found in
thee are bound together, which have fled from far.   Therefore
said I, I will weep bitterly ; labour not to comfort me, because
of the spoiling of the daughter of my people.   For it is a day of
trouble, and of treading down, and of perplexity by the Lord
God of hosts, in the valley of vision, breaking down the walls,
and crying to the mountains.   And Elam bare the quiver with
chariots of men and horsemen, and Kir uncovered the shield.
And it shall come to pass that thy choicest valleys shall be full
of chariots, and the horsemen shall set themselves in array at
the gate. . . .   And in that day did the Lord God of hosts call to
weeping, and to mourning, and to baldness, and to girding with
sackcloth : and behold joy and gladness, slaying oxen and killing
sheep, eating flesh, and drinking wine—Let us eat and drink, for
to-morrow we shall die ! " (Isa. xxii. 1–13).   As the host of the
enemy gathers round about the place, there is a general rush
of the inhabitants to their housetops, to see the strange sight.
Some of the rulers endeavour to escape, but are seized and
bound by the archers.   Others doubt what to do, for it is "a
day of trouble and perplexity."   The valleys are seen to be full
of chariots, and the horsemen set themselves in array at the
gate.   Elam bears the quiver, and Kir uncovers the shield.
Some cry to the mountains, and fill the city with tumult.   Others,

reckless in their despair, like sailors in a shipwreck, fall to feast·
ing, and set up a ghastly show of merriment, kill sheep and
oxen, broach their wine-casks, and shout one to another—" Let
us eat and drink, for to-morrow we die." The king, however,
has taken such precautions as were possible. He has repaired
the breaches of the city of David (ibid. vers. 9, 10), and looked
to the armour of the house of the forest (ibid. ver. 8). He has
"stopped the waters of the fountains, and the brook that ran
through the midst of the land, saying, Why should the kings of
Assyria come and find much water?" (2 Chron. xxxii. 3, 4).
He has "strengthened himself, and built up all the wall that
was broken, and raised it up to the towers, and another wall
without, and repaired Millo in the city of David, and made
darts and shields in abundance, and set captains of war over
the people, and gathered them together to him in the street of
the gate of the city, and spoken comfortably to them, saying,
Be strong and courageous, be not afraid nor dismayed for the
king of Assyria, nor for all the multitude that is with him : for
there be more with us than with him : with him is an arm of
flesh ; but with us is the Lord our God to help us, and to fight
our battles" (ibid. vers. 5–8). And his words had the effect of
calming the people, and inducing them patiently to endure the
siege, for how long we know not.

But at length a time came when it was impossible to endure
any longer. Sennacherib, leaving Jerusalem blockaded, had
removed to Lachish,[1] perhaps with the object of meeting and
crushing any Egyptian force that should attempt to raise the
siege ;[2] when Hezekiah found himself compelled to ask for
terms. He sent an embassy to the Assyrian king at Lachish
with the words—" I have offended ; remove from me ; that
which thou puttest upon me I will bear" (2 Kings xviii. 14).
The reply which he received was favourable. Sennacherib
consented to spare the city on the payment of a sum of thirty
talents of gold and three hundred talents of silver, which
Hezekiah with difficulty collected by emptying both his own
and the Temple treasury, and at the same time stripping off
the plates of gold with which some of the Temple doors were
overlaid (ibid. vers. 15, 16). According to the Assyrian monu-

---

[1] 2 Kings xviii. 14.

[2] The Egyptians would necessarily approach the city by way of the low
Philistine plain, where Lachish lay.

ments,[1] the Jewish monarch was not content with the bare payment of the indemnity required, but sent in addition a number of precious articles — carbuncles and other gems, couches and thrones of ivory, the horns and skins of buffaloes, warlike weapons, male and female musicians, several of the palace eunuchs, and even some of his own daughters, as secondary wives of the Great King. Sennacherib returned to Nineveh with his spoil, and with his captives, having, as he thought, wholly crushed the dangerous rebellion which had threatened the Assyrian power in south-western Asia.

But Hezekiah had no intention of sinking permanently into the position of an Assyrian feudatory. The garrison of Jerusalem was intact, and he had still hopes of aid from Ethiopia and Egypt. It would seem that scarcely were the soldiers of Sennacherib withdrawn from his country, than he sent in all haste ambassadors laden with presents to the Court of Memphis, and entreated that a strong force of horsemen and chariots might be sent into Palestine without delay, promising that, if they were, he would shortly renew the struggle.[2] Perhaps he was received into alliance ; at any rate hopes of assistance were held out to him (2 Kings xviii. 21, 24) by the great monarch, on whom Egypt now depended, or by his subordinates. Certainly he took heart, and began to think and say, "I have counsel and strength for the war" (ibid. ver. 20). He had not, however, formally revolted,[3] when, intelligence of his proceedings and intentions having reached Nineveh, Sennacherib determined to precipitate matters, and, quitting his capital, marched at the head of all his forces for a second time into Palestine. Regarding Egypt as his really formidable enemy, he took the coast route, and leaving Jerusalem on one side, pressed southward through the Philistine plain, till he was stopped by the resistance of Lachish, which he besieged, but for a long time without success. While thus engaged, he seems to have thought that possibly he might frighten Jerusalem into surrender by a threatening embassy. Accordingly he sent three of his chief officers—the Tartan, or chief general, the Rabsaris, or chief

[1] "Eponym Canon," p. 135, ll. 30-35.

[2] See Isaiah xxx. 1-7, which is best regarded as belonging to this period of the history.

[3] This appears, especially, from such a passage as Isaiah xxxiii. 8, where Sennacherib is taxed with "breaking his covenant" with Hezekiah.

eunuch, and the Rabshakeh, or head cupbearer—accompanied by a strong escort, to the Jewish capital, with instructions which they faithfully carried out. The Rabshakeh, who could speak Hebrew, took the word. Standing near the wall, on the north side of the city, he addressed in a loud voice the deputies whom Hezekiah had sent to meet him, and in a scathing speech, wherein pride, and disdain, and irony were skilfully blended, sought to impress those who heard him with a sense of the irresistible might of Assyria, and with the utter hopelessness of their cause. "Hezekiah," he said, "had no ground for his rash confidence. He thought that he 'had counsel and strength for the war.' But what was the counsel, and what was the strength? Was it anything more than Egypt, that 'bruised reed,' which always pierced the hand of those who leant upon it? Hezekiah talked of trust in Jehovah ; but had he not him-self angered Jehovah by tearing down the high places, where He had been worshipped for so many centuries? Jehovah would be against Hezekiah, rather than with him. Indeed, Jehovah had revealed Himself to Sennacherib, and had com-missioned him to 'go up against Judah and destroy it.'" Hezekiah's deputies at this point begged that further speech might be in the Syriac dialect, which they understood, instead of the Hebrew, which could not fail to be comprehended by the soldiers upon the wall. But the reply was only more exaspera-ting. "Sennacherib had not sent his envoys to confer with the king only or with his ministers, but to address the people." And then the people were directly addressed. "Let them not be deceived by Hezekiah, let them not hearken to him—rather let them submit themselves, and send the king of Assyria a present, and then they might rest in peace until the king came, and removed them to a land like their own land, where they might live and prosper. What deliverance could they expect? Where were the gods of Hamath and of Arpad, of Sepharvaim, Hena, and Ivah? What god in all the countries had delivered his country out of Sennacherib's hand, that Jehovah should deliver Jerusalem out of his hand? Let them be sure that that which had been would be again. There would not be one solitary exception to a universal law " (2 Kings xviii. 19-35).

The words of the envoys were received by the people in dead silence, Hezekiah having so commanded (ibid. ver. 36). The three deputies tore their garments in horror, and reported what

14

had happened to the king.   Carried away by their example, he too "rent his clothes and put on sackcloth" (2 Kings xix. 1) in an "uncontrolled outburst of grief."[1]   Sennacherib's envoys, finding that they had effected nothing, returned to their master, and reported that both king and people were obdurate.   Hezekiah, having first sent his officers to inform Isaiah of the crisis that had arrived, and to ask his prayers on behalf of the nation, himself took refuge in the Temple, to pour out his heart before God.   The answer to his prayer was delivered to him, through his officers, from Isaiah.   A score of times had the prophet already intimated in the way of metaphor and imagery the escape of Judah and the downfall of the Assyrian.   At one time the image used had been "the rock of Zion amid the raging flood.   At another, it was the lion of Judah, roaring fiercely for its prey, undismayed by the multitude of rustic shepherds gathered round about to frighten him (Isa. xxxi. 4). At another, it was the everlasting wings of the Divine protection, like those of a parent bird brooding over her young against the great Birdsnester of the world, whose hand was in every nest, gathering every egg that was left, till no pinion should be left to flutter, no beak left to chirp (ibid. x. 14 ; xxxi. 5).   Or again, it was the mighty cedar of Lebanon, with its canopy of feathering branches, which yet should be hewn down with a crash that should make the nation shake at the sound of his fall ; while the tender branch and green shoot should spring up out of the dry and withered stump of the tree of Jesse, which should take root downward, and bear fruit upward"[2] (ibid. x. 33, 34 ; xi. 1 ; xiv. 8).   But now a more explicit declaration was vouchsafed.   "Thus shall ye say to your master—Thus saith Jehovah, Be not afraid of the words which thou hast heard, with which the servants of the king of Assyria have blasphemed me.   Behold, I will send a blast upon him, and he shall hear a rumour, and shall return to his own land ; and I will cause him to fall with the sword in his own land" (2 Kings xix. 6, 7).

There was now a pause.   Sennacherib at Lachish had heard that the great lord of the south, Tirhakah, who had encouraged Hezekiah to revolt, was about to move to his assistance, and, having probably reduced Lachish,[3] had marched against Libnah,

[1] Stanley, "Lectures on the Jewish Church," vol. ii. p. 410.   [2] Ibid.
[3] See Layard, "Nineveh and Babylon," p. 150.

a city at no great distance, the possession of which would, he
thought, strengthen his position. Here his envoys found him
(ibid. ver. 8), and communicated to him the failure of their embassy. Enraged at the intelligence, but deeming it imprudent
to march against Jerusalem at once, while Tirhakah might be
approaching, he contented himself with sending Hezekiah a
letter, repeating the threats of his ambassadors, and suggesting
that Hezekiah's God might be "deceiving" him (ibid. ver. 10).
Hezekiah went into the Temple, and "spread" the insulting
letter before the Lord (ibid. ver. 14). It has been very gratui-
tously supposed that he entered the Holy of Holies, and laid the
letter before the Divine presence in that "dark recess."[1] But
Ewald is probably right in his view, that he merely "spread it
out in prayer before the altar" of burnt offering.[2] The object
was, no doubt, to waken God's anger against the Assyrian
king by exposing, as it were, to His sight the outrage and insult
offered to Him.[3] Once more the answer to his prayer came to
him from the lips of the prophet. "Thus saith the Lord God,"
he was told,—"That which thou hast prayed to me against
Sennacherib, king of Assyria, *I have heard*. This is the word
which the Lord hath spoken concerning him : 'The virgin
daughter of Zion hath despised thee and laughed thee to scorn ;
the daughter of Jerusalem hath shaken her head at thee.
Whom hast thou reproached and blasphemed? and against
whom hast thou exalted thy voice, and lifted up thine eyes on
high? Even against the Holy One of Israel. . . . But I know
thy abode, and thy going out, and thy coming in, and thy rage
against Me. Because thy rage against Me and thy tumult
is come up into Mine ears, therefore I will put My hook in thy
nose, and My bridle in thy lips, and I will turn thee back by the
way by which thou camest.' . . . Therefore, thus saith the
Lord concerning the king of Assyria, He shall not come into
this city, nor shoot an arrow there, nor come before it with
shield, nor cast a bank against it. By the way that he came,
by the same shall he return, and shall not come into this city,
saith the Lord" (2 Kings xix. 20–33). The promise seems to
have been enough for the pious king. He felt that "his

Stanley, *l. s. c.*
"History of the Jewish Church," vol. iv. p. 183, Eng. tr.
[3] Compare the action of Judas Maccabæus (1 Mac. iii. 48).

strength was to sit still " (Isa. xxx. 7).   He waited, and the next day brought him the happy intelligence that he was indeed delivered, and had nothing more to fear.

"In *that* night "—the night after Hezekiah had received Isaiah's message—" the angel of the Lord had gone forth, and smitten in the camp of the Assyrians," before Libnah, " an hundred fourscore and five thousand ; and, when men arose early in the morning, behold, they were all dead corpses." The great Assyrian host that lay encamped so near—not ten miles off, probably—was no more, was annihilated.   Death had come down upon the camp in the darkness without noise or disturb- ance, and had swept by far the greater number [1]—all probably but a few thousands, or a few hundreds—away.   The remnant had fled, together with the king, and were hastening back to Nineveh.[2]   Jerusalem was effectually relieved ; Judæa was saved—saved to outlast the empire which had so long menaced her with destruction.

Moderns have indulged in many vain speculations as to the *manner* of the destruction.   An Ethiopian attack, a sudden violent storm, a pestilence, and the simoom,[3] have been sug- gested.   But the Biblical narrative lends no support to any of these theories.   A far better conception of the scene and its surrounding circumstances is that of the English poet, who has thus depicted them :

" The Assyrian came down like the wolf on the fold,
    And his cohorts were gleaming with purple and gold ;
    Like the leaves of the forest when Summer is green,
    That host, with their banners, at sunset were seen.
    Like the leaves of the forest when Autumn hath blown,
    That host on the morrow lay withered and strown.
    For the Angel of Death spread his wings on the blast,
    And breathed in the face of the foe as he passed :
    And the eyes of the sleepers waxed deadly and chill,
    And their hearts but once heaved, and for ever grew still !
    And there lay the steed with his nostril all wide,
    Though through it there rolled not the breath of his pride.
    And the tents were all silent, the banners alone,
    The lances unlifted, the trumpets unblown.

---

[1] Assyrian armies rarely exceeded 200,000 men.
[2] Joseph. " Ant. Jud." x. 1. § 5,
[3] See the "Speaker's Commentary," vol. iii. p. 113.

And the might of the Gentile, unsmote by the sword,
Hath melted like snow in the glance of the Lord!"[1]

With this event, this perfect and entire relief from the danger
that had for years threatened him, the public life of Hezekiah
may be said to have come to an end. He probably did not
survive by many years the retreat of his great antagonist ; and
he seems not to have been engaged in any further war. His
successful defiance of the power of Assyria added, no doubt,
greatly to his *prestige;* and "many brought gifts unto the Lord
to Jerusalem, and presents to Hezekiah, king of Judah, so that
he was magnified in the sight of all nations from henceforth"
(2 Chron. xxii. 23).

In his private life Hezekiah was visited with more than one
affliction. Though twenty-five years of age at his accession to
the throne (2 Kings xviii. 2), and no doubt married long previously,[2] he had, up to his fourteenth year, no offspring.[3] Childlessness was always felt as a sore trouble by an Israelite, and to
one in Hezekiah's position it would be especially grievous, since
it would lead probably to a disputed succession, and would
involve a forfeiture of the great privilege promised to descendants of David (Acts ii. 30). Still, there was the possibility
that a son might yet be born to him ; but in the fourteenth year
of his reign that hope seemed to disappear, when suddenly
Hezekiah was struck down by a dangerous sickness, which had
every appearance of being a sickness "unto death" (2 Kings
xx. 1 ; Isa. xxxviii. 1). Then his cup of sorrow seemed to be
full. "He turned his face from the light of day to the blank
wall of his chamber." He expostulated with God, pleaded his
righteous deeds, and "broke into a passionate burst of tears."[4]
The Jews of Hezekiah's time had not the assurance of a happy
future life, which is among the blessed privileges of Christians
to-day. If the grave was not the end of all things to them, it
was the entrance into a dim and shadowy life, into a land of
silence, where God was not praised, and none could hope for
His truth (Isa. xxxviii. 18). To Hezekiah death was not only
the loss of this world's joys, but the loss of peace (ibid. ver. 17)
and of the Divine Presence (ibid. ver. 11). No wonder, there-

---

[1] Byron, "Hebrew Melodies" (Works, vol. ii. pp. 31, 32).

[2] The kings of Judah usually married at about the age of eighteen, or
earlier.   [3] Joseph. "Ant. Jud." x. 2, § 1.

[4] Stanley, "Lectures on the Jewish Church," vol. ii. p. 416,

fore, that he grieved, **and** grieved bitterly, when Isaiah, who
stood by his side, uttered the solemn words, " Set thine house
in order, for thou shalt die, and not live " (2 Kings xx. 1).   He
"wept with a great weeping" (ibid. ver. 3).   He lamented his
lot, like Antigone.[1]   He said in the cutting off of his days—" I
shall go to the gates of the grave; I am deprived of the residue
of my years ; I shall not see the Lord in the land of the living ;
I shall behold man no more with the inhabitants of the world.
Mine age is departed, and is removed from me like a shepherd's
tent ; I have cut off like a weaver my life ; He will cut me off
with pining sickness ; from day even to night wilt thou make an
end of me " (Isa. xxxviii. 10–13).   But in the midst of his grief
he prayed.   " O Lord, I am oppressed," he said ; " undertake for
me " (ibid. ver. 14).   The cry reached the Almighty ear, and the
response was instant.   Isaiah had left the royal presence and
was returning home ; but, before he could quit the palace, the
word of the Lord came to him, and the original sentence was
revoked.   " Turn again," said the new voice—" Go and say to
Hezekiah, Thus saith the Lord, the God of David thy father, I
have heard thy prayer ; I have seen thy tears ; behold I will
add unto thy days fifteen years " (ibid. ver. 5).   " On the
third day thou shalt go up unto the house of the Lord " (2
Kings xx. 5).   Hezekiah, relieved but still anxious, asked for
a sign of the coming deliverance ; and the prophet was instructed to announce that this request also was granted, and
even to give the prostrate monarch a choice of signs.   " Shall
the shadow on the dial of Ahaz go forward," he said, " ten
degrees, or go back ten degrees?"   And Hezekiah answered
him, " It is a light thing for the shadow to go down ten
degrees : nay, but let the shadow return backward ten degrees.
And Isaiah cried unto the Lord, and he brought the shadow ten
degrees backward, by which it had gone down in the dial of
Ahaz" (ibid. xx. 9–11).   In some mysterious manner, in some
way that is not revealed to us, the flight of time was (or at any
rate seemed to be) arrested—nay, not only arrested, but rolled
back—the shadow, which had begun to descend the steps on
the " dial of Ahaz," showing that the day was on the decline,
changed its course of procedure, and ascended them, returning
ten degrees, or ten steps, above the point which it had previously reached on its downward way.   The cause of the

[1] Sophocl "Antigone," ll. 798–930.

phenomenon is wrapped in obscurity ; but the fact is delivered
to us by an eyewitness (Isa. xxxviii. 8), and can scarcely be
doubted. It was noised abroad, and attracted attention in
foreign lands, where it was regarded as a "wonder" well
worth inquiring into (2 Chron. xxxii. 31). An attempt has
been made to show that it might have been produced by an
eclipse of a peculiar kind ;[1] but the explanation is not altogether satisfactory. Refraction of the sun's rays is another
possible cause ; but refraction to the extent required would be
very strange and abnormal.

In any case, the sign given him was fulfilled to Hezekiah's
entire satisfaction, and his recovery was rapid and complete.
In three days he was able to make his appearance in the
Temple, and to sing the song of thanksgiving which is recorded
in the Book of Isaiah (chap. xxxviii. 10–20). In a short time he
resumed the active duties of his station, bent upon utilizing to
the utmost the fresh lease of life which had been granted him.
It was probably now that many of those works were undertaken
which kept his memory so long in good odour among the Jewish
people, as the collection of Proverbs of Solomon hitherto not
put upon record (Prov. xxv. 1), and the arrangement of the
water supply of Jerusalem on a new system (2 Chron. xxxii. 30 ;
Isa. xxii. 9, 11). Research is still busy with these remarkable
constructions,[2] the extent of which is only now beginning to be
fairly estimated. Evidently a long term of years was requisite
for the elaboration of so vast a scheme, involving the excavation in the solid rock of numerous shafts, tunnels, and
aqueducts.

It was perhaps in the year following his illness that Hezekiah
received an embassy from a new and unexpected quarter. The
great city and kingdom of Babylon had been hitherto known
to the Jews by reputation only, as the place from which the
Assyrians had "gone out" (Gen. x. 10, 11), and where the
speech of man had been confounded (ibid. xi. 1–9). Of its
long struggle with Assyria[3] they probably knew nothing, and
very little of its power and resources. Now, they were suddenly

[1] See the Essay of Mr. Bosanquet in the "Journal of the Asiatic
Society," vol. xv. pp. 286–293.

[2] See the "Quarterly Statement of the Palestine Exploration Fund" for
January, 1889, pp. 35–52.

[3] G. Smith, "History of Babylonia," pp. 86–89, 94–97, 100–108, 110–
114, &c.

brought into contact with this strange and distant people, which had thought it worth while to send ambassadors to Jerusalem from what must have seemed "the ends of the earth" to Hezekiah. Probably, the embassy was an imposing one. The wealth of Babylon was unbounded, and would enable her to make a display quite equal to any in which Assyria was accustomed to indulge. Shortly, she became known as "the golden city" (Isa. xiv. 4), "the glory of kingdoms" (ibid. xiii. 19), "the beauty of the Chaldees' excellency" (ibid.) Now, we may suppose, having an object, or objects, to gain, she would set herself off to the best advantage. Her envoys would exhibit all the pomp of Oriental magnificence ; they would come with a large train, and bring with them rich presents. " Merodach-Baladan," they would declare, "son of Baladan, king of Sumir and Accad, king of the four countries, king of Babylon, and conqueror of all his enemies,[1] had sent them to greet his brother, Hezekiah, king of Judah, to congratulate him on his recovery from severe illness, and to make inquiry concerning a wonder which was reported as having been done in the land " (2 Kings xx. 12 ; 2 Chron. xxxii. 31). Merodach-Baladan was, in fact, seated on the throne of Babylon at the time. He had revolted from Sargon in the first year of that monarch's reign, had repulsed all Sargon's efforts to reduce him, and still maintained his power and authority unimpaired. He is acknowledged as king by Sargon himself,[2] by Polyhistor,[3] and by Ptolemy.[4] The real motive of his embassy was probably political—a desire to conclude an alliance with a prince who, like himself, was in revolt against Assyria. This desire, though not openly proclaimed, was intimated to the Jewish king, who encouraged it by displaying to the ambassadors all the riches stored up in his treasuries (2 Kings xx. 13). We are not told whether an alliance was actually concluded, and may conjecture that for the time being both parties were contented with the establishment of friendly relations.

But there was one individual in the country who was far from

[1] Compare "Records of the Past," vol. v. pp. 73, 74, 84, &c.
[2] Ibid. vol. viii. pp. 26, 45, 48, &c.   [3] Ap. Euseb. "Chron. Can." i. 5.
[4] See G. Smith, "Eponym Canon," p. 105 ; Clinton, "Fasti Hellenici," vol. i. p. 278 ; Bunsen, "Egypt's Place," vol. i. pp. 726-728. The work of Ptolemy which contains his "Canon" is the "Magna Syntaxis," a work not very easily procurable.

feeling satisfaction or contentment at what had been done. No sooner were the ambassadors departed than Isaiah demanded an audience, and rebuked the king's ostentation and folly. What had he done? He had thought to purchase a friend—he had in reality offered a temptation to an enemy. Babylon, and not Assyria, the prophet was now commissioned to declare, would prove Judah's most dangerous adversary, and ultimately her destroyer. " Hear the word of the Lord," he exclaimed to Hezekiah. " Behold, the days come, that all that is in thine house, and that which thy fathers have laid up in store unto this day, shall be carried unto Babylon : nothing shall be left, saith the Lord. And of thy sons which shall issue from thee, which thou shalt beget, shall they take away; and they shall be eunuchs in the palace of the king of Babylon" (2 Kings xx. 17, 18 ; Isa. xxxix. 5–7). It was a strange and unexpected reve-lation, and Hezekiah cannot but have felt a shock of surprise when it was made to him. But he received it with calmness and submission. " Good," he said, " is the word of the Lord which thou hast spoken" (2 Kings xx. 19); and then, after a pause, he added—"Is it not good, if peace and truth be in my days ? " Can I ask for more, that is, than to be assured that the punishment will not come in my time, but will merely fall, some day or other, on my descendants ? Am I not bound to be thankful that I am spared, and allowed to live out the term of years which has been granted me without having to contend with a new enemy ?

There was another point of view, in which Hezekiah may have thought the announcement made to him satisfactory. Hitherto he had no offspring. Now he was told, that *of the sons which should issue from him, which he should beget*, there would be captives taken, who would be carried to Babylon. The curse of childlessness was therefore to be removed from him; his wife, Hephzi-bah—happily named [1] (Isa. lxii. 4)—was to bear him at least one son ; his seed was to sit upon the throne of David ; and the Messiah might be, as in fact He was (Matt. i. 9, 10), among his posterity. Here was additional compensation for the doom predicted—here was a gleam of light flashing forth from the darkness, a blessing wrapt up in

---

[1] Hephzi-bah means literally "my delight is in her." Loosely, it may be said to mean " the Delightful" (Stanley, " Lectures," vol. ii. p. 420).

the curse pronounced, a blossom put forth from the rod of punishment !

And, within the space of a year or two,[1] the implied promise received fulfilment. Hephzi-bah brought forth her first-born, and it proved a "man child." No doubt the joy of the parents was great, and overshadowed by no prevision of their darling's future apostasy. They called their child Manasseh, implying, that now all their domestic troubles were forgotten (Gen. xli. 51), and perhaps anticipating that the name might prove attractive to the remnant of the Israelites. Whether Manasseh's birth was followed by that of any more children is unknown to us. The character of Hezekiah's later life depends on chronological considerations. Undoubtedly he enjoyed a time of rest and peace for some years before his decease ; but, if the Assyrian dates are followed, the time of rest and peace was but short. His *prestige* must certainly have been great at his death. Besides smiting the Philistines (2 Kings xviii. 8) and for a time exercising authority over half the kingdom of Samaria (2 Chron. xxx. 1, 10, 18 ; xxxi. 1), he had defied the power of Assyria, and maintained his independence, with complete success. We can quite understand that he "was magnified in the sight of all nations" (ibid. xxxii. 23) ; for the discomfiture of Sennacherib's host was an event which must have attracted universal attention, and have struck all the neighbouring nations with astonishment.[2] When he died, at the age of fifty-four, "all Judah and the inhabitants of Jerusalem," we are told, "did him honour" (ibid. ver. 33). As the catacomb of David, the general resting-place of the kings of Judah, was now full, he was buried, either on the ascent to it, or in an excavation at a higher level than the other graves, though within the precincts of the catacomb (2 Chron. xxxii. 33). "His burial forms a marked epoch in the royal interments,"[3] terminating the series that commenced with David. The later princes had to provide themselves with sepulchres entirely unconnected with the ancient burial-place. (See 2 Kings xxi. 18, 26, xxiii. 30 ; 2 Chron. xxxiii. 20.)

[1] Manasseh, being twelve years old at his father's death (2 Kings xxi. 1.), must have been born in his father's seventeenth year. The embassy of Merodach-Baladan belongs probably to his fifteenth year.

[2] Compare the notice of it which Herodotus derived from the Egyptians (Herod. ii. 141).   [3] Stanley, " Lectures," vol. ii. p. 419.

CHAPTER XXX.

MANASSEH.

MANASSEH succeeded his father, Hezekiah, at the age of twelve. He had, no doubt, been carefully brought up during his father's lifetime ; but it would seem that, almost immediately afterwards, he fell under evil influences, which completely carried him away, and caused him to become, not merely a patron of polytheism, but a fanatical hater of the religion of Jehovah. There was always among the Jewish nobles a considerable party which disliked the severity and strictness of the Mosaic code, and leant towards the laxer morals and the gayer ceremonial of the heathen. This party, which had shown its power in Judæa in the later part of the reign of Joash (2 Chron. xxiv. 17–22), and again during the entire reign of Ahaz (2 Kings xvi. 2–18 ; 2 Chron. xxviii. 1–25), probably chafed in secret under the godly rule of Hezekiah, and looked with anxious longing for the time when, under a weaker monarch, they might recover their ascendancy, and inaugurate a fresh period of license and self-indulgent laxity. To them it seemed a fortunate circumstance that the new king was such a mere boy, and they hastened to secure his person, to take the direction of his training, and to imbue him with their own sentiments. Few boys of twelve can resist the efforts of grown men bent on corrupting them, and whatever seeds of true religion had been implanted in the young prince's mind while Hezekiah lived, they were, probably without much difficulty, eradicated, or at any rate stifled and overpowered, by the novel and agreeable teaching of his new instructors. Manasseh, when he assumed the reins of government, at about the age of eighteen,[1] was a rank idolater, an approver and admirer of all the various creeds and practices which prevailed among the surrounding nations, wholly inimical to only one form of worship and one religion—that in which he had been brought up.

First of all, it would seem,[2] "he built up again the high places which Hezekiah his father had destroyed" (2 Kings xxi. 3 ; 2 Chron. xxxiii. 3)—restored, that is, the ancient worship on hill tops and mountain tops, so dear to the people, but so seductive and so dangerous, which Hezekiah had been the first Jewish monarch to absolutely put down (2 Kings xviii. 4), though other good kings had attempted the task before him (2 Chron. xiv. 5 ; xvii. 6). All over the country, worshippers were allowed, instead of bringing their sacrificial beasts to Jerusalem—"the place which God had chosen to put His name there" (Deut. xii. 21)—to offer them upon the rude provincial altars that had come down from remote times, with a ceremonial equally rude, and perhaps not over-edifying. The offering was supposed to be made to Jehovah (2 Chron. xxxiii. 17) ; but one can easily conceive how, in the absence of any priestly supervision, the delicious shades and the still solitudes might tempt to impure doings, and tend to degrade the Jehovistic worship to the level of the neighbouring polytheisms.[3]

Manasseh next "reared up altars for Baal, and made a grove, as did Ahab king of Israel" (1 Kings xxi. 3)—that is to say, he re-introduced into Judah the utterly licentious worship of Baal and Ashtoreth which the weak Ahab had brought into Israel

---

[1] Eighteen seems to have been the age when a Jewish prince was regarded as attaining his majority (2 Chron. xxxiv. 8).

[2] The writers of Kings and Chronicles both assign to him this as his first act.

[3] "Innocent as these vestiges of ancient religion might seem to be," says Dean Stanley, "they were yet, like the Golden Calves in the northern kingdom, and on exactly similar grounds, inconsistent with the unity and purity of the Mosaic worship, and had an equal tendency to blend with the dark polytheism of the neighbouring nations" ("Lectures," vol. ii. pp. 400, 401).

from Phœnicia **to** please the wicked Jezebel (1 Kings xvi.
31–33), and which Judah had only known for two brief spaces
under Athaliah (2 Kings xi. 18) and under Ahaz (2 Chron.
xxviii. 2). He brought the worship of Baal actually into the
Temple (2 Kings xxiii. 4) ; set up the *Asherah*—the emblem of
Astarte—there ; and established close to the Temple those
abominable houses which sheltered such as lent themselves to
the shameful rites wherewith that divinity was supposed to be
honoured (ibid. ver. 7).

Further, he "worshipped all the host of heaven and served
them " (1 Kings xxi. 3). In each of the two Temple courts
altars were raised to the honour of the heavenly bodies (ibid.
ver. 5), and incense, perhaps victims, burnt upon them. Sacred
horses were dedicated to the Sun, together with chariots, and
were kept in the immediate vicinity of the House of God (1
Kings xxiii. 11). This Sabaism, which seems to have been a
new thing in Judah, though practised earlier in the kingdom of
Israel (2 Kings xvii. 16), was a form of superstition, derived
perhaps from Arabia, which became very popular, spreading
from the king to his subjects, who in Jerusalem and elsewhere,
on the flat roofs of their houses, erected private altars of brick,
" from which little clouds of incense were perpetually ascend-
ing "[1] in honour of the Sun, and Moon, and Twelve Signs of
the Zodiac (Jer. xix. 13). The novelty awoke enthusiasm,
These were the gods, whom, in the last period of the Jewish
state, the people specially "loved, whom they served, after
whom they walked, whom they sought, and whom they worshipped " (ibid. viii. 2), in preference to all others.

Manasseh also "caused his sons to pass through the fire in
the valley of Hinnom " (2 Chron. xxxiii. 6)—*i.e.*, offered at least
one, perhaps more, of his children as sacrifices to Moloch,
according to the horrid ritual of the Ammonites and Moabites,
who deemed such offerings the most acceptable that could be
made to the Supreme God. Ahaz had done the like [2] under
his difficult circumstances. Manasseh, seemingly without any
strong pressure of danger, " reopened the furnace of Tophet
on an enlarged scale,"[3] and not only sacrificed a son of his
own (2 Kings xxi. 6), but encouraged the people generally

---

[1] Stanley, "Lectures," vol. ii. p. 421.
[2] 2 Kings xvi. 3 ; 2 Chron. xxviii. 3.
[3] Stanley, "Lectures," *l. s. c.*

to "slay their children in the valleys under the clifts of the rocks" (Isa. lvii. 5), and make the institution of child-murder a regular portion of their religious service. [1]

He also "observed times, and used enchantments, and dealt with familiar spirits and wizards" (2 Kings xxi. 6; compare 2 Chron. xxxiii. 6), or, in other words, "plunged into all the mysteries of sorcery, auguries, and necromancy." [2] Magic occupied an important place in the regards of the upper classes in Assyria, Babylonia, and Egypt. At Babylon the interpretation of omens was reduced to a science.[3] Manasseh, in his extreme syncretism, condescended even to this low form of superstition, "consulted wizards," and claimed to have his own special "familiar spirit" (2 Chron. *l. s. c.*), thus falling back into a shamanism with which no previous king is taxed excepting Saul (1 Sam. xxviii. 7-20), and which in Saul was the culminating offence that brought down upon him God's judgment.

Thus far, the weak and misguided king may have persuaded himself that he was acting as a mild and tolerant monarch, gratifying the inclinations of large classes of his subjects without inflicting injury upon any. But now his conduct took a darker tinge. "Manasseh shed innocent blood very much, till he had filled Jerusalem from one end to another" (2 Kings xxi. 16; comp. chap. xxiv. 4). He set on foot a persecution of the adherents of Jehovah, and raged against them with all the fierceness of an Ahab or an Epiphanes. A veritable "reign of terror" commenced. "*All* the righteous men among the Hebrews," says Josephus,[4] "did he savagely slay." Among the chief sufferers were those of the Prophetical order. "Day by day a fresh batch of them was ordered to execution. It seemed as if a devouring lion were let loose against them (Jer. ii. 30). From end to end of Jerusalem were to be seen the traces of their blood. The nobles who took their part were thrown headlong from the rocky cliffs of the city (Psa. cxli. 6, 7). It was in this general massacre that, according to a Jewish tradition, of which, however, there is no trace either in the Sacred Books or in Josephus, the great Prophet of the time,

[1] See Jeremiah vii. 31, 32; xix. 2-6; xxxii. 35.
[2] Stanley, "Lectures," vol. ii. p. 421.
[3] See "Records of the Past," vol. v. pp. 169-176; vol. xi. pp. 135-138.
[4] Joseph. "Ant. Jud." x. 3, § 1.

Isaiah, now nearly ninety years old, was cruelly slaughtered." [1]
The details in the Talmud are evidently untrustworthy,[2] but
the allusion in the Epistle to the Hebrews (chap. xi. 37) to
martyrdom by "sawing asunder" is so far consonant with the
main fact of the narrative as to lend it a certain credibility.
Manasseh's crowning sin, we may well believe, was his judicial
murder of Isaiah, his father's friend, perhaps his own instructor,
whom he condemned to be sawn asunder for his faithfulness to
the God of Israel.

Meanwhile, so far as foreign enemies were concerned, Judæa
enjoyed an interval of profound peace. Sennacherib, from the
date of the destruction of his host, carefully avoided all contact
with the nation of the Jews ; and thus Manasseh had reigned
for nearly twenty years before any necessity arose for him to
consider whether he should follow the example of his father in
his defiance of the Assyrian power, or, like his grandfather,[3]
should tamely submit to it. We need feel no surprise that he
preferred the latter alternative. Ahaz was his model in the
internal conduct of his kingdom ; why should he not follow
him also in its external management? Therefore, when
Esarhaddon, Sennacherib's son and successor, about the year
B.C. 680, made an expedition into Palestine with the object of
re-establishing Assyrian influence in the south-west, Manasseh
seems to have submitted to him without a murmur, and to
have resumed that position of Assyrian tributary which Hezekiah had succeeded in throwing off. On a broken cylinder of
Esarhaddon's, containing a notice of his second year, we find
"Manasseh, king of Judah," mentioned, together with the
kings of Tyre, Edom, Moab, Gaza, Askelon, Ekron, Gebal,
Arvad, Ammon, Ashdod, and ten Cyprian monarchs, in a connection that implies his subjection to the Empire of Assyria.[4]

Later on, however, the Jewish monarch seems to have
repented of his tame submission, and to have been guilty of
acts which his Assyrian suzerain regarded as rebellious. Perhaps he entered into negotiations with Tirhakah, or Tehrak,

[1] Stanley, "Lectures," vol. ii. p. 422.
[2] Isaiah is made to enter into a strife of words with Manasseh, and then
to take refuge from him in a hollow cedar-tree, which closed upon him for
his protection. The executioners proceeded to saw the tree asunder, and
so killed him.   [3] 2 Kings xvi. 7-18.
[4] "Eponym Canon," pp. 139. 140, ll. 12-27

king of Egypt and Ethiopia, who was an active enemy of the
Assyrian power, and anxious to detach the princes of Palestine
from their allegiance. A Tyrian revolt against his authority,
whereto Tirhakah was a party, is mentioned by Esarhaddon as
falling in his tenth year.[1] Manasseh was perhaps involved in
it. At any rate he displeased his Assyrian suzerain, probably
about the year B.C. 672, and an army was sent against him
under Assyrian captains, which, according to Josephus,[2]
ravaged his territory, and got possession of his person by
stratagem. His captors treated him with great severity. They
passed rings though his upper and under lips, and, attaching
thongs to them, so led him away prisoner,[3] and brought him
into the presence of Esarhaddon at Babylon, where that
monarch is known to have frequently held his court.[4] There
for some time he remained in captivity, probably from day to
day expecting a sentence of death, since the Assyrian monarchs
generally executed rebel kings ; but at length, in answer (as he
believed) to the fervent prayers which, in his affliction, he
addressed to Jehovah (2 Chron. xxxiii. 12, 13, 19), the royal
clemency was shown to him. Not only was he released from
prison, but Esarhaddon once more received him into favour,
and even sent him back to Jerusalem, there to reign again as
tributary monarch. Such clemency is not wholly unexampled
in Assyrian history ; but the parallels that can be adduced are
few ;[5] and we may fairly assume that Esarhaddon was actuated
in the business by policy rather than by compassion. He was
contemplating a serious struggle for supremacy with Egypt,
and it was of great importance to him to have so strong a
fortress as Jerusalem, and one situated so near the Egyptian
frontier, held for him by a trusty adherent. He must have
believed in gratitude as a powerful constraining motive, and
have thought that a forgiven enemy would be the surest friend.
Manasseh, as far as is known, did not disappoint him. The
only Palestinian power which deserted Assyria in its struggle
with Egypt seems to have been Tyre.[6]

[1] "Eponym Canon," p. 142, ll. 12, 13.   [2] "Ant. Jud." x. 3, § 2.

[3] See 2 Chronicles xxxiii. 11, and compare the author's remarks on the
passage in the "Speaker's Commentary," vol. iii. p. 370.

[4] "Ancient Monarchies," vol. ii. p. 194.

[5] "Egypt and Babylon," pp. 27, 28.

[6] "Eponym Canon," pp. 144, 145.

According to the author of Chronicles, the repentance of Manasseh in his captivity at Babylon was a true repentance, and was fully maintained after his return to his kingdom. Manasseh, he says, in his second reign, "took away the strange gods, and the idol" (*i.e.*, the Ashêrah) "out of the house of the Lord, and all the altars which he had built in the mount of the house of the Lord, and in Jerusalem, and cast them out of the city : and he repaired the altar of the Lord, and sacrificed thereon peace-offerings and thank-offerings, and commanded Judah to serve the Lord God of Israel" (2 Chron. xxxiii. 15, 16). Josephus is more diffuse. "When Manasseh returned to Jerusalem," he says,[1] "it was his endeavour to put away, if it were possible, even the very recollection of his previous sins against God, since he desired to repent of them, and to be as scrupulous as possible in all that had to do with religion. So he both sanctified the Temple, and purified the city of Jerusalem ; and it was henceforth his sole aim to show himself grateful to God for his deliverance, and to continue in the favour of God for the rest of his days. And he was also minded to teach the people to do the like, remembering what a calamity he had only just escaped by an opposite course of life. He likewise repaired the altar, and offered on it the customary sacrifices, as Moses had commanded." It is certainly surprising that the writer of Kings has left no record either of Manasseh's captivity, or of his repentance ; but the circumstantial narrative of Chronicles is not therefore to be rejected.[2] It was attested by that larger "Book of the Kings," to which the author of Chronicles so often appeals, and it had also the support of another writing extant when the Chronicler wrote, and known as "the Words of Chozai," or "the Sayings of the Seers"[3] (2. Chron. xxxiii. 18, 19). It has also in its favour the fact of the existence in the Septuagint of a Greek "Prayer of Manasseh" suitable to the supposed circumstances[4]

---

[1] Joseph. "Ant. Jud." x. 3, § 2.

[2] Ewald passes it over without a word. Stanley, on the contrary, accepts it (1) as resting on sufficient evidence, and (2) as valuable doctrinally ("Lectures on the Jewish Church," vol. ii. p. 424).

[3] The present text must certainly be translated "the words of Chozai," but it is suspected that the text has been corrupted. (See the "Speaker's Commentary," vol. iii. p. 159, note 7.)

[4] See the Apocryphal Book entitled "The Prayer of Manasseh."

—a prayer admitted into the *full* Canon of the Sacred Books by both the Anglican and the Lutheran communions.

But Manasseh, though he might repent of the past, could not really undo it. He had slain most of the more godly among the people, and had left only the profane and the idolatrous. He had made havoc of the Prophetical order, silenced the warning voices, and let a generation grow up without any sound religious teaching. After the murder of Isaiah, no new prophet seems to have been raised up until the reign of Josiah had begun.[1] Hence, his Reformation failed to reach the hearts of the nation. In spite of his persuasions and commands, the people could not be weaned from the High Place worship which he had at one time encouraged (2 Chron. xxxiii. 3), but " did sacrifice still in the high places " (ibid. ver. 17), swore by the name of Malcham (Zeph. i. 5), and worshipped the host of heaven upon the housetops (ibid). There was no genuine reaction from the idolatry of Manasseh, as there was from that of Ahaz, no real turning of the people to God with true and unfeigned repentance.

Manasseh, during his later years, made great efforts to place Jerusalem in security by strengthening and increasing her defences.[2] He " built a wall without the city of David on the west side of Gihon-in-the-Valley, even to the entering in of the Fish-Gate ; and compassed about Ophel, and raised it to a very great height, and put captains of war in all the fenced cities of Judah" (2 Chron. xxxiii. 14). The times were troubled— Cimmerian and Scythian ravages had perhaps begun in Western Asia ; Babylon was growing in power ; Media was pressing upon Assyria on her eastern frontier ; Egypt had rebelled and shaken herself free from her Assyrian conquerors ; in Asia Minor Gyges was aiming at the consolidation of an empire. War was in the air, and it was only prudent on the part of the Jewish monarch to take measures of precaution against probable, or even possible, enemies. He does not appear himself to have contemplated any aggressive struggle, or even any revolt ; but it was important to be secure from attack, in case attack should come ; and to his judicious precautions it may

---

[1] See Jeremiah i. 1 ; Zeph. i. 1. Even Habakkuk is thought to have written later than the beginning of Josiah's reign (Ewald, " History of Israel," vol. iv. p. 302 ; Stanley, " Lectures," vol. ii. p. 425).

[2] Joseph. "Ant. Jud." *l. s. c.*

have been owing that Ashdod, and not Jerusalem, was, under Psamatik I., about B.C. 640, assailed by the forces of Egypt. [1]

Manasseh died after a reign of fifty-five years, at the age of sixty-seven, and was buried in Jerusalem; but, as there was no more room in the burial-place of David, a tomb was made for him in his own palace garden, in a portion of it known as "the garden of Uzzah." He left his throne to his son, Amon (2 Kings xxi. 18).

[1] Herod. ii. 157.

CHAPTER XXXI.

AMON.

Age of Amon at his accession—Influence under which he fell—Duration of his reign—His idolatries and other evil practices—General condition of the people in his reign—Conspiracy against him within the walls of the palace—His death and burial.

AMON,[1] who was but twenty-two years old on the death of Manasseh, his father (2 Kings xxi. 19), must have grown to manhood during the time that Manasseh, having repented of his early idolatries, was doing his best to re-establish the pure worship of Jehovah in Judah, and to repress, discourage, and destroy all the many superstitious practices that he had formerly introduced (2 Chron. xxxiii. 15, 16). But, unfortunately, Amon fell wholly under the influence of that heathenizing party in the State which had warped the mind of Manasseh to evil in his younger days,[2] and had disliked and obstructed (ibid. ver. 17) his reformation. No doubt, as soon as this party saw that it had lost its hold upon the father, it would make every effort to obtain control over the son, and would use all the arts of flattery, misrepresentation, and cajolery to effect its purpose. Amon would be told that his foolish parent was in his dotage; that the Jehovistic prophets and priests had worked on his fears, and driven him to adopt views which, when his intellect was in full vigour, he had repudiated; that it was only priests, and old women, and men whose manliness had departed from them, that still clung

---

[1] Amon (אָמוֹן) has been compared with the name of the Egyptian god Amen; and Manasseh has been thought to have named him after that deity; but there is no other appearance of Manasseh having leant towards the religion of Egypt.

[2] See above, pp. 203, 204.

to the decaying forms of an effete superstition. He would be urged to assert himself, not to follow a vacillating guide, who "built again the things that he had once destroyed," but to take his own independent line, and head a party antagonistic to the Court party. Amon yielded himself to these persuasions, and was no sooner installed in power than he sat himself to undo, in every point, his father's recent reformation, and restore matters to the exact position which they occupied before his father's Babylonian imprisonment.

Though his reign lasted but two, or, at the utmost, twelve years,[1] he seems to have completely succeeded in this endeavour. He turned the Temple once more into a high place for Baal, set up an *Ashêrah* there, re-established the worship of the host of heaven on altars in the two Temple courts, built altars on the upper chamber of Ahaz (2 Kings xxiii. 12), restored the horses of the Sun to their position near one of the entrances to the Temple (ibid. ver. 11), set up "houses of the sodomites" close by the house of the Lord (ibid. ver. 7), re-lighted the fires of Tophet in the valley of the children of Hinnom (ibid. ver. 10), rebuilt the high-places round about Jerusalem and in all the cities of Judah, and caused incense to be burnt on them to the Sun, and Moon, and the zodiacal signs, and all the host of heaven (ibid. ver. 5), allowed the outbuildings of the Temple to fall into disrepair (2 Kings xxii. 5), filled Jerusalem with altars, and with molten and graven images set up above them (2 Chron. xxxiv. 3, 4), probably renewed the enchantments and the dealings with familiar spirits which Manasseh had first allowed (2 Kings xxi. 6) and then put down : "in *all* the way that his father walked in he also walked," and "served the idols that his father served, and worshipped them" (ibid. ver. 21) ; "and humbled not himself before the Lord, as Manasseh his father had humbled himself" (2 Chron. xxxiii. 23), but persisted in evil, and ever "trespassed more and more" (ibid.). If in anything he fell short of his wicked father, it was in respect of persecution. No martyrdoms are assigned to him. On the contrary, it is always "the innocent blood which Manasseh had

[1] The Alexandrian text of the Septuagint has "twelve" for "two" in 2 Kings xxi. 19 ; and in one computation of the chronologer, Demetrius, the reign seems to be reckoned at twelve years. But the "two" of the ordinary text of Kings is confirmed by 2 Chron. xxxiii. 21 and by Josephus ("Ant. Jud." x. 4, § 1).

shed" that is spoken of, and declared to be above all else the cause why Jerusalem was destroyed, since God would not pardon it (2 Kings xxi. 16; xxiii. 26; xxiv. 3, 4).

The general corruption of the people under the evil influences of Amon's reign seems in no degree to have fallen short of that reached in Manasseh's time. The picture drawn in Zephaniah and in the early chapters of Jeremiah represents this state of corruption, which necessarily continued on into the first years of Josiah. Zephaniah finds Jerusalem "filthy and polluted" (chap. iii. 1); her princes are "roaring lions," her judges are "evening wolves" (chap. iii. 3); her prophets are "light and treacherous," her priests "have polluted the sanctuary" (chap. iii. 4); her people worship Baal and the host of heaven (chap. i. 4, 5); they do not seek Jehovah (chap. i. 6) or believe in His power to do good or ill (chap. i. 12), but "swear by Malcham" (chap. i. 5). Jeremiah cannot find a man in all the city "that executeth judgment, that seeketh the truth" (Jer. v. 1). He sees oppression rampant (chap. vii. 6). All are "grievous revolters, walking with slanders; they are brass and iron; they are all corrupters" (chap. vi. 28). They "steal, and murder, and commit adultery, and burn incense unto Baal, and walk after other gods" (chap. vii. 9); nay, they "assemble themselves by troops in the harlots' houses" (chap. vii. 7); they "are as fed horses in the morning, every one neighing after his neighbour's wife" (chap. vii. 8). "From the least to the greatest of them every one is given to covetousness" (chap. vi. 13); "as a cage is full of birds, so are their houses full of deceit" (chap. v. 27); "from the prophet even unto the priest, every one dealeth falsely" (chap. vi. 13).

The falsehood, deceit, and violence almost universally prevalent, extended to the very palace of the king. We are not informed of the motives of the conspirators, or of their ultimate aims and intentions, but simply learn from the curt and dry record of Amon's reign, which is all that has come down to us, that a conspiracy was formed against him among his immediate attendants, and that they "slew him in his own house" (2 Kings xxi. 23). The murder was certainly not caused by any general dissatisfaction with Amon's idolatrous practices; for "the people" rose up against his murderers, "and slew all them that had conspired against king Amon," and gave him honourable sepulture in the burial-place which Manasseh had constructed in the palace garden, in the part known as "the garden of Uzzah" (2 Kings xxi. 24, 26). Here Amon rested, together with his father, Manasseh; and here was afterwards interred the last king whose body found a sepulchre in Jerusalem, the brave but unfortunate Josiah. If Amon died, as is probable, at the early age of twenty-four, **his sins may be to some** extent **excused by his youth.**

CHAPTER XXXII.

JOSIAH.

IT was fortunate for Josiah that his father died so young, since he in this way escaped the corrupting and degrading influences which would otherwise have been brought to bear upon him as he passed from youth to manhood. He was but "eight years old when he began to reign" (2 Kings xxii. 1), and had thus remained still almost wholly under the charge of his mother, as was the Jewish usage. She is mentioned with some particularity by the author of Kings (ibid.), as if she was a person of importance. Her name was Jedidah, which means "Beloved," and she was the daughter of Adaiah of Boskath, a Judæan town not far from Lachish, on the border of the Philistine country.[1] We may perhaps ascribe to her careful training and pious zeal the decidedly religious bent of Josiah's character, which began to show itself in the eighth year of his reign, when he was no more than sixteen (2 Chron. xxxiv. 3).

At first Josiah's religion was strictly personal. He "began to seek after the God of David his father." He began, that is, amid all the idolatry that surrounded him, and that was still encouraged by the princes and rulers, who had the actual conduct of affairs during his minority, to seek after, and try to realize, communion with the true God of Israel, the God of his

[1] Josh. xv. 39.

fathei David, whose psalms were perhaps known to him, whose fame at any rate had descended to his time as that of a worshipper of Jehovah, a pure Monotheist, a hater of idols.[1] In thus setting his heart he may have been encouraged by a certain number of kindred spirits, present in Jerusalem at the time— by Hilkiah the high priest, by Shaphan the scribe, by Huldah the prophetess, wife of Shallum, keeper of the wardrobe ; possibly by Zephaniah the prophet, the descendant of Hezekiah, his own cousin.[2] With Jeremiah at this date he is not likely to have had any contact, since Jeremiah dwelt at Anathoth in Benjamin, and did not receive his call till five years afterwards, in the thirteenth year of Josiah's reign (Jer. i. 2 ; xxv. 3).

Four years later, when he had attained the age of twenty, and the actual administration of affairs had devolved upon him, the young king proceeded from the cultivation of personal piety to the revival of true religion in all its purity, and in all its magnificence, throughout the country (2 Chron. xxxiv. 3). His first care was to " purge Judah and Jerusalem," i.e., to put down, remove, and eradicate all the open and flagrant idolatries, which his father Amon had re-introduced after they had been abolished by Manasseh, and which had now been allowed to flaunt themselves in the eyes of men for thirteen or fourteen years. Their character may be seen by the complaints of Zephaniah,[3] and of Jeremiah in his earlier ministry.[4] Baal was openly worshipped in the Temple itself, which was polluted also by the idolatrous emblem of Astarte. The host of heaven was adored upon the housetops. The fires of Tophet glowed in the valley of Hinnom, and the offering of innocent children to the horrid idol of Moloch was continued. Moloch was generally recognized as a god, and sworn by.[5] In Jerusalem, at every corner of the streets, there were images of heathen deities, and altars on which incense was burnt to them. The whole country was full of "high places," on which the Chemarim, or idol-priests. offered sacrifices. Josiah decreed a complete abolition of all these things. First and foremost, he cleansed the Temple. "The king commanded Hilkiah the high priest, and the priests of the second order, and the keepers of the door, to bring forth

[1] Psa. cxv. 4-8 ; cxxxv. 15-18.
[2] Zeph. i. 1. The " Hizkiah " of this passage is the same word which our Version ordinarily renders by " Hezekiah."
[3] Ibid. i. 4-9 ; iii. 1-4.   [4] Jer. ii.-xi.   [5] Zeph. i. 5.

out of the temple of the Lord all the vessels that were made for Baal, and for the grove, and for all the host of heaven, and he burned them without Jerusalem in the fields of Kidron, and carried the ashes of them unto Bethel. . . . And he brought out the grove from the house of the Lord, without Jerusalem, to the brook Kidron, and burned it at the brook Kidron, and stamped it small to powder, and cast the powder thereof upon the graves of the children of the people. . . . And he took away the horses that the kings of Judah had given to the sun, at the entering in of the house of the Lord . . . and burned the chariots of the sun with fire. And the altars that were on the top of the upper chamber of Ahaz, which the kings of Judah had made, and the altars which Manasseh had made in the two courts of the house of the Lord, did the king beat down, and brake them down from thence, and cast the dust of them into the brook Kidron" (2 Kings xxiii. 4–12). He then proceeded to cleanse Judæa. "The high places that were before Jerusalem, which were on the right hand of the mount of corruption, which Solomon the king of Israel had builded for Ashtoreth the abomination of the Zidonians, and for Chemosh the abomination of the Moabites, and for Milcom the abomination of the children of Ammon, did the king defile" (ibid. ver. 13). "And he brought all the priests out of the cities of Judah, and defiled the high places where the priests had burned incense from Geba to Beersheba" (ibid. ver. 8). "And he defiled Topheth, which is in the valley of the children of Hinnom, that no man might make his son or his daughter to pass through the fire to Molech" (ibid. ver. 10). After this he proceeded beyond the borders of Judæa into the ancient kingdom of Samaria, and there in the first place broke down, and defiled, and stamped small to powder, the high place which Jeroboam had made for one of his calves at Bethel (ibid. ver. 15), and afterwards proceeding through the various towns and country districts of " Manasseh, and Ephraim, and Simeon, even unto Naphtali," he broke down with mattocks "the altars and the groves, and beat the graven images into powder, and cast down all the idols throughout all the land of Israel" (2 Chron. xxxiv. 6, 7 ; compare 2 Kings xxiii. 19).

After the destruction of idolatry the zealous king addressed himself, in the second place, to the re-establishment of the religion of Jehovah. The Temple, besides cleansing, needed repairs. Many of the walls and outbuildings were broken

down, the floors were in a bad condition, and " couplings "
were needed in various places.¹ Josiah sanctioned a collection
of money for the repairs, not only in the Temple itself, where
the system of Joash (2 Kings xii. 4–12) seems to have been
reverted to, but also throughout Judah and Benjamin, and all
the land of Israel (2 Chron. xxxiv. 9). The money gathered
was expended in the purchase of hewn stones and timber (ibid.
ver. 11), and in the payment of carpenters, and masons, and
bearers of burdens, and overseers of the work (ibid. vers. 10–13),
which continued probably over several years, since there was a
great deal to be done. From time to time the civil officers who
had the general management of the work proceeded to the
Temple, and there received from the high priest such monies
as had been collected since their last visit, which they made
over to the superintendents of the workmen, who thereupon
paid their wages to the men employed (ibid. vers. 8–10). On
one of these occasions, after the business transactions had been
concluded, Hilkiah, the high priest of the time, communicated
to "Shaphan the scribe," the chief of the civil officers, an important discovery which had been recently made—" I have found,"
he said, "the Book of the Law in the house of the Lord" (2
Kings xxii. 8). In making the repairs, in clearing out chambers,
or "removing accumulated rubbish,"² a roll of parchment or
papyrus had been found, which Hilkiah recognized as containing a copy of the Law, and which he, apparently, believed to be
the Temple copy ³—that which, according to the Law itself
(Deut. xxxi. 26), was to be kept "in the side of the ark of the
covenant," but which in the troubles of Manasseh's, or of
Amon's time, had been lost. He thought this discovery of
sufficient importance to be communicated to Shaphan, and
through Shaphan to the king (2 Kings xxii. 8–10).

To the king the Book was a revelation. No doubt he had
often before had portions of it read to him from Jewish Litur-
gies, and those who instructed him in the religion of Jehovah
could only do so out of the Law, in one shape or another, as it
had come down to them ; but the reading of the entire Law to
him in one continuous sitting was like the breaking upon him

¹ See 2 Chron. xxxiv. 11.
² So Stanley, "Lectures on the Jewish Church," vol. ii. p. 428.
³ "The testimony "—probably the Temple Copy of the Law—was placed
on the head of Joash when he was crowned. See above, p. 117.

of a wholly new light, as the reading of the entire New Testament was to many at the time of the Reformation. The extreme severity of God's judgments in the Law against all those
idolatrous practices to which his nation had so long been given,
the awful curses pronounced on disobedience, the terrible
threats levelled against sins that were most common, and
scarcely deemed sins, in his day, filled Josiah with a holy
horror with respect to the future of his people, whom he
perceived to have transgressed the Law in ten thousand ways,
and to be obnoxious to its worst threatenings. It was not for
himself, but for his people, that he feared. What might not be
coming upon them? The prophetess Huldah answered, that
all the evils mentioned in the Book of the Law *would* shortly
come upon the nation—there was no escape—but that, with
respect to Josiah himself, "because his heart was tender and
he had humbled himself before the Lord, when he heard the
words of the Book, and had rent his clothes, and wept before
God, therefore he should not see the evil day, but should be
gathered to his fathers before it came, and die in peace" (2
Kings xxii. 19, 20)—die, *i.e.*, before the real attack began which
would bring Jerusalem to destruction—the attack of Nebuchadnezzar, king of Babylon.

The king was not, however, satisfied with this personal ex-
emption from the coming woes ; he would still strive to save,
so far as it was possible, his people. If the nation must perish,
yet at any rate individuals might escape the curse, and he
would do his best to enlarge the number of such escapes. In
the first place, the Book of the Law should be made known as
widely as possible. The solemn reading of the Law once in
every seven years before all Israel, commanded in Deuteronomy
(chap. xxxi. 10–13), had certainly not been observed since the
accession of Amon, perhaps not since the accession of Manasseh. Josiah summoned a great meeting, and "recited aloud
the whole Law from end to end to an immense concourse
assembled in the Court of the Temple, in which every order
of the State, priests and prophets, no less than nobles and
peasants, heard the (practically) new Revelation from the lips
of the Royal Reformer, from his pillar at the entrance of the
inner court, beside the sacred laver, himself the new Lawgiver
of his people."[1] Nor did he deem this enough. The time

[1] Stanley, "Lectures," vol. ii. p. 429.

seemed favourable for one of those national vows, or renewals
of the Covenant, which had been in favour under former pious
kings,[1] whereby the people bound themselves to the observance
of the commands of God, and, as it were, rehearsed the original
covenant of Sinai.[2] The king called on the people to make
profession of religion, and to pledge themselves that they would
thenceforward "walk after the Lord, and keep His commandments and His testimonies and His statutes with all their
heart and with all their soul, to perform the words of the
covenant that were written in the Book" from which he had
read. And then, as one man, "all the people stood to the
Covenant" (2 Kings xxiii. 3).

This striking scene was followed by a Passover, such as had
not been celebrated "from the days of the judges that judged
Israel, nor in all the days of the kings of Israel, nor of the kings
of Judah" (ibid. ver. 22). From all parts of the land the people
flocked up to the renovated Temple, and joined with every
demonstration of gladness in the eight days' festivity prepared
for them. Thirty thousand males of full age attended. The
king gave them their paschal offerings, a lamb or a kid for
each, and furnished besides three thousand bullocks for thank-
offerings ; while the leading priests and the chief of the Levites
were proportionately liberal (2 Chron. xxxv. 7–9). The require-
ments of the Law were most completely carried out in all
respects ; the ceremonial of David and Solomon was revived;
"the singers the sons of Asaph were in their place, and the
porters waited at every gate" (ibid. ver. 15) ; the enthusiasm of
the crowd, to most of whom the Passover was perhaps a novelty,
was extraordinary. In after times even the great Passover of
Hezekiah (2 Chron. xxx. 1–26) was considered to have been
outshone by the festival of the eighteenth year of Josiah, which
had no parallel "from the time of the judges," or "from the
days of Samuel the prophet" (ibid. chap. xxxv. 18).

The remainder of Josiah's reign is, until its actual close,
shrouded in darkness. Thirteen years intervened between
his Passover and his death. Into this space of time (B.C.
621–608) probably fell the great Scythic invasion of Asia,[3]
which (so far as Syria was concerned) Psammetichus (Psamatik I.) met and stopped,[4] and the fall of the Empire of Assyria.

[1] As Asa (2 Chron. xv. 12) and perhaps Hezekiah (ibid. chap. xxix. 10).
[2] Exod. xxiv. 3–8.   [3] Herod. i. 103.   [4] Ibid. i. 105.

It is uncertain how far the Scythians troubled Judæa. Ewald's conjecture, that they besieged Josiah for some time in Jerusalem on their return from Egypt,[1] is wholly unwarranted ; and the slight mention which the invasion receives from the sacred writers renders it probable that Judæa Proper suffered but little from their ravages. Most likely they both went and returned by the usual coast route, only diverging from it at one point, to attack Beth-shan in the eastern Esdraelon plain, on the right bank of the Jordan. Here a number of them settled, and the town acquired the names of Scythopolis ;[2] but, however injurious they were to the more inland regions of Asia, Judæa and even Samaria seem to have suffered little evil at their hands. Ezekiel upon the Chebar saw and noted their devastations (Ezek. xxxviii. 2–13) ; but the contemporary prophets who lived in Judæa have no clear reference to them as among the persecutors of Israel.[3]

However, in B.C. 608, in the thirty-first year of Josiah's reign, a real danger of a serious character menaced the Judæan kingdom. The Assyrian Empire had fallen—Nineveh had been taken and destroyed—about the year B.C. 615. Babylon at once aspired to take Assyria's place ; but the whole of Western Asia was disorganized, and for some years Babylon made little progress. Neco, son of Psamatik I., who ascended the throne of Egypt about B.C. 610, found this disorganization continuing, and thought he saw in it an opportunity for his own aggrandizement. Syria seemed to invite him to lay hands upon her. Accordingly, in his third year, having made ample preparations, he marched at the head of his army into Palestine, probably along the coast route, with the design of measuring his strength against that of the Babylonians at Carchemish,[4] their great fort on the Euphrates, and, if victorious, of adding to his dominions the entire tract between the Euphrates and Egypt. He did not suppose that any of the petty monarchs of this region, whose dominions he had to traverse, would venture to say him nay— much less to oppose their petty levies to his huge host. But Josiah, when he heard of the Egyptian king's intention, seems

[1] "History of Israel," vol. iv. p. 230, Eng. tr.

[2] Plin. "H. N." v. 16 ; Syncell. "Chronograph," l. p. 405.

[3] The only supposed references are Jer. i. 13–15 ; vi. 2–5 ; and Zeph. ii. 4–6. In the last of these places only are they certainly spoken of, but it is as spoilers of Philistia, not Israel.   [4] 2 Chron. xxxv. 20.

to have thought himself bound, either by duty, or in honour, to offer resistance. It is possible that he had already accepted the position of Babylonian feudatory, and felt called upon at any risk to oppose an enemy of his suzerain. It is on the whole perhaps more probable that he acted as an independent monarch, who must in honour protect his own territories. It was not given him to penetrate the future; and he may have expected such Divine aid as had been given to Asa against Zerah the Ethiopian or to Hezekiah against Sennacherib. He therefore boldly took up a strong position, near Megiddo, on the ridge joining Carmel to the Samaritan highland, at the south-western edge of the plain of Esdraelon—" the battle-ground of Palestine." Neco would fain have persuaded him to retire, having, as he assured Josiah, no quarrel with him, but only with the king of Babylon. Josiah, however, held to his own view, and continued to block Neco's path. Neco was thus forced to fight. We have no details of the battle, but may gather that the Egyptians gained an easy victory; [1] drove the troops of Josiah from the field, and immediately proceeded on his march. Josiah, who in the course of the fight had been wounded by an arrow, was conveyed to Jerusalem in his second chariot (2 Chron. xxxv. 24), where he died of his wound in a short time. Great lamentation was made over him, and he was buried with all due honours in his own sepulchre, near the tombs of Amon and Manasseh (2 Kings xxiii. 30 ; 2 Chron. xxxv. 24). Jeremiah mourned his death in a special elegy, which continued to be sung by professional minstrels of both sexes till long after the return from the Captivity (2 Chron. xxxv. 25).

Josiah is perhaps the most blameless of the kings of Judah. "He did that which was right in the sight of the Lord, and walked in the ways of David his father, and declined neither to the right hand nor to the left" (2 Kings xxii. 2 ; 2 Chron. xxxiv. 2). "Like unto him was there no king before him, that turned to the Lord with all his heart, and with all his soul, and with all his might . . . neither after him arose there any like him" (2 Kings xxiii. 25). But he was certainly not a strong nor a very wise king; and his reign cannot be said to have advantaged his country.

[1] See Herod. ii. 159.

CHAPTER XXXIII.

JEHOAHAZ OF JUDAH AND JEHOIAKIM.

Accession of Josiah's second son, Shallum or Jehoahaz—Further conquests of Neco—His deposition of Jehoahaz—Feeling of the Jews with respect to Jehoahaz—Jehoiakim reigns as an Egyptian vassal for three years, B.C. 608–605—Character of his early reign—Battle of Carchemish, and first expedition of Nebuchadnezzar against Palestine—Conquests of Nebuchadnezzar—His return to Babylon—Fresh intrigues among the Palestinian monarchs—Revolts of Judæa and Tyre—Second expedition of Nebuchadnezzar, and execution of Jehoiakim—Estimate of his character.

JOSIAH at his death left behind him three sons—Eliakim, the eldest, who was twenty-five years of age (2 Kings xxiii. 36), Shallum (1 Chron. iii. 15) or Jehoahaz, the second, who was twenty-three (2 Kings xxiii. 31), and Mattaniah, afterwards Zedekiah, the third, who was a boy of the age of ten (ibid. xxiv. 17, 18). The Jews, on Josiah's decease, "took Jehoahaz," the second son, "and anointed him king in his father's stead" (ibid. ver. 31), either because they preferred him to Eliakim, or because the latter was beyond their reach,[1] and the circumstances of the time made an immediate appointment imperative. After defeating the Jewish army at Megiddo, Neco, king of Egypt, had pressed forward, and made himself master of the entire tract between Samaria and the Euphrates, had taken Carchemish, and had established his dominion over the various states and kingdoms of Northern Syria, Cœle-Syria, and Phœnicia. But his conquests had occupied him some time, and it was not until three months[2] had elapsed from the date of his victory over Josiah, that he again approached the Jewish frontier, and proceeded to arrange the affairs of the Judæan

---

[1] Jehoiakim may have taken part in the battle of Megiddo, and have been made a prisoner; or he may have been accidentally absent from Jerusalem when Josiah died.　　　　[2] See 2 Kings xxiii. 31.

kingdom as he thought fit. Josephus tells us that he sent for
Jehoahaz, to come to him at Hamath, and there seized his
person, and put him in fetters.[1] The statement of the writer
of Kings (2 Kings xxiii. 33) is in harmony with this, except that
"Riblah in the land of Hamath" is substituted for Hamath
itself. It is clear that Neco disallowed the right of the Jews
to appoint any one to the Judæan throne without his consent,
and that he put down Jehoahaz and carried him a prisoner to
Egypt (ibid. ver. 34), because his authority had been set at
nought by the election. He then gave the crown to Eliakim,
the eldest son of Josiah, who might seem to be naturally
entitled to it, but required him to change his name, probably as
a mark of servitude, and laid upon him a heavy tribute (ibid.
ver. 33).

Jehoahaz appears, during his short reign of three months, to
have endeared himself greatly to his subjects. He was not a
worthy successor of Josiah, for "he did evil in the sight of the
Lord, according to all that his fathers had done" (2 Kings
xxiii. 32) ; but he pleased the popular imagination, which saw
in him a "young lion," well trained to "catch the prey" and
capable of "devouring men" (Ezek. xix. 3). The hope was
entertained that he would raise the fallen fortunes of Judæa, and
recover her glories for her (ibid. ver. 5); and when this hope
was disappointed by his capture and deportation to Egypt, the
regret was excessive. Among others, Jeremiah himself bewailed
him. "Weep ye not for the dead," he said, *i.e.*, for Josiah,
"neither bemoan him, but *weep sore for him that goeth away;*
for he shall return no more, nor see his native country" (Jer.
xxii. 10). No Jewish prince before him had died in exile ; and
the prophecy that he should do so touched the nation's heart
with a feeling of deep commiseration. To have not only to
descend from a throne, but to be carried to a distance from the
land of one's nativity, and there to lead a joyless life, untinged
by any, the faintest, hope of a return, seemed a thing almost
too sad to contemplate. It was worse than even that "cutting
off in the midst of one's days," with which Hezekiah had been
threatened (2 Kings xx. 1 ; Isa. xxxviii. 10), and Josiah visited
(2 Kings xxiii. 29).

Jehoiakim reigned, as an Egyptian vassal, for three years in

[1] "Ant. Jud." x. 5, § 2.

tranquillity. The country was heavily taxed to content the greed of Neco (ibid. ver. 33); but otherwise had little to complain of, and enjoyed a semblance of prosperity. Jehoiakim employed himself in enlarging and beautifying the royal palace, which he "cieled with cedar, and painted with vermilion" (Jer. xxii. 14). His leanings were towards the heathenizing party, and he is pronounced to have "done evil in the sight of the Lord, according to all that his fathers had done" (ibid. ver. 37; compare 2 Chron. xxxvi. 5); but he scarcely seems to have gone the lengths of Amon or of Manasseh. One act of extreme cruelty is, however, recorded against him, even in the earlier portion of his reign. A prophet named Urijah, the son of Shemaiah, of Kirjath-jearim, "prophesied in the name of the Lord" against Judah and Jerusalem, soon after Jehoiakim ascended the throne, much in the same strain as Jeremiah did afterwards. His words roused the anger of the king, the nobles, and the army, who at once threatened his life. Urijah, alarmed at the danger, fled into Egypt, where he hoped to be safe; but he was relentlessly pursued, captured, and brought back to Jerusalem, by the command of Jehoiakim, who had him beheaded, and his body buried in the cemetery of the common people (Jer. xxvi. 20-23). The life of Jeremiah was about the same time threatened for similar reasons; but the influence of Ahikam, son of Shaphan, and of some other nobles, saved him from the fate of his brother prophet (ibid. vers. 16, 17, 24).

In the fourth year of Jehoiakim (B.C. 605) the crisis predicted by these "prophets of evil" arrived. Nebuchadnezzar, son of Nabopolassar, king of Babylon, in the last year of his father's reign,[1] led the forces of the Babylonian Empire to the far west, with the object of chastising the bold Pharaoh, who had laid his hand on provinces which Babylon regarded as her own, and of wresting them from the grasp of the usurper. Neco, aware of his intention, marched to meet him;[2] and the two armies came into collision at Carchemish on the Middle Euphrates, the site now known as Jerabus, or Jerabolus. "Egypt rose up as a flood, and her waters were moved like the rivers—I will go up, he said, I will cover the earth—come up, ye horses; and rage, ye chariots; and let the mighty men come

[1] See the fragment of Berosus preserved by Josephus ("Ant. Jud." x. 11, § 1).

[2] See Jer. xlvi. 7-9; Joseph. "Ant. Jud." x. 6, § 1.

forth—the Ethiopians and the Libyans, that handle the shield ; and the Lydians, that handle and bend the bow" (Jer. xlvi. 8, 9). On the other side was the mighty power of Babylon—the army seen in vision by Habakkuk, " terrible and dreadful— their horses swifter than the leopards, and more fierce than the evening wolves—their horsemen spreading themselves, and coming from far, and flying upon the prey as straight and as quick as the eagle" (Hab. i. 7, 8). Awful was the shock of battle—terrible "the day of the Lord God of Hosts, the day of his vengeance when he avenged himself of his adversaries—the day that the Lord God of Hosts had a sacrifice in the north country by the river Euphrates" (Jer. xlvi. 10). And complete was the discomfiture of Egypt. "They were dismayed and turned away back ; their mighty ones were broken to pieces ; they fled apace and looked not back ; they stumbled and fell towards the north by the river Euphrates" (ibid. vers. 5, 6). God "made many to fall ; yea, one fell upon another ; and they said, Arise, and let us go again to our own people, and to the land of our nativity, from the oppressing sword" (ibid. ver. 16). Pharaoh's valued mercenaries, Greeks and Carians,[1] were of no service— the "hired men" also were "turned back, and fled away together ; they did not stand, because the day of their calamity was come upon them, the time of their visitation" (ibid. ver. 21).

The hasty flight of Neco and his army left the whole of Syria open to the invaders. Nebuchadnezzar's host poured like a torrent over mountain and plain, from Carchemish to Aleppo, from Aleppo down the broad Cœle-Syrian valley, across the roots of Lebanon, over Galilee, Samaria, Judæa, Philistia, Edom, into Egypt. No one thought of resistance any more. Jehoiakim was only too glad to submit, and become Nebuchadnezzar's servant (2 Kings xxiv. 1) instead of Neco's, and pay his homage and his tribute to his new sovereign. The kings of Edom, Moab, Ammon, probably also those of Tyre and Sidon, did the same. Nebuchadnezzar, however, was prevented from punishing Neco as he desired, or completing his arrangements for the future government of Syria and Palestine, by intelligence which reached him as he was about to ascend the valley of the Nile. His father, Nabopolassar, had succumbed to his weight of years, and died at Babylon, in the twenty-first year of his reign,

[1] Herod. ii. 152, perhaps called "Lydians" in Jer. xlvi. 9.

towards the close of B.C. 605.   To avoid a disputed succession, it was of the greatest importance that Nebuchadnezzar should return to his capital at once.   He therefore broke up his camp, entrusted the bulk of his forces, together with his prisoners and booty, to some of his generals, with orders to return to Babylon by the usual circuitous route, through Cœle-Syria, and then by Aleppo and Carchemish to the Euphrates valley, while he himself, with a few light troops, crossed the desert and hastened to the capital by way of Tadmor or Palmyra.[1]

Arrived at Babylon, Nebuchadnezzar ascended the throne without difficulty, but the state of affairs seeming to require his presence in the East rather than in the West, he for some time left Syria and Palestine to themselves—a policy which was almost sure to result in fresh troubles.   A single defeat was not likely to have cowed the possessor of an old and powerful monarchy ; and the petty kingdoms of South-western Asia were almost certain to incline to that one of the two rival Empires which was not at the time their master.   Neco, under the circumstances, naturally encouraged this disposition, and it was not long before some of the petty kings openly revolted and declared themselves independent of Babylon.   Jehoiakim was the first to take the plunge.   In the fourth year after his subjugation, B.C. 602, despite the warnings of Jeremiah, he "turned and rebelled against" Nebuchadnezzar (2 Kings xxiv. 1).   At first the Great King was content to punish him by sending against him a few "bands" of Chaldæans, which, in combination with some of the neighbouring nations—as the Syrians, the Moabites, and the Ammonites, plundered and ravaged his territory[2]; but, about the year B.C. 598, Ithobal, king of Tyre, having also rebelled,[3] he became convinced that his personal presence was needed in the Palestinian region, and marched at the head of a large army into Syria.   The sieges of Tyre and Jerusalem were formed simultaneously ; but, while Tyre resisted with great obstinacy, Jerusalem very soon succumbed. Jehoiakim fell into Nebuchadnezzar's hands, was executed, and received at first "the burial of an ass" (Jeremiah xxii. 19) ; but his remains were afterwards collected, and interred in the sepulchre of Manasseh (2 Kings xxiv. 6).

---

[1] Berosus ap. Joseph. "Ant. Jud." x. 11, § 1.
[2] 2 Kings xxiv. 2 ; Ezek. xix. 8.   [3] Joseph. "Contr. Ap." i. 18.

Jehoiakim's character deteriorated as time went on. In his later years he was given up to covetousness, employed forced labour for the construction of his palaces, and was guilty of many acts of oppression and violence (Jer. xxii. 13, 17). "In the recollections of his countrymen, he was the last example of those cruel, selfish, luxurious princes, the natural product of Oriental monarchies, the disgrace of the monarchy of David."[1] Among his various crimes, that which will perhaps live the longest in human memory is his audacious act in cutting to pieces with a penknife the roll of Jeremiah's prophetic warnings, which was being read to him by the courtier, Jehudi, and his casting of the pieces into the brazier by which he was warming himself, until the whole roll was consumed (Jer. xxxvi. 23). It is hard to say whether folly or impiety had the larger part in this action, which only led to the re-inscription of all the words of the first upon a second roll, and the adding thereto of " many like words " (ibid. ver. 32).

[1] Stanley, " Lectures on the Jewish Church," vol. ii. p. 458.

CHAPTER XXXIV.

JEHOIACHIN AND ZEDEKIAH.

Jehoiachin made king by Nebuchadnezzar—His evil and short reign—He is carried captive to Babylon—Zedekiah, his uncle, made king in his place—Zedekiah's early efforts to introduce reforms—He succumbs to the influence of the nobles—Rebels and allies himself with Apries—Last invasion of Nebuchadnezzar—Siege of Jerusalem commenced—Advance of Apries—Siege raised—Renewed and final investment—Jerusalem taken—Capture and punishment of Zedekiah—His weak character.

FOLLOWING a practice not uncommon in the East,[1] Nebuchadnezzar, while executing the rebel king who had defied his authority, made no change in the natural order of succession, but placed his son, Jehoiachin or Jeconiah, upon the throne. Jehoiachin had reached the age of eighteen at his father's death[2] (2 Kings xxiv. 8), was married to several wives (ibid. ver. 15), and had at least one child (Jer. xxii. 28). His mother, Nehushta, was the daughter of El-nathan, one of the nobles of Jehoiakim's court, the same who had been sent in pursuit of Urijah the prophet, and had brought him back to Jerusalem (Jer. xxvi. 22, 23). She held the rank and position of Queen-Mother, an office of high dignity even in the last extremity of the royal house. Whether she had any influence over her son is unknown to us, but if so, its exercise had no salutary effect. Jehoiachin, like all the kings of Josiah's stock, "did that which was evil in the sight of the Lord" (2 Kings xxiv. 9; 2 Chron. xxxvi. 9), and provoked Jeremiah, after he had reigned a few months, to declare that he was "a despised broken idol, a vessel wherein there was no pleasure" (Jer. xxvi. 28). On

---

[1] See Herod. iii. 15; and compare the ordinary practice of the Assyrians ("Eponym Canon," pp. 129, 133, &c.).

[2] "*Eight* years old" in 2 Chron. xxxvi. 9 is clearly a corrupt reading.

him, as on Jehoahaz, went forth the sentence that he should be cast out of his own land, and carried into another country, where he was not born, and should die there" (ibid. vers. 26, 27). Nebuchadnezzar, probably suspecting him of an intention to revolt, sent an army against him under some of his generals, who laid siege to Jerusalem (2 Kings xxiv. 10), but were not allowed to have the glory of its capture. Nebuchadnezzar, after a brief delay, came up in person against the place, which was soon reduced to extremities and forced to surrender. The king, his mother, the eunuchs of the court, and the princes of Judah and Jerusalem, "went out to the king of Babylon" and placed themselves at his disposal (ibid. ver. 12). The Babylonian army entered the city, plundered the Temple and the royal palace of their treasures, rudely broke in pieces the vessels of gold which Solomon had made for the Temple service, and added them to the rest of their booty, but spared the fabric of the Temple and of the palace, and do not seem to have plundered the houses of the inhabitants generally (ibid. ver. 13). A multitude of captives were, however, seized and carried off, including the king, the Queen-Mother, the king's wives, the court eunuchs, " all the princes," the best soldiers of the army to the number of seven thousand, and a thousand craftsmen and smiths (ibid. vers. 14–16).

Still, the Babylonian monarch did not push the rights of the conqueror to the uttermost. It was his glory to be a " king of kings,"[1] and until a subject nation proved incorrigibly rebellious, it was, under the Babylonian system, allowed to retain its laws, its native rulers, and its nationality. He therefore, before returning to his capital with his captives and his rich booty, appointed to the vacant throne of Judæa a new monarch. This was Mattaniah, the third son of Josiah, who had now reached the age of twenty-one (2 Kings xxiv. 18), and was therefore regarded as fully competent to take the reins of government. Once more the condition was made, that the new king must take a new name, and Mattan-jah (= "Gift of Jehovah") changed his name to Zedek-jah (= " Righteousness of Jehovah"), perhaps with some reference to the prophecy of Jeremiah, that a time was coming when a king of the house of David should "reign and prosper," whose name should be "The Lord" (Jehovah) "our Righteousness" (Jer. xxiii. 5, 6).

[1] Ezek. xxvi. 7 ; Dan. ii. 37.

Both Zedekiah's old and his new name seemed to attach him
to the worship of Israel's true God ; and it might perhaps
have been expected that he would walk in the steps of his
pious father, Josiah, rather than in those of his unfortunate
and wicked brothers, Jehoahaz and Jehoiakim.   He did indeed
at first show signs of an intention to obey the Law of Moses,
and in his foreign policy to follow the counsels of Jeremiah : he
persuaded the nobler and the wealthier classes to make in the
Temple a solemn league and covenant with Jehovah, binding
themselves to set free all those of their nation whom, in spite
of the Mosaic ordinance to the contrary (Exod. xxi. 2 ; Lev.
xxv. 39–41), they were holding in permanent slavery (Jer.
xxxiv. 8–10) ; and he sent a peaceable embassy to Babylon,
with advice to the Jewish exiles there to be quiet subjects of
the Great King, and "seek the peace of the city whither they
had been carried away captive, and to pray unto the Lord for
it" (ibid. xxix. 3–7).   He also went himself to Babylon in his
fourth year, B.C. 594 (ibid. li. 59), probably to renew his fealty, and
to disabuse Nebuchadnezzar's mind of any suspicions that he was
entertaining respecting him.   The oath of allegiance, which he
had taken at Jerusalem on his appointment to be king (Ezek.
xvii. 13), was most likely on this occasion repeated, and the
king returned to his capital more than ever pledged to be a
faithful vassal of the Babylonian crown.

He had, however, by this time fallen completely under the
influence of the party at Jerusalem which opposed Jeremiah,
and regarded him as a coward and a traitor.   Trust in Egypt
had revived with the accession to the throne of a young and
enterprising prince, by name Uapra or Hophra.[1]   Nebuchadnezzar had perhaps suffered reverses in the far East.   At any
rate, Syria and Palestine were once more stirred with the hope
of shaking themselves free from the Chaldæan yoke, and prophecies were floating about[2] that the Babylonian power was
about to fall (Jer. xxviii. 1–11).   Many of the petty kings whose
territories bordered on Judæa sent ambassadors to Jerusalem
to induce Zedekiah to join them in open rebellion (ibid. xxvii.
3).   Zedekiah himself sent ambassadors to the court of Hophra,

---

[1] Herodotus calls the king "Apries" (ii. 161), and this name is commonly
used by historians.

[2] Compare Joseph. "Ant. Jud." x. 7, § 2, with Jer. xxvii. 16, and xxviii.
2–4.

offering his alliance, and asking that a large body of troops might be sent to his assistance (Ezek. xvii. 15). A secret treaty was probably made, and about B.C. 589, in the ninth year of his reign, the Jewish king took the last fatal step, and, despite the warnings of Jeremiah, broke his fealty,[1] and openly raised the standard of rebellion against his suzerain (2 Kings xxiv. 20 ; 2 Chron. xxxvi. 13).

The forces of Nebuchadnezzar were immediately put in motion. Ever since his expedition against Jehoiakim (B.C. 598), he had been maintaining an army on the coast of Syria, which had been for ten years besieging Tyre ; but this body of troops could not be spared from its uncompleted task. Nebuchadnezzar deemed it necessary to come in person " with all his host" (2 Kings xxv. 1) from Babylon, and to sit down before Jerusalem in full strength. He was no doubt aware that Judæa was not his only, or indeed his principal, enemy in this quarter. Moab, Ammon, Philistia, Edom, were all of them more or less hostile ; and behind these secondary powers, which by themselves would not have been very greatly to be feared, stood the towering form of Egypt, the strength of which could not as yet be accurately estimated.[2] At a certain point of his advance, he came to a spot where the route which he had hitherto followed divided, the left-hand road leading to Rabbath, the capital of Ammon, and the right-hand road to Jerusalem. Here the king experienced a momentary doubt. Standing at the parting of the ways, he had recourse to divination in three forms—by means of arrows made bright for the purpose, by means of images, and by inspecting the entrails of victims (Ezek. xxi. 20–22). All the omens were in accord, and pointed to Jerusalem, whither accordingly he came. While his army ravaged Judæa far and wide, capturing all the provincial strongholds, except Lachish and Azekah (Jer. xxxiv. 7), he himself, with his best troops, invested the capital. Mounds were raised against the walls, especially toward the north, moveable towers were brought up, the place was assailed with battering-rams, and engines of various kinds, slingers and

[1] Note the frequent reference to this as a heinous crime in Ezekiel (ch. xvii. 15, 16, 18, 19 ; xxi. 25 ; &c.).

[2] Egypt, it must be remembered, employed in her army negroes from the Soudan, as well as large bodies of Greek and Carian mercenaries (Herod. ii. 152, 163, &c.).

archers drew continually nearer, more and more galling the
defenders with their weapons; resistance was beginning to
slacken, a successful defence to appear hopeless, when suddenly the hopes of the besieged were greatly raised and those
of the besiegers depressed, by the intelligence that Apries had
come forth from Egypt at the head of his army, and was
advancing to the relief of the beleaguered city." [1] Nebuchadnezzar judged the movement so important that he immediately
broke up his camp, raised the siege, and marched away southwards to meet the new enemy (Jer. xxxvii. 5). Many thought
that the siege was altogether at an end, that the Babylonians
were gone never to return, and that Jerusalem had nothing
more to fear from them. Jeremiah combatted this feeling, but
with small effect. A foolish confidence had succeeded to an
extreme despondency (ibid. ver. 9): it was expected that Apries,
with his "mighty army and great company" (Ezek. xvii. 17),
would prove more than a match for Nebuchadnezzar, would
defeat his forces, and drive him out of the country.

But the result was far otherwise. Egypt proved herself once
more the "bruised reed" (2 Kings xviii. 21) whereto it was
folly to trust. Either her army declined the battle which the
Babylonians offered,[2] and withdrew from Palestine without
striking a blow, or else it was defeated and forced to retreat.[3]
Judæa gained nothing by the movement beyond a brief respite,
which enabled a certain number of the inhabitants to fly to the
neighbouring mountains (Ezek. vii. 16), and others to seek a
refuge in foreign countries (ibid. vi. 8). Within a very short space
the Babylonian monarch returned, as Jeremiah had prophesied
he would (Jer. xxxvii. 8–10); the city was again invested, the
engines brought up against the walls, and the attacks renewed.
At last Zedekiah began to despair, and sought the counsel of
the prophet, whose warnings he had hitherto scorned (ibid.
xxxviii. 14). Jeremiah assured him that, even now, if he would
make his submission to Nebuchadnezzar, it would be accepted,
his offences against his suzerain would be pardoned, and
Jerusalem spared. But the king could not bring himself to
accept the advice given him. He was afraid of the treatment

---

[1] Jer. xxxvii. 5–7.

[2] This is the conclusion which we should naturally draw from Jer. xxxvii.
7; but it is not directly asserted.

[3] So Josephus ("Ant. Jud." x. 7, § 3).

which he might receive, not so much from the Babylonians, as from those of his own subjects who had deserted to them (ibid. ver. 19). Accordingly, he persisted in his resistance, and made no attempt to open negotiations with his enemy.

The end was now approaching. With the one brief interval caused by the advance of Apries, the siege had lasted a year and a half (Jer. lii. 4–6). The supply of food was at length exhausted. "Famine and its accompanying visitation of pestilence ravaged the crowded population within the walls. . . . It was only by a special favour of the king that a daily supply of bread was sent to Jeremiah in his prison from the baker's quarter, and at last even this failed. The nobles, who had prided themselves on their beautiful complexions, 'purer than snow, whiter than milk, ruddy as rubies, polished as sapphires' (Lam. iv. 7), had become ghastly and black with starvation. Their wasted skeleton forms could hardly be recognized in the streets. The ladies of Jerusalem, in their magnificent crimson robes, might be seen sitting in despair on the dunghills. From these foul heaps were gathered morsels to eke out the failing supply of food (ibid. ver. 5). There was something specially piteous in the sight of the little children, with their parched tongues, fainting in the streets, asking for bread, crying to their mothers for corn and wine (ibid. ii. 11, 12, 19). There was something still more terrible in the hardened feeling with which the parents turned away from them. The Hebrew mothers seemed to have lost even the instincts of the brute creation, to have sunk to the level of the unnatural ostriches that leave their nests in the wilderness. Fathers devoured the flesh of their own sons (Ezek. v. 10; Baruch ii. 3) and their own daughters. The hands even of compassionate mothers were known to have sodden their own children, the merest infants just born (Lam. ii. 20; iv. 10)." [1]

As the famine and pestilence increased, the defence became weaker. At length, on the ninth day of the fourth month, in the eleventh year of Zedekiah, when the siege had lasted within a day of eighteen months, about midnight according to Josephus,[2] the invaders succeeded in forcing an entrance into the town. Nebuchadnezzar had by this time removed to Riblah, whence he could superintend the operations against Tyre,

---

[1] Stanley, "Lectures on the Jewish Church," vol. ii. p. 470.
[2] Joseph "Ant. Jud." x. 8, § 2.

as well as those against Jerusalem. In command at Jerusalem he had left six of his high officers, Nebu-zar-adan, the captain of the host, Nebu-shasban, the chief eunuch, Nergal-shar-ezer, the Rab-mag, another Nergal-shar-ezer distinguished by no title, Samgar-Nebo, and Sarsechim (Jer. xxxix. 3, 13). These princes entered the city with the army, on the north side, where the wall was most assailable, and took their station "in the Middle Gate" (ibid. ver. 3), but whether of the Temple[1] or of the city is uncertain. A promiscuous slaughter then began. The Temple was invaded, and "the priest and the prophet slain in the sanctuary of the Lord" (Lam. ii. 20), together with the brave young Levites, who formed the ordinary Temple guard (2 Chron. xxxvi. 17). The courts of the Temple, and the streets, ran with blood. Neither age nor sex was spared. "The young and the old lay on the ground in the streets ; the virgins and the young men fell" equally "by the sword" (Lam. ii. 21)—there was "no compassion upon young man or maiden, old man or him that stooped for age" (2 Chron. xxxvi. 17). The other horrors usual at the sack of towns were not wanting. "They ravished the women in Zion, and the maids in the cities of Judah : princes were hanged up by their hand, and the faces of elders were dishonoured" (Lam. v. 11, 12). Every worst woe befell the devoted city, which drank the cup of God's fury to the dregs.

Meanwhile, the king, with his bodyguard, his wives and children, and a certain number of the princes, made a desperate effort to escape. There was a gate, probably a small postern, towards the south of the city, opening into a narrow alley "between two walls," which conducted by the way of the royal gardens into the Kidron valley, and so to the steep descent to Jericho and the Jordan. This gate appears to have been unwatched. In the dead of the night, or at any rate before the breaking of the early summer dawn, the fugitives, with such of their worldly possessions as they could carry (Ezek. xii. 12), stole away along the narrow passage unobserved, reached the Kidron valley, and hurried on down the steep path, intending no doubt to take refuge in the wild mountain region beyond the Jordan (Jer. lii. 7). They had escaped the notice of the Babylonians, but were betrayed by their own countrymen. Jewish deserters, seeking

[1] Stanley supposes the Middle Gate of the Temple to be meant ("Lectures," vol. ii. p. 472).

to curry favour with the conquerors, gave information of the flight and its direction.[1] Immediate pursuit was made, and in the open Jordan plain not far from Jericho, the fugitives were overtaken and seized. There does not appear to have been any fight. " All Zedekiah's army was scattered from him " (2 Kings xxv. 5), his guard, *i.e.*, had melted away upon the march, each man seeking his own safety ; and when the enemy approached, the last remnant scattered and fled. Zedekiah, his wives and children, and a handful of attendants, "faithful among the faithless found," were made prisoners and carried to Nebuchadnezzar at Riblah. There a solemn trial was held and judgment pronounced. His attendants and his sons were put to death before his eyes ; and then, when he had seen the gruesome sight, his own eyes were put out. After this, " the king of Babylon bound him in chains, and carried him to Babylon, and put him in prison till the day of his death " (Jer. lii. 11). A Jewish tradition states, that at Babylon he was compelled to grind in a mill, like an ordinary slave.[2]

Zedekiah was a weak, rather than a positively wicked, king. In the earlier years of his reign, he showed a decided leaning towards justice and equity, if not even towards true religion. The liberty which he proclaimed to the Jewish slaves wrongfully kept in servitude by their masters, was a step, at any rate, in the right direction (Jer. xxxiv. 8–10), and, had it been vigorously followed up, might have brought a blessing upon the nation. His secret attachment to Jeremiah (ibid. xxxviii. 10, 16, 24–28), which clearly appears in the narrative, is an indication of some amiability of character ; and it is always to be remembered in his favour, that he certainly saved Jeremiah's life. On the other hand, his weakness was deplorable, and had results almost as fatal as any that could have followed from actual wickedness. Zedekiah's subserviency to the " princes " is marvellous, and utterly contemptible. He lets them not only dictate his foreign policy, but overrule him in matters where right and justice were in question. Their influence was allowed to re-establish the wrongful slavery, which, in the early part of his reign, he had put down (Jer. xxxiv. 11) ; and it was their hostility to Jeremiah which caused him those intense sufferings known by the king to be undeserved, but which he contented

[1] Joseph. x. 8, § 2.
[2] See Ewald, " History of Israel," vol. iv. p. 273, note 5.

himself with mitigating when they threatened the prophet's life (ibid. xxxvii. 15–17 ; xxxviii. 4–13). Zedekiah's fear of personal ill-usage at the hands of the Jewish deserters was also contemptible, and certainly ought not to have been allowed to influence him in deciding the grave question, whether the public interest would be most promoted by a surrender or by continued resistance (ibid. ver. 19). His repudiation of his oath to serve the King of Babylon faithfully, admitted, no doubt, of some defence from a perverted casuistry, and we must not forget that even Christian monarchs and Christian casuists have held that

> "Vows made in pain are violent and void "—

but the higher morality of the Jewish prophets pronounced his perjury one of his worst crimes, and wholly inexcusable (2 Chron. xxxvi. 13 ; Ezek. xvii. 15–20 ; xxi. 25). Moderns will perhaps view with even more disfavour the misgovernment and perversion of justice by the upper classes which he permitted, and did scarcely anything to check. His nation undoubtedly mourned his loss (Jer. xxxiv. 5), but it was rather as "the Anointed of the Lord" (Lam. iv. 20), and the last of the "lion whelps" of Judah (Ezek. xix. 2, 5, 6), than as a leader who had been of any service to them, either against their domestic or their foreign oppressors.